Overcoming Abuse: Embracing Peace. What a treasure-trove of help and hope! This author tackles one of the toughest topics on Earth—the tragedy of abuse. Davison knows that most people throughout the world are ignorant about the why's of abuse and especially the what-to-do's.

The pervasiveness of domestic violence is appalling (1 in 3 women worldwide). The *prevalence of childhood sexual abuse is heartbreaking—we must intervene.*

Thankfully, these insightful pages are filled with a plethora of Scriptural principles and *practical strategies ready for us to apply—to set the captives free. Consequently, to help us and to help us help others, we all need these books.*

June Hunt
Broadcaster, Hope for the Heart
Author, *Counseling Through Your Bible Handbook*

Reina Davison provides essential hope to abuse victims and valuable guidance to those who counsel and care for them. Overcoming Abuse Embracing Peace Volume I, II, and III are unique contributions to the understanding and treatment of abuse trauma. These are must have tools for counselors, caregivers, and abuse sufferers alike.

Major General Bob Dees, U.S. Army, Retired
Author, *The Resilience Trilogy and Resilience God Style*

Reina Davison's books are shrouded in truth. I held my breath as I read *Overcoming Abuse: Embracing Peace* Volume I and II. It's a necessary, but painful topic and Davison handles it with grace, courage, and wisdom. Naming the abuse—calling unhealthy behaviors out for what they are—puts power, hope, and the possibility of healing into the hands of the victim and those who desire to help. Written in a forthright style, these books are must reads. They are steeped in honesty and compassion, giving readers ample opportunity to reflect on and apply what they are uncovering in the pages.

Vicki Tiede
Vicki Tiede Ministries
Author of *When Your Husband is Addicted to Pornography: Healing Your Wounded Heart*

If women and children are ever to count as equals with men -- and abuse is one of the pivotal matters --, the change must come about in our time. With this in mind, Reina Davison's *Overcoming Abuse: Embracing Peace* Volume I, II, and III strike us as a compassionate enterprise of the first importance. May it flourish for years to come.

Julia O'Faolain, Novelist
Lauro Martines, Historian

The subtitles for Reina Davison's books are not exaggerations. The word 'encyclopedic' is accurate. These *Overcoming Abuse* companion volumes I, II, and III provide helpers and victims alike with a wealth of important insights into the tragic problem of abusive relationships and how to deal with them.

Abuse is a difficult problem for churches and church leaders to address. In the first place, abuse is not as simple as it might seem to the casual observer. It is complex, secretive, and entrenched. Simple exhortations or solutions do little more than allow the abuse to continue. Second, while abuse has significant spiritual causes, the role of psychological and emotional factors requires deeper and more nuanced understanding. Abuse is not a problem for mere spiritual formation strategies. It requires a comprehensive and professional set of interventions before it will give way to peace and freedom for the victim. Third, the church has a long history of male-dominated leadership. One of the most tragic consequences of this gender imbalance is that well-intentioned 'helpers' in the church often give more credence to the reports of males than to the plaints of women. Too often the church blames the victim for the abuse without taking into consideration the entire scope of the issues involved.

These books contain first-person accounts of victims that grip your heart. The tragedy that these victims have endured is immense. Yet we can all learn by listening to their stories and taking their experiences seriously. The massive problem of abuse in relationships, even those within the church, require all of us to be informed and equipped to deal effectively with it. The Overcoming Abuse volumes go a long way to do just that.

James R. Beck, Ph.D.
Senior Professor of Counseling
Denver Seminary

Overcoming Abuse Embracing Peace

VOLUME I

YOUR ENCYCLOPEDIC GUIDE TO FREEDOM
FROM ABUSE

Reina Davison

NEW HARBOR PRESS
Rapid City, SD

Copyright © 2020 by Reina Davison.

All rights reserved. No part of this publication may be reproduced, distributed or transmitted in any form or by any means, including photocopying, recording, or other electronic or mechanical methods, without the prior written permission of the publisher, except in the case of brief quotations embodied in critical reviews and certain other noncommercial uses permitted by copyright law. For permission requests, write to the publisher, addressed "Attention: Permissions Coordinator," at the address below.

Davison/New Harbor Press
1601 Mt. Rushmore Rd.
Rapid City, SD 57701
www.NewHarborPress.com

Ordering Information:
Quantity sales. Special discounts are available on quantity purchases by corporations, associations, and others. For details, contact the "Special Sales Department" at the address above.

Overcoming Abuse / Reina Davison —1st ed.
ISBN 978-1-63357-310-9

This book is a work of non-fiction. Unless otherwise noted, the author and the publisher make no explicit guarantees as to the accuracy of the information contained in this book and in some cases, names of people and places have been altered to protect their privacy. The information, ideas, and suggestions in this book are not intended as a substitute for professional advice. Before following any suggestions contained in this book, you should consult your personal physician or mental health professional. Neither the author nor the publisher shall be liable or responsible for any loss or damage allegedly arising as a consequence of your use or application of any information or suggestions in this book. Because of the dynamic nature of the Internet, any web addresses or links contained in this book may have changed since publication and may no longer be valid.

The author has researched data and sources which are believed to be reliable information that is in accordance with the professional code of ethics and current standards of practice at the time of publication. In the event of the possibility of human error or changes in the medical and mental health sciences, neither the author nor the editor and publisher, or any other parties who were involved in the process or publication of this book guarantees that the information contained in this work is complete and flawless in respect to accuracy and they are not responsible for accidental omissions, errors, or any outcomes which result from the use of the information in this book. Readers are encouraged to consult with Scripture, continue the research contained in this book, and to confirm with additional sources.

All Scripture quotations are taken from the New King James Version®. Copyright 1982 by Thomas Nelson, Inc. Used by permission. All rights reserved.

Cover art by Victoria Aleice.
Author photo by Tessa Klingensmith.

*Dedicated to my Heavenly Father,
Who created woman, and Whose
Word instructs that women are to be
loved as Christ loved the Church.*

Contents

FOREWORD 1

ACKNOWLEDGMENTS 5

NOTE ON SELECTED TERMINOLOGY 9

AN INVITATION FOR
THE BEST USE OF THESE BOOKS 15

PART I

SEVEN TYPES OF ABUSE 21

    Abuse Defined 21

    Am I Being Abused? 24

    Dysfunctional vs. Functional Family 26

    Emotional Abuse 32

    Neglect and Types of Neglect 39

    Emotional Neglect 40

    Physical Neglect 42

    Educational Neglect 43

    Medical Neglect 43

    Financial Neglect 43

Consequences of Neglect 44

Physical Abuse 46

Rape 48

Child Sexual Abuse 57

Economic Abuse 58

Spiritual Abuse 72

PATTY'S STORY 77

PART II

THE ABUSER:

EVERYTHING YOU EVER WANTED TO KNOW 93

Personality 93

Abuser Characteristics 95

What Makes an Abuser Abusive? 99

The Abuser's Self-View 102

The Abuser's Profile 105

What's it Like to Live with an Abuser? 120

The Abuser-Parent Profile 129

The Abuser and Anger 137

The Abuser and Mental Illness 141

The Abuser as a VIP & VEP 143

The Abuser and Disrespect 148

The Abuser—The Controller 150

The Abuser—The Silencer 155

Contents

    To Love and Control—'Til Death do us Part 157

    Why Abusers Won't Change 167

    The Abuser, Judicial System, & Society 181

MARY'S STORY 189

PART III

THE VICTIM:

EVERYTHING YOU EVER WONDERED 203

    Victim Characteristics 203

    Abuser Dating Warning Signs 205

    Identity Theft 235

    Victim Isolation 238

    To Love and To Cherish—'Til Death do us Part 240

    Children as Secondhand Victims 243

    The Victim and Self-Defense 257

    Divorce and the Victim of Abuse 268

    Post-Traumatic Stress Disorder (PTSD)

    & the Victim 301

    A Safety Escape Plan (SEP) 303

    Forgiving Yourself & the Abuser 326

ESMERALDA'S STORY 339

ENDNOTES 349

RESOURCES 351

OTHER BOOKS BY REINA DAVISON 357

FOREWORD

WHEN REINA DAVISON INITIALLY asked me to provide a Foreword for the *Overcoming Abuse* book series, I was flattered, to be sure, but I did wonder quietly what our respective professions had in common, and how I could best introduce a book on a subject matter with which I was, mercifully, not terribly familiar. My career, after all, has been in the realm of clinical medicine, as a practitioner of Critical Care. For the better part of four decades, my days have been spent at the bedsides of the critically ill and dying in the intensive care unit of military and civilian hospitals. These patients are terribly ill, deeply broken physically and emotionally, and yes, spiritually. In many cases, their illness has befallen them because of inadvisable choices they have made in their lives; in others, illness has come unbidden, if you will, seemingly at random. Regardless, the devastation of their affliction is great, and their suffering, unknowable.

But clinically, I have not been acquainted with victims of abuse—or have I? Of course, I knew a few victims...a friend or a relative, one in particular, now long deceased (by suicide), about whose "situation" my mom had told me. And, "situations," as we called many things back then, were not openly discussed. Isn't that the case for many of us—we know *about* someone who is a victim of abuse, but not much more.

But Davison reassured me...she had heard me lecture on things medical through a spiritual lens; we have this much in common, that we trust in a Lord who is acquainted with grief and suffering, *our* grief and suffering, into which He entered, and enters, completely, and in which He is present to meet us and to be, finally, the only Source of healing and restoration.

Thus encouraged, I read the manuscripts—and it didn't take long before several dimensions of this work began to stand out. The first of these is Davison's breadth and depth of experience as a counselor and friend to the victims of abuse. She is a keen clinician, one who speaks authoritatively on her field of practice. She is knowledgeable in the subject of abuse, perceptive of the nuances of the illness, and familiar with pertinent literature on the subject. Like an astute physician, she is not fooled by the nuances of victims' symptoms, nor by the subconsciously illusive turns of the history that the abused will give, nor by the psychopathology of the abuser. Nor by the shroud of, well, frank *ignorance and denial* of abuse, which is individually and societally symptomatic of the disease itself and of its deep evil.

So it began to dawn on me that her line of work is not terribly divergent, after all, from my own. Victims of abuse are critically ill, and desperately so, and in need of their own form of *intensive care*. Davison provides precisely that: care for the victim and a resource for those who would care for them. And, like any great advocate, she is an educator—not only of the victim and their counselors, but of her readers. These books are nothing short of revelatory for those of us who, hitherto, "may only have known about" a victim, whether because we did not know the signs or manifestations, or because these were "situations" about which one doesn't speak. Perhaps *I have* met a number of

FOREWORD

people—friend, relative, or patient—who have been victims, secretly suffering, and I never knew, because I hadn't been aware. These books raise consciousness.

The second dimension that caught my eye was Davison's faithfulness to the biblical teaching of the redemptive work of Christ and of the active and very real presence of the Holy Spirit to heal and restore. Davison's text is punctuated with the personal accounts of victims. Their path to healing is never "fake," as in the well caricatured tossing away of a no-longer-needed set of crutches, but of the complex, often tedious, but fundamentally important healing process that occurs over time and as a result of sound therapy, patience, and much prayer. The Holy Spirit is no less present and active in these long and difficult processes than in the dramatic healing of the paralytic at the Beautiful Gate (Acts 3:1-10). Davison's is not an appeal to a vague secular "spirituality," but to the mighty Triune God. The hope she offers is rock-solid.

The third key dimension of these books for me is their inherent and urgent relevance for the Church. It has always been incumbent upon the Church universal and the Church local to be sensitive and responsive to the deep brokenness of her members. Inasmuch as the Apostle Paul understands the institution of marriage itself to be the visible symbol of Christ and His church (Ephesians 5:32), we see perhaps no greater consequence of the fall of humankind than abuse, marital discord, dysfunction, and rupture. But do some churches strain to keep a marriage intact at the expense of the well-being or even the life of a victim of abuse? Davison is not shy to address this head-on. If the recognition, diagnosis, intervention, and counsel of abuse victims are not on the heart and in the pastoral care ministry of a church, then that church has work to do. Davison's books should find their way onto every pastor's desk, and into seminary curricula.

Ministry to victim and to abuser, like medical treatment of critically ill patients, is not for the faint of heart. Ministry and treatment are all about the rolling up of the sleeves of our hearts and minds, the speaking openly about the unspeakable, and entering into the thick darkness of compassion as we come alongside victims and abusers in the hard work of redemption, remembering, all the while, that thick darkness is the very place where God Himself is known to dwell. The prayers of the afflicted do certainly rise to the throne of God. Reina Davison has given practical wisdom of life and hope to those who are in deep and abiding need.

Allen H. Roberts II, M.D., M.Div., M.A. (Bioethics)
Professor of Clinical Medicine
Georgetown University Medical Center

ACKNOWLEDGMENTS

A HEARTFELT THANK YOU to the abusers and victims of whom these books are written; it is regrettable that there had to be abusers and victims for these books to be written, but the hope is that out of these tragic abusive relationships, victims will be reached and many lives will be saved. A wholehearted thank you to each Overcomer for responding in a humanitarian way by pouring out your heart and allowing your story to be shared in these books.

Thank you, colleagues—too many to acknowledge, but you know who you are because you sacrificially gave of your time to disclose your professional experiences in the community, with the government, the judicial system, with abusers and the victims of abuse.

Thank you, Hershall Seals, for taking time out of your schedule on some beautiful summer days and actually painting alongside Victoria Aleice on your own canvas as she created the covers for Volume I, II, and III, of the *Overcoming Abuse: Embracing Peace* book series. Thank you, Victoria Aleice, for painting the book covers with the exact vision I proposed to you; an oil painting with purple clouds (as purple is the official color for domestic violence awareness) depicting the darkness of the trauma of abuse on the bottom which then flows into an ombre lavender, fading into white clouds and sun (SON) rays streaming down at the top to represent the healing from darkness (abuse victim trauma) that turns into light (an Overcomer light of Christ).

Thank you, Dr. Roberts, for taking time out of your busy life to meticulously research and read the manuscripts for the *Overcoming Abuse: Embracing Peace* book series, and then writing a foreword. Thank you for caring about this ministry medically, educationally, and spiritually.

Thank you, Mary Ellis Rice, for poring over the *Overcoming Abuse: Embracing Peace* manuscripts and for proofreading, along with providing your welcomed suggested edits. From day one, in spite of your full agenda, you cared about the mission of this project and up until the day that you returned the manuscripts to me—you fulfilled what you said, "I want to do my best work."

To the New Harbor Press publishing assistants. My heart wells up with gratitude toward the thought of each of you being called to do this work for the abused, many years ago; before I even knew of you. As we all know, nothing is a surprise to our Master. The fact that each of you as a team member has been divinely appointed to be a part of this project was orchestrated long ago. I respect your gifts and servanthood toward this ministerial work. I am certain that there are others that unbeknownst to me are or will be a part of the production and delivery of these books and for them I am also grateful. However, I want to take a moment right now to recognize those that I am aware of who have contributed to this work. Thank you Rick Bates-Managing Editor, Pauline Harris-Editor, Steve Nordstrom-Project Manager, Bob Swanson-Typesetting, and Graphic Designer-Natalie Reed. May your service to the abused and helpers of the abused be rewarded a hundredfold!

ACKNOWLEDGMENTS

Thank you to all of my educational, clinical, and spiritual mentors past and present who have selflessly given of your time, wisdom, planted seeds in me, trained and coached me. Your mentoring is an eternal gift which I will treasure and continue to pass on.

My deep appreciation goes to my family of origin, and a tribute to my late parents for their influence in my life. I'm grateful to my immediate family and dear friends who have supported the writing of these books by lovingly standing back, allowing me the flexibility and space, and for praying, so that God's perfect timing would develop the books.

NOTE ON SELECTED TERMINOLOGY

FOR THE PURPOSE OF readability and in an effort to select short universal terms, I have elected to use the words *abuse*, *abuser*, *spouse*, and *victim*. Abuse is used as a term that can involve all forms and levels of victim and family violence: emotional, physical, sexual, economic, and spiritual. This book is not intended to be offensively sexist when the male gender is referred to as the abuser and the female gender is referred to as the victim. My true desire and motive for this book is that it becomes a manual for the victim and any person that is interested in helping with the devastation of family violence.

To maintain a clear and simple discussion throughout the book, I at times refer to the husband or wife as the *spouse*. When referring to the *perpetrator,* I have selected the shorter term, *abuser*, not because I believe that every man who has problems with controlling behaviors is an abuser, but because it is a word that applies to any man who has consistent, ongoing problems with disrespecting, devaluing, and controlling behaviors toward his spouse.

When I refer to a spouse it's not to imply that premarital abuse doesn't exist; in most cases the abuse begins *before* the marriage and goes undetected or ignored until the consummation of the marriage. I have elected to use the term *he* to refer to the abusive spouse. This is not about denigrating men—it's the *mindset* of abusive men that the research addresses, not their manhood. The term *he* is used because the term describes the majority of the research done on relationships in which power and control are misused by men. The research in the June 28, 2013 U.S. Department of Justice, Bureau of Justice Statistics Report documented ninety-five percent of victims of domestic violence are women.

When writing about the woman that is being abused, I use the term *victim,* not because I view that woman as a helpless dupe but because it is a term that applies to any woman suffering from some act(s) of violence that has led her to have severe recurring feelings of intimidation, humiliation, confusion, anxiousness, fear, and/or depression. In selecting women as my victimization sample, it is not to infer that men are not abused.

If you are a man that is in an abusive relationship with your wife, there is information in this book for you as well. Wives that abuse their husbands share the same socialization, background, history, and dynamics as abusive men do. Female abusers use the same tactics, rationalizations, and excuses for their behavior as male abusers. Husbands that are consistently abused by their wives have the same characteristics as wives that are victims of abuse. So read on; you will just have to change the gender language to fit your experience as an abused husband.

In order to incorporate every potential counselor (that may have an opportunity to work with family violence), I have selected the term *professional* or simultaneously the word *helper* as

NOTE ON SELECTED TERMINOLOGY

opposed to using the title of each mental health practitioner and clergy member. The word "professional" is not used to infer that laypeople are not capable of ministering or working professionally with victims of abuse. The "professional" or "helper" is referred to in the masculine pronoun for the sake of uniformity and word simplicity (applies to both female and male professionals).

The narrative stories that are recounted in this book are all authentic. They are the victims' personal experiences and perceptions of abuse, as told to this writer. They are offered for the victim to recognize and easily identify the various types of abuse via another victim's story; and for the victim to be inspired and encouraged that she too can be healed from the trauma of abuse. Each story has their given name left out, and the victim (now an *Overcomer*) has selected a name with which to be identified. For her protection and privacy, other identifying factors are not disclosed.

The abuser's name and all identifying data have been changed. Any similarities to a reader or circumstances of an individual are simply a resemblance as each of these biographies have been tape recorded, reviewed by the subject, and documented for publication with the subject's signed consent. Permission has been obtained from all research study subjects and case scenario examples cited in this book; if any similarities are recognized, it is purely coincidental. The color purple is the official, symbolic color for family violence; it is used in the book cover, in memory of those victims known and unknown that have been killed by their abusers.

The name "God," His proper names, and pronouns referring to God are capitalized out of reverence to Him. Since capitalization is like italicization—it's a method that suggests "importance" and emphasis—I have elected not to extol satan's name, thus his name is not capitalized. Because God the Father, God the Son, and God the Holy Spirit are One in the same trinity,

I am referring to the three of them simultaneously when I'm speaking of our Heavenly Father, since they are each equal as one God (Genesis 1:1-2, 1 John 5:7, John 10:30, Matthew 3:16-17, Matthew 28: 18-19, 2 Corinthians 13:14).

The word *Overcomer* is capitalized as a proper noun and given importance because the word represents Jesus; it is also set apart from the other text for emphasis. All Scriptural quotations are from The Holy Bible, New King James Version. The same Scriptural references may be quoted in parts of this book in order to expand on the verse, use it in a different context, or facilitate comprehension through a different example.

When referring to the victim's *soul*, I am referring to her emotional and moral sense of identity. When speaking of the victim's immaterial being, which is the nerve center for her feelings and sentiments, I speak of her *heart*. I am not using the term soul in a theological form as her immortal part of her being. Conversely, when I refer to her spirit, I am then speaking about her mood or immortal and eternal soul. The Spirit (Holy Spirit) is always capitalized.

The term *mindful* is used to describe the process of becoming aware of one's thinking as related to the mental technique of *mindfulness*, not as in a religious ritual, but as conscious mindful observations of one's thoughts, experiences, and behaviors.

It is a tough calling to comprehensively document years of observing and working with the lives of victims and abusers, and it is even tougher to write in a language that depicts their life through their eyes.

Those of us therapists and others who write about the taboo subject of abuse and report the darkness and the evil that victims encounter dare to open Pandora's Box and risk public scrutiny and credibility in the same way as the victim. To speak and transparently write about the devouring consequences of

NOTE ON SELECTED TERMINOLOGY

abuse trauma in a society that silences victims of abuse invites controversy.

It has been my sincere desire throughout the writing of this book to put into words only the precise expressions and descriptions from the dialogues of the victim, abuser, and society—to depict what I've listened to, witnessed, and worked with.

> "May He grant you according to your heart's *desire*,
> And fulfill all your purpose.
> May the LORD fulfill all your petitions."
> Psalm 20:4

AN INVITATION FOR THE BEST USE OF THESE BOOKS

THE OVERCOMING ABUSE VOLUME I, II, and III encyclopedic guidebooks were created through the work done with individuals experiencing the dynamics of family abuse. My clinical sources for these books are the victim and the abuser. Both my research and experience with these soldiers, clients, inmates, and patients have consistently indicated the same end results: No matter what class, cultural, ethnic, or racial background they come from, the dynamics of the victim of abuse remain the same; the dynamics for the abuser are consistently the same. There are universal characteristics among the hundreds of victims and abusers that my colleagues and I have researched and worked with in the past four decades. Samples of case scenarios from victims who have willingly voiced their stories of abuse are included at the end of each part of the books to encourage you so that you too can overcome your abuse! So you too, can help the abused.

It is my intent to share in these books a body of knowledge on the trauma of abuse. My goal is to encourage women in abusive relationships to receive this message: that there is hope, and that the cycle of abuse can be stopped *before* it begins with the next generation. The purpose of these encyclopedic guidebooks is to empower women who are involved in an abusive relationship into permanent recovery—to be set free from the cycle of abuse and their abuser. These books teach women how to identify an abuser in order to prevent them from getting involved in an abusive relationship(s) again. Secondly, imbedded in that effort is my goal to empower families and our society as a whole with an awareness and understanding of family violence through education on the trauma of abuse.

Will the abuser be happy that the victim is reading these books? Absolutely not, so these books are best kept a secret between the victim and her support system. There are good and bad secrets to keep; this is a good secret to keep. Whether you have the books in electronic copy or in book form, you must take safety precautions in preserving the books. It may be easier/safer for you to download your book to your tablet or into your TracFone smart phone (see Resources for TracFone information). If you feel that you can't maintain a private password for your e-books or that you have no private place to keep a copy of these books in your home, rather than living in fear that your abuser will discover them, take them to work. If that's not an option and you feel most comfortable asking someone to store them for you, then ask a friend. Or, put book covers on them and ask your church secretary/librarian if you can confidentially keep them in an undisturbed area at the church (be creative!).

If you are uncertain as to whether your spouse's behavior should be classified as abusive, glance through Volume I Part I of

AN INVITATION FOR THE BEST USE OF THESE BOOKS

this book, which can help to clarify the definition of abuse. Even if your spouse's behavior doesn't fit the definition of abuse, if your spouse is consistently controlling and disrespectful, there is still a problem. Having a disrespectful and controlling relationship with your spouse is a problem. Controlling spouses fall on a range of behavioral tactics (as discussed in Volume I Part II Abuser Characteristics) from exhibiting only *some* tactics to exhibiting *most* of them. All the recurring thoughts and feelings that a victim experiences may still have an unhealthy effect. Abuse ranges from *mild* to *severe*; nevertheless, all abuse has the same impact on the victim (See Volume I Part III, Victim Characteristics). Additionally, examples of abusive relationships are cited throughout the books with stories of women who were once victims of abuse but now lead recovered lives—free from abuse. These stories are case scenarios that will not only help you to answer the question of whether your spouse's behavior is abusive, but they will also encourage you to realize that abuse is a preventable and treatable health problem which you can overcome!

Not all of the information written in these books will pertain to your abusive relationship. If there are parts of the books in which I describe the abuser or the victim, and those parts do not fit or apply to you or your relationship, it's alright to skip to the part that does apply. Not everyone has the same lifestyle; read what is most helpful to *your* specific circumstances or abusive relationship. I do not wish at any point in these books to cause you discomfort by telling you how your situation is. You are already bombarded with mind-control games; you don't need another person to tell you how you should think or act. I don't want to become a part of that very unhealthy pattern to which you have been subjected.

At the same time, I do not recommend that you skim read the books, as this can lead to a misinterpretation of the contents and message. Use each book as a guideline. Listen to what our Heavenly Father has inspired me to write and you to read. If it doesn't speak to you or your situation and does not re-create the abusive dynamics as they are played out in the particulars of your household, it doesn't apply. These books are structured in an encyclopedic topical form to allow you to identify the information you are searching for and to refer back to the sections that you can read later. They were created to conveniently accommodate an opportunity for you to access information quickly if you are in a crisis state.

Even if you skip the parts that do not apply, one truth does remain the same for all households that experience abuse: an abuser will alter your lifestyle and your mind so that *everything* becomes focused on him. The strategic way out of this abusive torment is to take charge of your person! Focus on you, and if children are involved, your children's well-being as well. It is imperative that you reclaim your person, stop dwelling on your abuser, and instead use that energy to *overcome* your abuse. Overcoming abuse is a daunting journey. I say it is a journey, not to further stress you, or to suggest that it is a never-ending rite of passage, but to communicate to you that it is a *process*. Processes that can, miraculously through supernatural power, evolve—and can be resolved! You must no longer carry this burden of an abusive relationship alone. The Lord invites you to lighten your burden (actually commands you to unburden yourself) when He says, "Take My yoke upon you and learn from Me, for I am gentle and lowly in heart, and you will find rest for your souls. For My yoke *is* easy and My burden is light" (Matthew 11:29-30). Our burdens are made lighter through His companionship!

After confiding in the Lord—the Good Shepherd ("I am the good shepherd." John 10:11a, "The LORD *is* my Shepherd; I shall not want" Psalm 23:1), you must follow up by confiding in *someone else* about your abusive relationship. It is like getting

AN INVITATION FOR THE BEST USE OF THESE BOOKS

an under-shepherd (a supportive assistant). If the sheriff has an undersheriff (deputy), so can you! Confiding in the Good Shepherd and someone else provides you with an under-shepherd; it is your first step to getting free and overcoming abuse.

You may feel guilty for speaking negatively to anyone about your spouse or ashamed of your spouse's abusive behavior. You may fear the person whom you tell will scrutinize you as to *why* you continue to tolerate this abuse. Perhaps the concern may be that you will not be believed because, after all, your spouse is such a hard-working family man in the eyes of the Church, employer, or his community. Regardless, in order to *heal* and to obtain *peace*, surrendering your abusive burden to the Lord and seeking support while reading these books is absolutely *necessary*. Some women (particularly those that have been coerced into near isolation) will feel extremely uncomfortable reading these books, which may generate unbearable feelings that have unconsciously or consciously been blocked. These books may initiate leaving the comfort zone of *denial* when overwhelming realizations about your abuse are brought to the surface. In spite of the fact that your trust level is tender and has been violated by those that have abused you, I still highly recommend that you consider contacting someone you trust, as an *under-shepherd*. If it's safe, reach out to this trustworthy person.

Pray about who that person may be, and then make the contact. This person may be a friend, family member, pastor, pastor's wife, church member, counselor, or an organization (organizations are listed under "Resources" at the end of this book). I realize *trusting* someone as a support system is extremely difficult for some women because there is a *fear* of the reaction and judgment from that person (when you tell them your secrets about being mistreated by your spouse). However, having a support system is a *vital* part of problem-solving and accountability.

Having this support will expedite your healing process in overcoming your abuse.

Consequently, these books are written in three volumes. Volumes I and II are written for you—the abused. Volume III is for lay people and those in the helping professions who are the support system for victims of abuse. There is no rule that you as a recovering victim of abuse cannot proceed to read Volume III; vice versa, if a helper wants to grow in the knowledge of the dynamics of abuse, the abuser profile, and the characteristics of victims of abuse, he/she can read Volume I and II.

So, let's get started and move forward on this journey to overcome your abuse!

> **"God *is* with you in all that you do."**
> **Genesis 21:22**

PART I

SEVEN TYPES OF ABUSE

Abuse Defined

WHAT IS "ABUSE," AND how do I know if I am being abused? Most family violence researchers and abuse experts, such as psychotherapist and author, Susan Forward, Ph.D., answer this question by defining abuse as: "any behavior that is intended to control and subjugate another human being through the use of fear, humiliation, and verbal or physical assaults."

Abuse can happen to *any* of our female next of kin because abuse knows no socioeconomic class, education, culture, race, or creed. There are many different types and levels of abuse: emotional, physical, sexual, economic, and spiritual. Abuse can range from mild sarcasm and ridiculing, to severe, physical attacks. Just like when a child is abused and the abuse impairs the child's ability to develop and grow normally, in the same way a spouse's abusive behavior interferes with and damages the *victim's* potential to grow. Abuse is abuse—it does not matter how often it occurs. The fact that it occurred makes it abuse. There are legalistic terms that are used to describe the abuse that has occurred, such as: one-time event (lost control of temper and hasn't attacked since then), infrequent (only loses temper when undergoing stressful events), and substance-related (only loses temper when under the influence of drugs and/or alcohol).

Unfortunately, these terms can play into the victim's and public's mindset regarding minimizing the trauma to the victim and the criminal act of abuse. I have had several victims share their trauma over *the one-time* abusive incident by which, years later, they never regained the trust in their spouse, even after forgiving him, for fear he would attack again. One patient's abuser did indeed attack again to her death—fifteen years later when he lost his temper after being given a pink ticket at work. These legalistic terms can unduly infer that because the abuse is not ongoing, that the victim remains unharmed and not at risk for future harm. These suggested terms to define and categorize abuse lead to the victim's and society's *normalization* of abuse as a part of working out the relationship. Further, these suggested types of abuse that a victim may have encountered fail to recognize the *atmosphere of terror* that is common to most abusive relationships, an atmosphere that is not conducive to working out the relationship.

Most of the time if a victim is involved in an abusive relationship, it is accepted as "normal" because she doesn't know any different and assumes that's just the way it's supposed to be. By the time the victim realizes that she is involved in an abusive relationship, she hardly notices it because it has become an ordinary occurrence in her marriage. She has been desensitized to the difference between a loving, healthy marriage and an abusive one. In some cases, the victim has been conditioned to adapt to abusive relationships because that's all she has ever known. Perhaps she was raised in an abusive environment or has never experienced being treated with respect in a romantic relationship. Whichever the case may be, it is the abuser, *not the victim*, who *creates* the abusive relationship. The abuser creates the abusive relationship through certain behaviors and attitudes such as undermining and ridiculing the victim's complaints of mistreatment, by emotionally or physically intimidating her, or sexually assaulting her.

What behavioral tactics does your abuser use to intimidate *you*? Depending on the abuser's personality profile, he may use one or several of the following tactics:

Swearing, sarcasm, inducing guilt, interrupting whenever you express your thoughts or feelings, sulking, stonewalling and giving you the silent treatment, out-shouting/yelling, giving you the middle finger, pointing his finger consistently at you like a gun, distorting/twisting what you say, not listening/refusing to respond, accusing you of doing what *he* does, yelling and when you ask him *not* to yell he says you're the one that started the yelling simply because you're defending yourself from *his* yelling attacks, using a tone of final authority, locking you in/confining you, disconnecting your home phone or confiscating your cellphone.

Frequent criticism that is harsh and undeserved, being a martyr as if he's the victim, cracking jokes/laughing out loud at your comment/opinion/perspective, when you confide in him he turns your grievances around to use against you, focuses on *your* faults when you address a concern, accuses you of thinking the way that he thinks, changing the subject to *his* grievances, smirking, rolling his eyes, using contemptuous facial expressions, bad-mouthing you to friends and/or family, soliciting friends' and/or family's support to turn against you, building up and showing his affection to your children/family members/friends as preferred over you, or totally denying and distorting what is happening or happened in an earlier interaction (reversing reality).

In order to sustain your reality, maintain a journal. Document your experiences with your abuser so that when your abuser attempts to drive you insane with his suddenly "good person" composure or uses his head games, you can do a reality check by back-tracking who *you* really are, what *he* really says, and how *he* truly behaves.

Am I Being Abused?
If any of the aforementioned abuser behavioral tactics are present in your interactions with your spouse, *you are* involved in an abusive relationship.

Let's verify your conclusion through a personal exercise. Stop reading right now and instead track down the abusive behavior patterns in your relationship. Take a sheet of paper and fold it into three columns. Or, if you're able to privately use your phone, create three note columns. This may sound very elementary, but it's powerful in its astounding results. Label column one "abusive behavior," column two "what I felt," column three "how did I deal with it?" Take a thorough inventory and think back as early as you allow yourself to recollect. Write down in the list which abusive behaviors you have experienced (that are like the behavioral tactics that have been discussed).

Do you find an abusive behavioral pattern? Do you see how you usually felt? Did this abusive behavior consistently cause you to feel disrespected, devalued, and controlled? Did you do anything about it? If the answer is "no," why? Perhaps you pretended it did not happen or hoped it would not happen again, or maybe it was easier to think that it would eventually take care of itself. Or maybe, when you attempted to do something about it, he escalated and the situation got worse, so you backed off from bringing it up again. Maybe his in-between "good" hours or days gave you false hope that he was no longer going to disrespect,

SEVEN TYPES OF ABUSE

devalue, and control you. Is it possible that you felt powerless to address the problem with your abuser?

What excuses have you given to yourself or others about your spouse's abusive behavior toward you? In some form of denial, you might have thought or stated, "I'm just having a bad day and he had a hard day at work," "It's my fault," "I deserved it," "I should not have instigated him with my complaint about his attitude," "That's just the way he is and it's not up to me to change him," "I should be grateful because he's a good provider, he's good to the kids, and he's just tired," "Don't be ridiculous, my spouse has never hit me or hurt me that way, he's just had a rough childhood, and he can be a little controlling when he gets angry, that's all," and "I just need to *forgive* him is all."

The *truth* is that the list that you created in this exercise is real, and right now, what you need to do with the list is to allow yourself to *admit* that you are in an abusive relationship. It is painfully difficult, but do the following anyway. Number one: push away all of the excuses in your mind—do not justify or minimize your spouse's abusive behaviors toward you. Number two: do not rationalize that it was really not that bad—and after all, it could be worse. Look at your list. Indeed, all of those abusive behaviors *happened*, and it is as bad as you felt. See for yourself; look at column number one and two. Keep this list where you can confidentially look back on it whenever your abuser refuses to see your view, denies his abusive behavioral pattern, or attempts to confuse you.

If you don't have the energy or don't want to devote time to doing this personal exercise to create your list, use a litmus test to identify if you're in an abusive relationship. Have you ever smelled the stench of a dead rat? If not, think about the worst smell that you have ever encountered. Got that well-thought-out smell? Would you say that your relationship smells like a dead rat (or other repugnant odor) *or* the fresh fragrance after a rainfall?

Being involved in an abusive relationship can emotionally, physically, and spiritually drain you. Sometimes you may even feel mentally depleted and unbalanced after experiencing the harrowing effects of cruelty. What you are feeling is *normal* for someone who is being abused. Abuse is similar to being consistently interrogated. This inventory list is not intended to be maintained as a list of wrongs but to be used by you as a support system, a reality therapy tool. It is also to serve as a reminder that a functional marriage and family does *not* have patterns of abusive behaviors. Functional marriages and families have boundaries in place as to how they will respectfully relate to one another. It's tempting for victims and society to be desensitized from what a functional relationship is like if dysfunctional (abusive) relating has been ignored or accepted as the norm. Before identifying and defining the various types of abuse, let's be clear on the difference between a dysfunctional and functional family.

Dysfunctional vs. Functional Family
The June 28, 2013 U.S. Department of Justice, Bureau of Justice Statistics reported that four women and three children die each day as a result of abuse. The U.S. Office on Violence Against Women (OVW) confirms that domestic violence is the leading cause of injury to women in the U.S. This is a nationwide study; the size of the study and the number of deaths speak to the definitiveness of the findings. What is one of the factors that allows abuse to occur and persist? Dysfunctional families. As has already been mentioned, many abusive spouses and victims have been programmed from childhood with deeply malingrained abusive behavioral patterns. For instance, the sons of violent parents have a rate of spousal abuse one thousand percent greater

than those of non-violent parents. Only ten percent of violent couples have a family history that was nonviolent.

It is predicted by research statistics that in *most* of the couples who are involved in abusive relationships, one or both spouses have had a dysfunctional family background. A person raised in a dysfunctional family may suffer from any of the various types of abuse. A dysfunctional family usually deviates from the social behavior expected of society's norms; these behaviors tend to be negative, abnormal influences which impair individuals' and society's functioning. The term "dysfunctional family" basically refers to a family that relates to one another in immature, improper ways, ultimately impairing the growth and relational skills of a family member(s). This impairment may affect *all* family members even if there's only one family member that is identified as having a problem. Problems in a dysfunctional family are either denied, evaded, or are handled inappropriately or in destructive ways.

The term "functional family" refers to a family that practices mature and balanced relational skills between parents and their children, *respecting* one another's individuality and encouraging the development and growth of each family member. The key word is *respect*—each family member is consistently *respectful* of one another regardless of differences. Personality and abilities, or lack thereof, are differences in functional family members that are celebrated, not shunned. Respect includes role-modeling as parents and family members, as well as the ability to use common courtesies like "thank you," "you're welcome," "please," "I'm sorry," or "I made a mistake; please forgive me."

Using common courtesies naturally extends itself into a *clear* definition of boundaries. Dysfunctional parents and their family members do not initiate an apology and *almost never* seek forgiveness or offer forgiveness. It is extremely difficult for a dysfunctional family member to admit to making a mistake(s) as they feel *entitled* or *deny* overstepping boundaries. Clear boundaries include being sensitive and adhering to the private emotional or personal space of each family member. Each member has a defined role as an individual and is appreciated for this, as expressed by treating each one with courtesy and apologizing when courtesy is not demonstrated and boundaries are crossed. Whenever a problem is identified in a functional family, parents and family members will address the problem openly, confide in one another, and offer unconditional supportive guidance.

In functional families, parents support one another when addressing problems. Parents of functional families work together as a co-parenting team; these parents find solutions to family problems together and thus have a special marital bond. Functional parents encourage siblings and other relatives to nourish their relationships through sharing times together and problem solving any miscommunication one-on-one, instead of interfering and getting in the middle of their problems. Functional families feel emotionally safe and free to share their thoughts, feelings, and aspirations without fear of induced guilt or rejection of their communication. If a problem(s) arises, no matter how stressful or traumatic, functional families work together to be supportive, heal, and recover, encouraging one another to restored spiritual, emotional, and physical health. This response, as opposed to a *negative reaction,* lets each family member know that it's acceptable and appropriate to become independent at each age milestone, but it's also acceptable to return to the family for spiritual, emotional, and/or physical safety when nurturing through problem-solving is needed.

Changing and growing is allowed and embraced in functional families, whereas in dysfunctional families there is an overprotective supervision (control) and family members are *not* encouraged or allowed to navigate independently through their chronological milestones. Dysfunctional family members prefer symbiotic relationships through which they can be enmeshed with the family member. Dysfunctional parents and family members use two forms of control: through *indifference* (direct or indirect neglect or ignoring) of the family member, or the constant bossiness and *interfering* with the family member's daily life activities as they are organized and preferred. A dysfunctional parent/family member stops any talking from happening by not allowing anything to be said through interruptions, joking, sarcasm, creating confusion, being critical, intimidating, instigating arguing, or simply saying, "I'm done with all the talking!" (and sometimes just walking away). Sometimes, there's a disowning of the family member and a request made not to ever talk to them again.

A family member from a dysfunctional family just wants to be allowed to talk and cry whenever experiencing hurt feelings, for feelings to be validated, to stop being told what to do with every moment of their life, and to be allowed to emotionally grow up; they just want to feel free to be themselves as they are able to be with total strangers. In functional families, there is a mutually respectful trust that is established from childhood to adulthood. Dysfunctional parents do not trust their children to grow into adulthood independently of their ongoing surveillance. Functional parents do protect their children, but they do so without false concerns and undue prohibitions; they teach their children chronologically along the way about life, vices, how to make healthy choices, and how to protect themselves as they become independent individuals.

In dysfunctional families there is usually a parent that interacts in inappropriate, highly anxious, immature, destructive ways, thereby disrupting the family system, while the other parent passively allows the dysfunctional parent to carry on at the expense of family members. In some extremes, both parents are openly dysfunctional toward one another and the family as a whole. Dysfunctional families don't make use of opportunities to improve communication whenever there's a misunderstanding; they operate under a defensive argumentative stance. The simplest way to identify a dysfunctional family is to notice that they live by an unspoken and unwritten rule: no speaking about thoughts and feelings is permitted. If they speak, they use an accusatory, guilt-inducing "you" statement such as, "You hurt me!" instead of the functional use of an "I" statement such as, "I feel hurt." Some dysfunctional families use the silent treatment on one another for indefinite periods when angry or holding a grudge toward a family member(s). Mostly, *if* they talk, it is not in a normal tone but through scolding harshly and yelling, which usually ends up either in a screaming rage, agitation, and/or with physical aggression.

It is also typical in dysfunctional families that a family member(s) may not receive celebration, praise, or recognition for an accomplishment(s). Functional families routinely acknowledge their family member's achievements even just to communicate worth—to convey how much that family member is valued. Compliments are naturally and genuinely given in functional families; they are restricted in dysfunctional families. Dysfunctional family members may compliment and even brag about a family member to others, but they will not give the personal recognition directly to the family member. Dysfunctional families spend limited amounts of bonding time together, whereas functional families cherish their special times around one another and make efforts to plan meals, events, projects, and recreational times together; functional families work and play together.

Functional families are generous with hugs, saying, "I love you" to their loved ones; it does not come naturally for dysfunctional family members to hug or express love verbally. In some dysfunctional families, members are not told that they are loved, but they are expected to assume that they are. Some dysfunctional families are rigid and expect their family members to be perfect and don't allow room for mistakes and growing; they are authoritarian and punitive when mistakes are made. Functional families have a balance in making room for mistakes and expect the family member to learn from natural consequences. They don't rescue; they set limits on any patterns of breaking the expected norm.

Some dysfunctional families go the other extreme and praise the negative and "out of the norm" behaviors of their family members; they are quick to rescue and defend their next of kin even when knowing that their loved one has done something wrong. These types of dysfunctional families appear to be functional on the exterior because they don't ever show discord or symptoms of being disgruntled; everyone likes being around their family because they seem to always get along so well. They refute any conversation focusing on family problems and prefer to deny and to coddle any family member that is being identified as having a problem. That coddled family member's maturity and future growth is impaired because they are not ever able to take full responsibility for their irresponsible behaviors as they can count on being rescued and blaming another for their responsibility. It is a customary norm in this type of coddling dysfunctional family to request of anyone that approaches them about resolving a family problem that it's *never* to be brought up again. Their typical family one-liner is, "And, we shall never speak of this again!" When a parent silences a family member or other with "and we shall never speak of this," it is a power-control tactic to intimidate, an unhealthy need to be the one in control of the others' expressions, natural thoughts, and feelings.

Crying is discouraged in most dysfunctional families; family members are to "quit the crying" when upset about an incident. It's as if in dysfunctional families there's an unspoken commandment not to show or speak out thoughts and feelings. This, in turn, denies personal growth and stunts the emotional maturity of family members. This puts these family members at risk for isolation whenever experiencing stress or pain; they tend to make themselves invisible. These family members spend most of their lives (sometimes unbeknownst to them) searching for the nourishment of genuine, healthy communication without reproach, intimidation, lying, induced guilt, humiliation, intense rebuttal/argumentativeness, unusual distortions, rejection, and projections. Dysfunctional family members are unable to self-disclose angry thoughts or hurt feelings in a respectful way; however, they long to be heard, understood, and to be taken seriously, as they do suffer inconceivably from this deprivation. Functional families accept when someone is hurt or angry and allow crying. These families have learned how to express and receive their deepest pain and disappointments in a respectful, managed manner instead of having a shouting match or physically attacking one another.

The following is a list of the seven types of abuse that are most commonly experienced by victims in dysfunctional relationships:

Emotional Abuse
Emotional abuse consists of a *regular pattern* of behaviors exhibited by the *abuser* which are *mentally* hurtful to the victim. This pattern of verbal and emotional abuse systematically humiliates and degrades the victim's self-worth. The abuser's behaviors or comments may include consistently insulting, ridiculing, or belittling the victim. The abuser may threaten the victim with bodily harm if she does not do as he expects. The abuser usually wears down the victim with demeaning criticisms and fault-finding remarks such as "you're worthless, stupid, slow, silly, ugly, skinny, fat, lazy, lame, and useless" or may call her foul

names. The abuser may choose not to overtly call her names and instead make negative remarks aimed at rejecting the victim. An abuser may overtly make consistent, favorable remarks about others to exclude or communicate to the victim that she's not favored. Abusers can degrade a victim while smiling and disguise their offensive remarks in the form of a joke then comment that she is just "imagining something negative was said or done," is "too sensitive," "can't take a joke," or "I was just being sarcastic, I really didn't mean it." Abusers' insults can be about the victim, and/or her family, heritage, culture, race, social class, or friends.

All of the abusers' offenses may be done privately or both privately and in front of others, as well as both online and offline using electronic devices (digital abuse). Whether privately or publicly, the abuser is relentlessly saying that she can't do anything right. This is a crime of the heart that the abuser commits against the victim; he attacks her heart daily. The abuser is saying persistently that she is unfit as a spouse, mother, or any other role that she attempts to engage in. An abuser pretends to be listening when the victim is talking and will later not recall a word she said, but he remembers what others say to him. Listening to *him* is more important, as he feels entitled to her full attention. Abusers humiliate their victim by having to repeat what they have already said. They use the excuse that they "forgot" what the victim said, when indeed it was ignored or never heard. The abuser is usually insensitive; he does not validate and prefers to ignore the victim's feelings. Some abusers whisper threats or use intimidating gestures such as glaring, frowning, raising eyebrows, getting closer to the victim's face, or purposely brushing past her and having her walk behind him en route to home, tightening his facial muscles, and turning red with rage while eyeballing the victim, or other nonverbal language to communicate to the victim that she can anticipate negative consequences when she gets home.

Abusers can be very demanding and nitpicky. Some will also make trivial demands which are nonsensical, but if those demands are not met, the victim suffers the consequences. What follows is a series of other trivial demands because when the original trivial demand does not satisfy him, the rules keep changing, and changing, to the point that the victim does not know *how* to please her demanding abuser's expectations. Abusers steer and monopolize the victim's conversation with inconsequential details. The abuser elaborates on paltry things and the victim can't seem to get away from his paltriness of mind. An abuser will make the victim feel like she is going "crazy." There are times when the abuser says kind words to the victim, and within the same breath, he immediately takes back the nice things he said and gives her a mouthful of hateful words.

The victim may confront the abuser about his behavior or ask the abuser a question, and she remembers his answer. However, in the next hour or day he may deny ever saying or doing it. After multiple incidents whereby the abuser denies that he has said or done something, even though these have been important times and the victim has full recollection of these occurrences, the abuser begins to cause her to doubt her own judgment. It becomes difficult for the victim to resolve this realm of confusion that she finds herself in; she's so out of balance with deciphering all of his mind-games. The abuser thrives in keeping her off-balance and in bringing her down—as that is his aim. Over and above, the victim's trust level of the abuser begins to deteriorate. Trust is a strong requirement for a healthy marital relationship; the mindset that the abuser brings into the marriage makes him impossible to trust and get along with. The victim has to nearly shut down in order to avoid arguing about every little detail of their lives.

To add to her dejection, an abuser will betray her confidences. A spouse is supposed to be one's confidante, so it's natural to trust him and make oneself vulnerable when revealing the inner self. Abusers violate trust—without consent they expose the victim to others in her presence or absence; this is a form of emotional abuse. The abuser may withhold warmth, affection, appreciation, approval, or attention, even when the victim is hurt or ill. An abuser will tell others how proud he is of her, but he won't tell her. In some cases, the abuser makes over other women by gazing at them, openly flirting with them, or flaunting infidelity. The abuser may also justify infidelity through a passive-aggressive method of "just having friends" via email or his social media accounts. This type of abuse may include the abuser's participation in the use of pornographic outlets through the internet or literature. Covert abusers are prone to have "emotional affairs" through their addictions, which they justify in their minds as not infidelity because the actions don't involve attaching themselves to a person but rather an inanimate outlet such as spending most of their free time on gambling, watching television, or favored hobbies. As a result of this emotional abuse (neglect), the victim often feels invisible, unwanted, devalued, and undeserving.

Some abusers engage in a combination of emotionally-abusive acts, and others reserve infidelity as their prime choice for emotionally abusing their wife. The abuser may be a hard-working provider and well-mannered gentleman in every area as a husband—except with infidelity. A victim of infidelity is deeply chagrined by the abuser. Infidelity is a form of abuse that immediately targets the victim's sense of self-worth and leads to all of the symptoms of abuse: hurt, humiliation, anxiety, helplessness, depression, hopelessness, distorted self-blame, and a state of confusion. The abuser is not the only contributor to the victim's state of confusion, but the victim may receive counsel from others that are not knowledgeable about infidelity being an emotional attack on the victim. Their undermining of the severity of her infidelity abuse only serves to confuse her traumatic feelings with the denying of her spouse's abuse.

The trauma of infidelity is as devastating and damaging to the victim as a physical attack. Infidelity by the abuser puts the victim's and children's health and well-being at risk. Those lay persons or professionals that label infidelity as a "mistake," "one-night stand," "midlife crisis," or blame it on the abuser's dysfunctional background deny the truth that the abuser made a willful choice based on his disrespect, self-entitlement, and control of the victim. Not acknowledging that the infidelity is emotional abuse toward the victim and recommending that the couple in the abusive relationship work through the infidelity to recreate their marriage is the *same* as recommending that they work through his physical assaults of her. Some persons will advise that forgiving and forgetting is recommended and that infidelity actually *strengthens* the marriage *and* the relationship with the children. Their basis for this recommendation is the assumption that infidelity can transform a marriage into a better marriage. There is no evidence that a marriage can be strengthened or transformed for the better by a victim being violated and emotionally attacked. But there is evidence that a victim's life can be transformed for the better when she leaves her abusive relationship. Infidelity abuse or any other emotional abuse *does not* strengthen a marriage.

Infidelity kills the trust level that the marriage foundation is based on; the victim grieves that loss whether the infidelity is a one-time or ongoing occurrence. Some will state that she should forgive her spouse because, after all, he has only been unfaithful one time. Forgiving the abuser does not erase the memory or trust that was lost. Some will state that the victim has not truly forgiven if she maintains the memory of the emotional abuse. She's *not* responsible for her brain's function that stores memory. She is only responsible for choosing not to dwell on that memory which will always be there. It is a traumatic memory. It is not a memory like yesterday's sunset; it's a memory of deception, an intimate betrayal which has caused emotional destruction. It is not up to others to save a victim's unhealthy, abusive marriage. Others may not save the marriage, but they can assist the victim in saving herself from herself.

Whether the abuser engages in infidelity once or more than once is *insignificant*—what is of overarching *significance* is that he chose to emotionally abuse the victim. In the same way that it would be determined if he had physically assaulted her, the diagnosis of his physical assault of her would not change if he assaulted her once or several times—assault is assault. Infidelity is infidelity. Infidelity is not about soulmates; it is about sin mates engaging in a self-gratifying, bogus relationship. It *is* emotional abuse, whether the abuser engages in an extramarital affair emotionally, physically, or over the internet with another person(s), animal (bestiality), or through pornography (virtual infidelity). In situations whereby the victim experiences recurring cycles of infidelity, the abuser may voice guilt, remorse, and even repentance which leads the marriage to function well periodically; but then as usual, there are *other* episodes of infidelity abuse which intermittently arise and interfere in the healthy functioning of the marital relationship.

This reoccurring emotional abuse through infidelity is a direct result of the abuser's refusal to acknowledge the pain he is preying on the victim and their children. This is an emotional statement the abuser makes regarding his insensitivity toward the victim and his family's suffering. Infidelity is a manipulative, deceptive, self-serving, calculated, emotional abuse tactic of the abuser. Like all humans, the abuser has a conscience. An abuser is not forced to be unfaithful to his wife; he can choose respect for his wife and say "no" to infidelity. The abuser is not only electing to disrespect his wife but also disrespecting the woman with whom he's having an affair by offering his married self to her as if she deserves an abuser. Some folks in society think that infidelity (adultery) is only about a biblical commandment. They are not aware that there are U.S. laws on adultery and that in some states it is a crime. In the military adultery is a punishable criminal offense under the Uniform Code of Military Justice (UCMJ) no matter in what state or country the affair takes place. Adultery in the military is defined as sexual relations between the person who is married and someone who is not their spouse or if the person is unmarried but has sexual relations with a person who is married or legally separated. Legal separation from their spouse is not a legal defense to adultery.

My colleagues and I have worked with victims who have been told that reconciliation with the abuser after an infidelity episode(s) is an act of courage and that it's an honorable thing to do for the sake of the marriage and the children. However, we have not met any victim that has been emotionally abused through infidelity that described herself with feelings of self-respect and courage. The victims that have elected to return to the abuser after infidelity generally feel humiliated, betrayed, and afraid. They fear losing their home life security/lifestyle, and they fear that he cannot be trusted and that he will be unfaithful again—there is no valor in that. There is no bravery in reconciling with an abuser. The woman who elects to reconcile with her emotional abuser becomes an unwitting victim of mental wife abuse. Whether it is infidelity or any other type of abuse, a woman who is abused no longer feels safe in the presence of her spouse or in her home. When safety is threatened or compromised, it is called abuse. When the victim is encouraged or instructed to reconcile with her emotional abuser, it promotes an unhealthy dependence on him. This makes for a co-dependent, unhealthy marriage whereby he emotionally controls her, and she feels a need to allow it instead of choosing an abuse-free life. (See Volume I Part III for an amplified definition of a codependent relationship.)

Some abusers may go to the other extreme and never be unfaithful to their wife but instead smother her, monopolize her time, and are irrationally, insanely possessive or jealous. Sometimes the possessiveness is obsessive and veiled with concern for the well-being of the victim. Occasionally, he may stalk her. The abuser may isolate the victim and forbid her to socialize with others, visit family, go to school, work, and make any plans or decisions. This isolation creates a dependent atmosphere—away from a support system—where the victim can be programmed to be willing to accept her maltreatment. Emotional abuse can involve manipulation of the victim, forcing her to do things she does not want to do. This can include hurting or threatening to hurt the children or pets, and threatening abandonment while blackmailing to take the children and/or property away. The abuser may make threats about killing himself, the victim, or her loved ones if she doesn't comply with his requests.

Neglect and Types of Neglect
Neglect is a passive-aggressive form of emotional abuse in which the abuser is responsible to provide care and protection for the victim but fails to provide such care. The expectation for care, protection, or emotional responsiveness may exist as a result of an assumed responsibility or a legal or contractual agreement, such as a marital and parental commitment. Neglect may include the failure to provide sufficient protection, nourishment, medical care, and economic support or the failure to fulfill other needs which the victim legitimately requests. Some examples of legitimate requests are as follows: when the victim makes a request that the abuser not stonewall her, not view pornography, not expose the children to inappropriate activities, or requests that he spend time with the children.

The term "neglect" applies when necessary responsible actions are passively or deliberately withheld by the abuser. Neglect basically means a failure of the abuser who is responsible to provide care or supervision to make a reasonable effort to protect his wife and children from abuse. The abuser's neglect subjects the victim to significant emotional distress, which leads to ongoing unreasonable discomfort and ultimately severe loss of personal dignity. This places the victim at risk for threatening her spiritual, emotional, and physical well-being. Most professionals identify five types of neglect when assessing a victim: emotional, physical, educational, medical, and financial.

Emotional Neglect
Emotional (psychological) neglect includes actions such as chronic disengagement from the victim while alone with the victim or in the children's presence, refusing or failing to provide needed mental health care, undermining the presence of the victim and the children, and withholding affection. Emotional neglect is typically the most complex and difficult circumstance to substantiate in a legal context and is usually reported secondary to other abuse or neglect types.

Abusive behaviors considered to be emotional neglectful maltreatment include:
- **Ignoring**—Consistent failure to respond to the victim's need to be listened to, nurtured, encouraged, and protected, or failure to acknowledge the victim's presence.
- **Rejecting**—Denying and actively refusing to respond to the victim's emotional, physical, economic, or spiritual needs. Not accepting the birth of their child, not acknowledging, or stating their child is not wanted.
- **Verbally Discounting**—Consistently minimizing the victim's verbal interactions.

- **Isolating**—Preventing the victim and children from having normal social contact with him.
- **Monopolizing**—Creating a climate of silence, awkwardness, inferiority, or discomfort in the home by playing on the victim's or children's feelings.

Emotional neglect involves saying things or behaving in ways that communicate to the victim that she is insufficient, only valued as far as the abuser's needs are concerned, and is basically unloved and worthless. The abuser can do this through various means: by being silent or silencing her, not allowing her to express her views or opinions, accusing her of harboring negative feelings, mocking, and denying or ridiculing what she says when she tries to communicate. Spurred on by a burning, spiteful, argumentative competition, he's always looking to be one better than the victim when she contributes her opinion. An abuser can quickly attack his victim through a jab in his malicious words; she can literally feel like he just stabbed her heart. The children seeing or hearing their mother being ill-treated is also a form of emotional abuse to both the child and the mother. This exposure to their mother's neglect exploits and may frighten the children, which may set them up for future destructive emotional problems. There are various types of abuse that on some level include emotional abuse. However, neglect can also occur on its own.

The following are some indications that the abuser is neglecting his wife and/or children. An abuser who is possibly guilty of victim or child neglect:
- appears not to care about the victim's and child's happiness or general well-being;
- openly/passive-aggressively and relentlessly berates, belittles, and blames the victim or child;
- expresses verbally/through actions that he shows little concern about the victim's or children's needs;
- indirectly or directly rejects the victim;

- refuses *any* guidance, assistance, or interaction regarding his problem of neglect.

The following are some signs that a victim and/or her children may be experiencing neglect:
- The child may exhibit behavior that ranges in extremes of compliance, passivity, assertiveness, aggressiveness, meekness, or neediness.
- A neglected child may mimic the abuser, such as silencing or parenting others, or may regress into an infantile mode, such as rocking back and forth, exhibiting frustrated head banging, or isolating self and curling up in a fetal position.
- The victim or child may self-mutilate or attempt to regain control of his or her life through overeating/undereating.
- The victim or child may become depressed, suicidal, or make an attempt at self harm.
- The victim or child may feel and/or say that they have no attachment to the abuser.
- The victim or child may periodically resort to day-dreaming or excessive use of the internet or audio/visual entertainment as an escape from the pain of neglect.

Physical Neglect
Physical neglect accounts for the majority of reported maltreatment. Physical neglect usually involves the abuser not being willing to provide basic necessities such as nourishment, clothing, and shelter. Failure or unwillingness to provide basic necessities threatens and endangers the victim's physical and mental health. Physical neglect includes the physical and emotional deprivation of the children through indirect or direct abandonment, inadequate supervision, invalid kicking out of a child from the home, or not providing for the children's safety and physical and emotional needs.

Educational Neglect

Educational neglect of a victim is when the abuser forbids the victim to pursue any form of spiritual or academic knowledge. The abuser may look upon the victim disapprovingly if she insists on growing educationally and may threaten her provision and well-being if she defies his refusal to allow her to learn. Educational child neglect involves the failure of the abuser to enroll a child of mandatory school age in school or provide appropriate home schooling or necessary special educational needs. This encourages the child to engage in truancy. Educational neglect deprives the child of acquiring basic life skills and leads to the display of disruptive behavior, learning disabilities, and school dropout.

Medical Neglect

Medical neglect is the failure or refusal to provide for the victim's or children's health care (even if financially able to do so), thus placing the victim or child at risk for infection, of being disfigured, disabled, or dying. Concern is valid not only when the abuser refuses medical care for the victim in an emergency or for an acute diagnosis, but also when he *ignores* medical or mental health recommendations for her or the children and they have a treatable chronic disease or disability, which results in significant deterioration or frequent doctor's visits or hospitalizations. Medical neglect leads to the victim's poor overall health and the risk of multiple medical problems for her and her children.

Financial Neglect

Although financial neglect is highly correlated with poverty, there is a distinction between an abuser's inability to provide the needed financial provision based on cultural norms (the lack of financial resources) and an abuser that knows the needs yet is reluctant or refuses to provide financially—and a spouse or parent that is not being intentionally neglectful. When victims and children are in need of nutrition, emotional support, educational, or medical services, and poverty limits the resources to adequately provide necessities for them, state or government programs and services are available to help provide for these needs. Non-neglectful spouses usually cooperate with these programs.

In the cases of intentional financial neglect, the abuser refuses to provide for healthcare insurance, but if he does, he refuses to pay the bills for the health services received by the victim and children. At this point the victim may have to seek assistance from the state and judicial system. A victim can seek assistance for herself and can ask a child protection service agency to step in and seek a court order for physical, emotional (mental health), educational, financial assistance, or medical treatment for her children in order to prevent a life-threatening illness, disability, or disfigurement. There are preventive wellness care programs for her children.

Consequences of Neglect
Neglect can carry on in the victim's life. These fall into many long-term symptoms, including low self-esteem, hoarding, eating disorders, depression, and even suicidal ideation. The various types of neglect *all* have mental or physical consequences. Information processing and brain functioning can also be affected by neglect. Neglect is mostly associated with the effects on the victim mentally, which can lead to the feeling of rejection and being unwanted. Neglect can affect the body physically by affecting health, sometimes leading to chronic medical problems.

Neglect is an emotional abandonment. It is a quiet disdain for the victim—which the abuser expresses through his emotional desertion. An abuser who neglects his wife and children has an unsung family. A neglectful abuser treats his victim coldly, with apathy and indifference, as she goes unnoticed and ignored, through his heart-rending rejection. The abuser overlooks the victim and brushes her aside with a failure to look after her, leaving her uncared for and offering to the children only a lack of proper care. The neglectful abuser is emotionless and careless about the victim's inner needs of her heart. An abuser that neglects is detached, poker-faced, and inexpressive. Negligent abusers are aloof and cold-blooded toward their victim—they are expressionless. Neglectful abusers pay no attention to the victim or children; this type of abuser makes certain that the marriage deteriorates and ends up in a place of disrepair.

A neglectful abuser conveys that he has disuse for the marriage—and the victim. This, in turn, prompts the victim to feel useless as a wife, and she begins to feel that she lacks something in order to measure up to his attention. The abuser's attitude is an air of unconcern and heedlessness regarding the victim and children. This disrespectful disregard and inattention to his wife and children leads them to feel emotionally deprived. The victim and children experience and feel untended to, undervalued, unappreciated and therefore maltreated. Ultimately the abuser's irresponsibility with his relationship to the victim and children leads him to become delinquent as a husband and father. The victim and children may end up feeling mentally forsaken.

Neglect can have severe psychological consequences. In general, in an abusive relationship, there is also neglect and unresponsiveness to the children's basic emotional needs. The abuser's detachment from the victim and children may destroy the marital attachment and can harm the children's development of bonding and attachment to the abusive parent. Neglect may cause children's expectations to be the same when they get older (repeating the cycle of abuse). A lack of parental availability can result in a child's immature coping skills with difficulties in problem solving and the proper development of social relationships.

Many pioneers and current seasoned professionals in the field of abuse believe that emotional abuse may have longer lasting effects on the victim than physical abuse. If a victim has been emotionally abused, it is clinically agreed that no other injuries to the heart are more painful to her. This is because when a victim repeatedly hears only destructive comments about herself, she may internalize these comments and allow them to become a part of her self-image. Patricia Murphy, Ph.D., a counselor and rehabilitation specialist, works with women to help them rebuild their lives after abuse. She states, "When we hear over and over that we are worthless and incompetent, we begin not only to believe it, but to hear it repeating over and over in our minds." In some cases, the victim leaves the psychologically-abusive spouse only to return to him in hopes that he will change as he says he will. Studies have been done on victims of abuse that have a history and pattern of multiple breakups and makeups, resulting in the victim's diagnosis of mental health challenges with anxiety and depression. These research studies find that victims of psychological abuse have an increased chance of experiencing anxiety and depression when the emotional abuse is left untreated and remains unresolved.

Physical Abuse
Physical abuse (even if it only happens once) is shoving, pushing, poking, shaking, throwing things, slapping, grabbing, biting, covering your mouth, pulling hair, hitting, blocking your path, holding you against a wall or piece of furniture, refusing to let you out of his car/refusing to get out of your car, restricting/restraining your coming and going, smothering/choking, kicking, burning, raising a fist at you, punching, headlocking, beating, rape, any form of contact with the victim's body with intent to control and intimidate, and any other act intended to injure, hurt, endanger, or inflict physical pain. Research results show that victims subjected to a pattern of physical abuse have

a greater chance of experiencing increased anger over their victimization the longer they remain in their victim role.

- The American Medical Association's research indicates that one out of three females is a victim of violence by a boyfriend or spouse at some point in their lifetime.
- The U.S. Surgeon General warns that assaults by male abusers are the number one cause of injury to females between the ages fifteen and forty-four.
- The government's research reports that 1,500 to 2,000 women are killed by their spouses and ex-spouses annually, equal to over one-third of all female victims of homicide with a history of abuse.

If those statistics don't alarm you or at least get you to thinking, let me share with you the following:

Professional research results conclude that annually over six million children witness their mothers being physically abused. In addition to the victim being traumatized, children that are exposed to their mother or loved ones being abused face a future with Post-Traumatic Stress Disorder themselves. Studies show that children who have been traumatized by observing abuse in their household do suffer higher rates of various distresses, including aggression, academic and behavioral school problems, and early childhood onset of Attention Deficit Disorder, depression, and substance abuse.

Some studies have indicated that physical abuse often either begins or intensifies during the victim's pregnancy. According to the Maryland Health Coalition Against Domestic Violence, Minnesota Center Against Violence and Abuse and a 2011 U.S. Senate Judiciary Committee report, of the one point three million victims of domestic violence, thirty-seven percent of female victims of domestic violence are pregnant at the time of abuse. Usually, the physical violence is directed to the abdominal area.

Factors attributed to the risk for pregnant victims include the abuser's fear of loss of control, jealousy toward the baby, reluctance to adjust to his new responsibility, and increased anger toward the victim and the baby. There are abusers who manipulate their victims to consider or force her into an abortion. The abuser then blames the victim for the abortion. If the abuser allows the pregnancy and there are other children in the home, they witness their pregnant mother being abused by their father. Some abusers purposely impregnate the victim through careless contraception or forbidding contraception as a way of increasing the victim's dependence and vulnerability, through her weakened bodily state of pregnancy.

Rape
Rape is another form of physical violence for some abusers. The abuser deliberately uses the sexual act as a weapon to ultimately attack the victim. Rape is one of the most violent acts of sexual abuse. It is a sexual violence that can begin to include sexually harassing, forcing unwanted sexual intimacy when the victim has said *no*, the abuser enforcing his coercive sexual fantasies, making the victim perform sexual acts with another person, making sexual threats, coercing the victim to engage in the sexual act in the children's presence, intimidating the victim by criticizing her sexual appearance or performance, incapacitating the victim through induced drugs or alcohol and sexually exploiting her, flaunting his previous sexual partners descriptively and demanding the same of the victim, exposing her to pornography against her will, trafficking the victim, and soliciting and/or forcing the victim into unwanted sexual activities without her consent. All of the above can eventually graduate into unconsented forceful stimulation, vaginal and/or anal penetration—rape. An abuser that rapes sees the victim as an opponent to be disabled and conquered. Rape is *not* about sexual attraction and arousal—it is

about an act of power, control, and violence. Some abusers prey on the already disabled and prefer to take advantage of women with disabilities. The National Sexual Violence Research Center reports that eighty-three percent of women with disabilities will experience sexual abuse in their lifetime.

In the 1970s, a psychiatric nurse, Burgess, and Holmstrom, a sociologist, studied the psychological effects of rape. Their research took place twenty-four-seven for a year in the emergency room of Boston City Hospital. Their observations noted a pattern of psychological reactions by rape victims which they named "rape trauma syndrome." In 1974 their study entitled "Rape Trauma Syndrome" was published in the American Journal of Psychiatry. Their conclusion indicated that the women experienced their rape as a life-threatening event; they typically feared mutilation and even death while being raped. The women disclosed that after being sexually assaulted they experienced insomnia or nightmares while sleeping; they felt easily startled and a sense of numbness or a desire to disassociate the rape from their conscience. Burgess and Holmstrom stated that some of the victims' symptoms were similar to those of combat veterans.

Rape is rape whether the abuser is a total stranger or a spouse. The aftermath symptoms are the same: shock, feeling completely invaded, betrayed if the abuser is known, embarrassed, humiliated, distrust, anxiety, fear, guilt, depression, denial, protecting the abuser, blaming self, feeling numb and misunderstood, anger, shame, feeling permanently damaged, stigma, degraded, losing sense of security and safety, threats from abuser to harm/kill victim/loved ones, threats of abandoning victim and children, silence, and isolation. The difference in spousal rape is that strangers generally vanish; however, with a spouse, the victim is still in danger of being attacked again. If the stranger is caught, the assault may be recognized as rape and brought to justice, while the same act committed by a spouse may not. Generally, this is the natural consequence for a victim of marital rape. *Most victims report that the rape marks a permanent change in their life.* The symptoms of the trauma of a victim of rape may appear as if she's mentally ill. However, not all victims appear or act the same. Some victims look weary from the long suffering they have withstood; their faces may look haggard and drawn. Others work diligently to conceal their plight; they don't look their part and make an extra effort to appear at their best for the abuser and the public.

The trauma of marital rape is further elevated and complicated because, by nature, the victim is highly vulnerable due to being raped by someone whom she trusted and sought protection and safety from—her spouse. If a victim decides to report her rape to the authorities, she may experience rejection from her prior support system (that now does not want to be associated with her). The victim gets further isolated in her sexual assault circumstances because family, friends, co-workers, and/or classmates are concerned about the victim being involved in a criminal investigation and how that will interfere or affect their own lives. In most cases, the victim of marital rape will not be believed nor provided with support because her spouse has an honorable status in the community. Spousal rape is a crime in all fifty U.S. states. However, some states have specific reporting requirements. For example, in some states, the marital rape must be reported within thirty days of the incident. It's important to check the reporting guidelines for each state as some have policies and procedures regarding the grounds for marital rape. Victim support surrounding marital rape allegations varies from state to state, and in general, some family members of the victim will not validate her claim and will often shun her for even making such an allegation. This denial and lack of support by the community and family only serves to compound the symptoms that the victim is experiencing.

SEVEN TYPES OF ABUSE

There are various reasons to explain or rationalize the lack of assistance to victims of rape. However, it is evident that those who come to the defensive rescue of a rapist are uninformed on the deep-seated characteristics of an abuser; it's in the same category of dysfunctional family members that rescue their friends or family perpetrators in the absence of clear educational knowledge about victims and the dynamics of abusers. Abusers portray a certain *"je ne sais quoi"* charm that victims and others (that don't know abusers)get pulled into. Some victims have been required to report the sexual assault within a certain period of hours after the rape so that a medical examination can be conducted to retrieve reliable evidence.

Most victims panic, feeling arrested by the trauma of the rape; they may not report it within the period of time to retrieve the evidence. Victims have to weigh out how reporting the rape and making it public knowledge will affect them at work, with family, and with any interpersonal relationships. Some victims, due to fear for their life, cooperate with the rapist and do not show outward physical signs of the rape. Some police have declined to file a report and request for an exam when the victim shows no evidence of her allegations. Sexual abuse is one of the crimes in which a victim can show no visible wounds. Even if the physical abuse escalates into a sexual assault (rape), the physical sexual parts of the body are so resilient; sometimes there are no visible signs that a victim has been forced into sexual intercourse.

Further, there are people in our society, including the police, that come from a belief system that believes a victim invites and instigates being sexually pursued. The victim has to deal with the "blame the victim" mentality, which infers that the victim most likely was promiscuous and led on the abuser. This is a significant reason why marital rape and other types of rape are so vastly under-reported and have become known as a *silent crime*. Perhaps the victim used poor judgment in how to act or dress herself, but even then, that does not give anyone a right to her body without her consent. In the past, and even in today's society there are folks that fall for the unfounded misconception that men that rape can't control their sexual drive, have a sexual addiction, or are mentally ill, and therefore the victim provokes the rape. Some folks, whether in the community, in positions of authority, or even on jury duty, may see the victim as responsible for her rape, but the truth is that no one has a right to sexually assault. Their erroneous belief system that the victim is to blame does not give consent to the abuser to rape her. How our society views sexual abuse and assault, whether by a stranger or by a spouse, deeply affects the healing and recovery of a victim of rape.

Amongst the numerous worrisome reasons that a victim of rape gives as to why she doesn't file a police report are the fears that she will not be believed and that the rapist will retaliate. The most dangerous times for a victim's life are when she reports her rape or when she attempts to leave. If the victim decides to report her rape, it is highly recommended that a victim secures herself with a Safety Escape Plan (see Volume I Part III) and an Emergency Protective Order (EPO). An EPO doesn't guarantee the victim against being raped again, but it does provide police protection by authorizing them to arrest the abuser if he violates the order. Violating the EPO will cost him a Class A Misdemeanor and can lead him to a confinement of up to a year and/or a hefty fine.

Please note that restraining your abuser by separating him from your presence *does not* equal to his learning his lesson and stopping his abusive nature. Even if your abuser were to be sentenced to some jail time, he will not have learned to stop his abusive ways. In fact, most jails or prisons where my colleagues and I have worked with abusers reek of ill repute toward females. An abuser will not learn to confront his problem with victim abuse while in jail. Some jail time may *temporarily* curb his appetite for abuse, but the best help available for an abuser includes a well-trained probation officer and the participation in an abuser program. The disclaimer is that some abusers never set foot in or never complete the abuser program unless court-mandated or legally required through their probation period. Why do abusers not accept the abuser programs? In addition to not wanting to let go of the benefits they gain by continuing to be abusive, they also have distorted, discrediting views about abuser programs— much like they have about their victims.

Some states have police chaplains on staff in the workplace, which provide support for the victim in her decision-making process of reporting her abuse. These trained law enforcement officers of various denominations can advise in a calm, empathetic way. Some states also have police pastors who ride in patrol cars with law enforcement officers to provide comfort and guidance for the victim and serve as a liaison between police and the victim (when appropriate and upon request). A victim can call to inquire if the police chaplain and/or police pastoral program is offered in her nearby vicinity and ask for police chaplain/police pastor assistance.

It's important that the victim of rape make an appointment with the Women's Crisis Center after obtaining the EPO so that it can be converted into a permanent protective order when the EPO expires. The permanent protective order is generally good for two years and is renewable. This is a free service available and provided for victims through the county attorney's office. Please, always remember that neither an EPO nor a permanent protective order will offer total protection. There's no document that can protect a victim against rape or any other form of abuse. If you know that you have been threatened and are in danger emotionally and/or physically, your best option is to go to a women's shelter or other anonymous location. You can receive a referral for a safe location to go to via telephone or electronically through a website (see resource list). You can remain confident that when you contact and speak with a shelter caseworker that person will completely comprehend your circumstances. Shelter caseworkers are like teachers who teach English as a second language; these caseworkers teach and speak abuse as a second language.

Some states pay for sexual assault exams. Most states' policies have been that if there is no police report filed, then hospitals are not required and cannot be legally made to provide free-of-charge sexual assault exams. In such a case, *if* the victim does not file a police report, she is responsible for paying all of the costs of a medical sexual assault exam. A victim that is being persuaded to file a police report in order to receive a free sexual assault exam can seek assistance from the Violence Against Women Association (VAWA). VAWA has changed the federal law whereby a victim can now receive a free forensic medical sexual assault exam regardless of whether she decides to file a police report or not.

There is no other free-of-charge medical care offered by the state for other lab tests, prescriptions, and mental or physical treatment of a victim of rape. This becomes an added burden for the victim to carry within the abusive relationship *especially* when there's a risk that the victim will develop a sexually transmitted disease (STD) from an unfaithful spouse and/or Post Traumatic Stress Disorder (PTSD) after the rape: which ranges between a fifty and ninety-five percent chance. The victim may recover with time, but if the sexual assault trauma symptoms linger and affects her functioning in daily life activities, then the impairment may be diagnosed as full-blown PTSD (which will require medical attention).

The best way to rule out concerns about the financial coverage of a sexual assault medical exam and other medical costs for treatment is to contact the local rape crisis center, victim assistance program, or police department. Regardless of financial cost, it is *always* recommended that a victim of rape receive an immediate forensic sexual assault exam. One of the reasons why it is highly recommended that a medical exam is done after a victim is raped (even if it's spousal rape) is because an abuser may have a medical history that the victim may not be aware of. The risk that a victim may contract an STD is always there in an abusive relationship. It is also important that a victim be aware that mental and/or physical symptoms of rape can remain dormant for extensive periods of time but manifest themselves years later through the immune system's breakdown. The immune system can deteriorate and no longer sustain the trauma, resulting in physical symptoms (e.g. headaches, respiratory or digestive problems, and other illnesses). This is why it is imperative for the victim of rape (as soon as she is able) to pursue mental and/or physical care—to protect her for the present *and* future with the appropriate supportive care.

It's not uncommon for victims to experience a re-traumatization from the community or the legal system's hostility toward her as a victim who is making allegations of rape. A victim of marital or stranger rape is usually unprepared to receive this type of hostility from a community that she thought could protect her from her source of danger. It is a rude awakening for most victims of rape. It becomes apparent to the victim that the community can't guarantee her rights to safety but guarantees rights to the abuser. Some communities and justice systems don't alleviate the post-traumatic symptoms that the victim of rape is inflicted with; on the contrary, she feels re-victimized. A victim of rape, who feels incriminated and overshadowed by the community and justice system may choose to drop her claim. Therefore, most marital rape remains private and confined to the home without acknowledgement from the community or restitution from the judicial system. The legal system can sometimes become an adversarial institution for the victim. For the victim to be evaluated for competence and provided with full justice, she must be understood and appreciated within her circumstances (this is generally bypassed during the legal process).

Some marital rape victims know this lack of support in advance and choose to keep the rape attack to themselves and grieve their shame, and physical and emotional pain in solitude. Other victims become so isolated in their own abusive world that they ultimately withdraw from their social world (friends, work, school, or other commitments). The predicament that a victim of spousal rape often finds herself in is not being provided with the opportunity to criticize or denounce the police, judicial, medical system, or community for their lack of help. This is information that victims and those assisting victims have experienced and reported. This phenomenon can be traced back to the solid truth that *all* of the individuals working in the above-mentioned capacities and organizations come from their own personal backgrounds and live in the same society that tolerates family abuse.

Having support, protection, and safety for a victim of rape is *crucial* to her recovery and healing. The best outlet that can influence recovery and healing for the victim of marital rape is seeking a rape crisis center that can validate her trauma and provide advocacy. This resource is instrumental in assisting the victim to report the incident, secure shelter, help with the administrative tasks, and accompany the victim to a clinic, hospital, the police, or a court system. Ultimately the victim may find her path to reconnecting with her community, but generally this can only happen if, through her work as an *Overcomer* (see Volume I Part V), she finds meaning in her traumatic experience and can therefore rise above the limits of her suffering and trauma.

SEVEN TYPES OF ABUSE

Child Sexual Abuse

Sexual abuse of a child consists of *any act* that manipulates or forces a child or minor to participate in sexual activities, regardless of whether or not the child is aware of what is happening. In the United States, child sexual abuse (CSA) is a crime. Sexual abuse of a child does not necessarily have to include violence. Sexual abuse may include touching the outside of clothing, rubbing, kissing, masturbating, penetration such as rape, and non-penetrative sexual activities. All of these activities are considered sexual assault because they are unsolicited and unwanted sexual stimulation.

Some non-contact activities are also in the category of sexual abuse. These include forcing the child to look at pornography or others physically performing sexual acts and encouraging the child to behave sexually. CSA can happen in an instant, online or offline, at home, in public places, and through electronic devices. Stay calm if you discover or your child reports he has received sexual content. Reassure your child that it's not his fault that he received the material; take a moment to teach your child about CSA predators. Tell him that you will protect him from CSA, beginning by removing all electronic devices and sexual content materials until the CSA problem is resolved.

It's very important that as much as you want to erase the content that you do not delete the sexual images/content from the electronic devices or discard the hard copies. Contact the authorities to report the content in your home computer and take the electronic devices or offline materials to the authorities as evidence to track the abuser down. It's difficult for law enforcement to trace the abuser without content, images, media, handprints, or DNA to identify the abuser. Grooming is also sexual abuse (this refers to preparing the child to engage in sexual activity). Child sexual abuse left untreated and unresolved can result in physical, psychological, and mental health symptoms.

Symptoms are manifested and diagnosed in childhood, adolescence, and/or adulthood. Symptoms include but are not limited to: shame, guilt, self-blame, PTSD, difficulty with interpersonal relationships, self-neglect, depression, anger, anxiety, eating disorders, body dysmorphia, self-mutilation, sexual dysfunction, cigarette/alcohol/drug abuse, gynecological disorders, physical inactivity, becoming obese to deter sexual advances, gender dysphoria, wearing provocative/over conservative attire, promiscuity, STDs, unplanned pregnancies, and prostitution.

The 2013 Domestic Violence Abuse statistical report from the Department of Justice reported that a child's exposure to the father abusing the mother is the strongest risk factor for transmitting violent behavior from one generation to the next. About sixty-five percent of those abusers that abuse the mother also physically and/or sexually abuse their children. For more information on child sexual abuse, see the following guidebooks in the Overcoming Abuse book series written for parents/caregivers/helpers and children: *Overcoming Abuse: Child Sexual Abuse Prevention and Protection* and *Overcoming Abuse: My Body Belongs to God and Me.*

Economic Abuse
Economic abuse, like *all* abuse, permeates throughout *all* socioeconomic classes. Economic abuse includes but is not limited to the abuser's rigid control and restraint of the household finances. Economic abuse involves the abuser's control of the financial assets which the victim disposes of as he interferes with her management of monies by his undue restriction of the disposing or management of their common financial assets. Economic abuse is the abuser's undue setting of prohibitions of the victim's and family's income. The United States Department of Justice defines economic abuse as, "Economic abuse involves maintaining control over financial resources, withholding access to

money, or attempting to forbid a victim's attendance to school/employment in an effort to create financial dependence."[1] In some cases there can also be various forms of economic abuse through coerced debt. "Coerced debt consists of non-consensual, credit-related transactions which occur in a violent relationship."[2] Examples of coerced debt include, but are not limited to:

- applying for credit cards, obtaining loans, or opening other financial accounts in a victim's name, or using her benefits to obtain credit or membership in his name;
- forcing the victim to obtain loans;
- using the victim's educational loan for personal/household expenses while she pays off the loan;
- forcing the victim to sign financial documents and not allowing her to read or review them beforehand;
- the use of threats or physical force to convince the victim to make credit-related transactions;
- refinancing a home mortgage or car loan without a victim's knowledge.

Some victims who elect to suffer the consequences of economic abuse purposely agree with the abuser's financial point of view; they placate him to avoid an argument (which leads to further abuse). This continuous economic deference to the abuser ultimately affects the victim's self-confidence and ability to become self-sufficient which further impedes her efforts to restore her identity. A victim's choice to stay in the economically abusive relationship (in order to preserve her children's and her own financial security) means that, as a mother, the victim will continue to experience the emotional and/or physical violence against her will and influence the children by their witnessing of her unequal, oppressive relationship. Many have asked the sixty-four-thousand-dollar question: "*why* does she *stay* with *him*?" Over ninety-four percent of victims of abuse have also experienced economic abuse. This means that on top of the risk of safety, a victim has difficulty finding a job, securing a place to live, or nourishing herself due to complete lack of economic self-sufficiency incurred by debt and/or personal credit records from the abusive relationship. Society sometimes has a measuring rod on their low tolerance for victims of abuse. Before judging the victim, it's important to note that there's always one more fact of which we may know nothing about.

One source of financial assistance that's not only available for the purpose of refuge and economic help with housing but is also there to provide guidance when applying for work or government assistance (e.g. food stamps), is a victim's shelter. This is a place where a victim not only has access to public resources available to her but is also where she can take time out to discover her own personal resources. According to Gondolf and Fisher's studies in 1988, the victims who make use of shelters are usually poorer and have lower education and job experience than other victims. *However*, that is not always the case as there are victims that, regardless of economic strata in a desperate move for their lives, flee to a shelter to take temporary refuge. A woman's shelter provides victims with the safety, resource information, and the time to do some clear thinking as they experience a newly-found functioning separately from their abuser.

Temporarily living in a shelter actually provides women of all backgrounds an opportunity to respect the differences in other cultures, races, socio-economic groups, and religious denominations. The one thing that *all* of the women in the shelter have totally in common is that they have all been severely abused. It's important to keep this commonality in perspective while at the same time giving each woman the space that she needs, respective to her own personal background. It is not a victim's place to define these women. The victim is there to restore *her own* peace of mind. Focusing on her lifestyle preferences and measuring the disparities between her and the shelter inhabitants will only bring on new conflicts to add to the abuse she has endured. A victim's purpose in a shelter is to begin to recover; she needs *all* of her energy to focus on the birth of *herself* as an *Overcomer* of her abuse.

While under economic oppression, the victim experiences the abuser's obsession with holding her accountable for any money that she spends. The abuser may sabotage the victim's efforts to earn her own income, and if he allows it, he makes her accountable or induces guilt when she spends the money that she has earned. The abuser may attempt to prevent the victim from establishing a career that would make her economically independent. If she does establish a career or has an occupation outside of the home, he may demand that she call in sick or not work the hours assigned by her employer. Many times, the victim is forced to miss work for fear that her distraught condition or evidence of her abuse may be observed at work. The abuser may elect to restrict the victim to an allotted monetary allowance or may withhold his or her earned income or credit card use. Some abusers deprive the victim of basic necessities such as nutrition, toiletries, medications, clothing, or shelter. At times, abusers are known to steal money or possessions from the victim.

There are upper- middle-class and upper-income class abusers which some of the public still assume *do not* engage in any type of family violence. This assumption is based on the *myth* that spousal abuse doesn't occur in the homes of highly-educated individuals with more than sufficient means of income. Nevertheless, all types of family violence are real in the homes of *all* abusers and victims whether they hold educational degrees or have any level of income.

The other reason there's an assumption that family violence is uncommon in the upper classes is because the spousal abuse statistics do not include the uncalculated innumerous incidents that go unreported by the upper-class. Most of the research is based on the lower- and middle-class victims that have called the police or shelters. The upper-class victims *do not* suffer any less or differently in their abuse; they're just a group of silent victims that sacrifice themselves in the name of maintaining the status quo. Many of these victims are married to prominent abusers, and some of these victims hold prominent careers themselves. These abusers are parsimonious nonetheless. Society has also made the gross assumption that upper-class victims can successfully liberate their own self through their power and monetary means. The result of these assumptions has led to the absence of the significant upper-class abuse statistics *and* the lack of awareness of the economic abuse that upper-class victims experience.

The upper-middle and upper-class victims that my colleagues and I have worked with include nurses, professors, journalists, media leaders, corporate administrators, professors' wives, corporate wives, political leaders' wives, doctors' wives and others. These victims were all married to abusers that had a higher education, and as couples they associated in the same circles with those of comfortable, grand, or wealthy lifestyles. They had their own social circle—a domestic circle—through which abuse was silenced. There are victims whose husbands own very lucrative businesses, yet they come to therapy venting how they are not allowed to make any purchases outside of food (or an explanation is required), and they live cautiously for fear of being furiously reprimanded by their spouses who hold a position that their finances are in dire straits, with no such evidence (quite the contrary). These victims usually pay cash for their sessions with money they have received through family gifts or other creative sources. One victim, unbeknownst to her spouse, held a part-time job off the books while he was busy with his business, so as to have cash for her personal toiletries, eye contacts prescription, and incidentals.

SEVEN TYPES OF ABUSE

The typical reason given by these victims for being bound to silence about their abuse was to protect their privacy and preserve their lifestyle. Upper-class victims that eventually come for treatment are those who are at their ultimate rock bottom and have gone past their barometer in fear for their life or that of their children. Occasionally, these educated well-to-do wives attempt to seek assistance from family, trusted friends, or a resource in the community *and* they have been received with disbelief, lack of understanding, and an inability to guide them to a Safety Escape Plan (SEP) (see Part III for SEP). Part of this dilemma is based on the victim's and abuser's reputation and being well known in the community; there's no place in the community that the victim can feel understood and that she can trust to provide her with confidentiality. Unfortunately, many victims of high economic means experience less access to victim assistance than the less privileged victims.

The socialization process of middle- to upper-class upbringing contributes to the victims' and abusers' thinking that it's not appropriate to call law enforcement on "family problems." Even when suburban or wealthy neighborhood wives have in desperation called law enforcement, somehow their powerful, abusive spouse manages to manipulate the law's involvement. The upper economic abuser has the means to defend his abusive acts with legal representation that covers his bases. There's a visible difference when my colleagues and I have had court hearings working with lower- or upper-class abusers and their victims. The attorneys and judges that are in the same educational and economic strata as the upper-class abuser not only invariably favor the abuser's defense but adhere to a tolerance for this abuser in denial that upper-class abuse does exist. There is a discrepancy in the measure of the power a woman of means and a man of means have in society, and the abuser therefore is more able to protect his privacy, rights, and economic resources.

Those economic resources buy the abuser's extra edge; they insulate the existence of his abuse toward his wife. Sometimes the very resources (judicial system, family violence programs, law enforcement) that are designed to help all victims renounce the upper-class victim and empower the abuser as a result.

There is a strong need for public and professional awareness about the undermining of upper-class abuse that continues to exist in our nation. An upper-class victim has *no* advantage over a lower-class victim in coping with or escaping from her bondage of abuse. The cover-up excuses used for the bruises or maltreatment at medical clinics, places of employment, or social activities are believed when used by upper-class victims but are seen as more suspicious when lower-class victims offer them up. Spousal abuse cannot be measured economically. Society needs to be educated on this dynamic: It's not about the commoner and the renowned victim—or being in the red or black—it's about unspoken economic victimization across the line. Upper-income victims feel overwhelmed internally with the conflict between how they feel within and the pressure to perform as normal around their peers and society. When an upper-class victim's devastating abuse is ignored, she is denied validation, support, resources, and assistance.

Marrying into economic privilege can become economic abuse for the upper-class victim just as easily as for the lower-class victim. Whether the victim has a career or not, the upper-income abuser uses money to threaten and control her. This economic abuse is strategically organized by the abuser. For example, if it's a two-income home, he will request that her income be used for household services or general merchandise; he makes sure that she never gets a return on her funds, whereas his income goes toward principal and builds financial equity. Major purchases are under his name, even if she has contributed to the purchase by working in and/or outside of their household. Major purchases go under his name because he gets the outstanding credit score while she doesn't develop a credit history.

Sometimes the victim has a benefit advantage of being able to apply for a loan, and even if the abuser is gainfully employed, he suggests she apply for the loan in her name. Once the loan is approved, he manages, through manipulating the billing office, to change the loan to his name because he is the head of household, and once again, her credit history is not built up. The abuser generally keeps their financial assets private; they are not shared with the victim except for gaining her signature for tax forms, or he might do it electronically without her signature (he signs her name to any refund checks). Her name is in all of his insurance policies, but she has no other information about those policies. Upper-income victims can be clueless about their stocks and bonds, or any assets, because the abuser controls all of the financial records. This type of abuser receives his mail at his office or at a post office box; he uses the family income to leverage his wife's financial dependence on him.

There are victims that are terrified by the idea of not being able to provide for themselves; these abusers use this vulnerability to exploit their wives with threats of becoming poor if they leave. Some of these abusers punish their wives by withholding or reducing their allowance. Abusers that control the victim financially through manipulating an allowance usually prefer to have total financial control of the household. There is no brainstorming and shopping together for household items. These abusers get to decide who gets to make purchases and what an acceptable purchase is. They get to plan the present and the future expenses. They surprise the victim with major purchases, but she may not get to do the same in return.

Economically, the abuser decides whether or not the victim is allowed to drive, go to school, or work outside of the home; her input on these matters is ignored. Regardless of the household level of income, the abuser usually benefits the most from the family finances because he typically has monetary dominion even over the victim's paycheck. An abuser is a control manufacturer of exploitation. The way an abuser views the matter of giving up his abusive nature is as follows: he would have to give up the financial and egotistic rewards he gets from exploiting the victim. Discussing family plans with an economic abuser becomes a bitter feud for most victims. An upcoming family or social event for which the victim is responsible to host usually means the abuser escalates in his tone. If the victim confronts him on his hostility toward her over the matter, he reminds her loudly that it's *his* money and he gets to choose where and how it will be spent. This is his way of putting her back in her oppressed state.

Like with the low-income victim, the upper-class victim also experiences the same extreme pressure from the abuser and society to keep a bad secret within the confines of their home. Upper-income victims, like other victims, are made to believe that they betray their spouse and children by not being silent about the abuse. The dynamic that plagues the upper-income victim is her own mind; she thinks that if she tells family or friends, they will think that she's ungrateful for her good provider. This is one of the main reasons that the upper-income abused wife refrains from reporting the abuse. She has consciously chosen her path to cooperate in this abusive relationship given the lack of knowledge on the dynamics of abuse and the social standing that she has to live up to.

An upper-income victim carefully analyzes her choice to participate in the abusive marriage—it is an economic decision to stay silent. This is not just about *traumatic bonding* with her spouse, it is also about her relationship with her lifestyle. In simple terms, *traumatic bonding* is a strong emotional and physical attachment between a victim and her abuser, formed as a result of the cycle of abuse (*traumatic bonding* or *trauma bond* is noticed in the victim stories cited in these books and defined in greater detail in Volume I Part III and in Volume III Part II). With very few exceptions, most upper-class victims have never experienced or even have a clue about abuse because they were not abused or raised in abusive homes. When these victims are asked if they noticed any abuse warning signs during their courtship, most of them say that they would not have known what to look for.

This is what makes it even more tragic for this class of victims, because their spousal abuse is unacknowledged by society, and on top of that, they are in shock and don't know how to process or cope with such disrespect and cruel maltreatment. This class of victim, as with any other victim, sincerely believes that in time they will be able to fix the abuser—he will change, and the marriage will be resuscitated. There's a fairy tale expectation that her abuser will love her, that they will ultimately have a romantic relationship like they used to and that he will take care of her. As with all abusers, the upper-class abuser manages to seduce his victim into thinking that the intermittent romantic, lavish times full of elation will be ongoing, and the victim is left with false fantasies that their marriage will thrive and is induced into staying.

In exchange for the lifestyle the victim receives from her abuser, she is expected to be obedient to his needs: look and dress attractively, behave properly, and parallel the lifestyle that her abuser is leading. These abusers justify their demanding tempers and entitled attitudes based on the financial support and all of the material luxuries and amenities that the victim receives. In the upper-class, the victim can go from one extreme to the other regarding her decisions about involving the children in the abusive relationship or not; the victim may either be deeply concerned about the abusive impact on them, or she may stay for fear of losing their lifestyle. Lifestyle is the part of what challenges upper-class victims whenever they seek domestic violence services. These victims' feelings regarding the loss of their lifestyle are discounted by service providers and most other victims who don't relate to a victim being concerned about loss of money and material things when they are struggling to just make ends meet, are seeking to protect themselves and their children, and *just* live.

Economic abuse in upper-income households are the epitome of an unspoken dysfunctional, co-dependent arrangement. The victim picks up on the economic ground rules from the abuser and learns to live with it. The affluent abuser brainwashes his victim into thinking that there's no possibility for her and the children to be able to financially survive without his provision; he makes her out to be a failure if she even tries to become independent of him. She does not want to be seen as a failure by her spouse or the community. The victim then resolves that she does not possess the courage, strength, skill, or intellectual capacity to have a life of her own outside of the marriage; with this in mind, she chooses to keep the economic abuse silent.

This dangerous silence serves to sustain the co-dependent relationship; she's unable to receive any take from others on the abuse she's enduring or any encouragement about her worth and capability. At this point, she has become voiceless—deaf and mute to her abuse. *When* and *if* she ever decides to do a cost-benefit assessment of her marital relationship, it is only then that she is able to recall some of her strengths, talents, and capabilities. This empowers a renewed potential in her. It's at this point that she is able to evaluate *how* the abuse has and is impacting her and her children's lives. She begins to look at the perks and privileges she has through her lifestyle and weighs them against the emotional and/or physical trauma she has sustained, the economic persecution, risks of safety and danger versus the approval of her family, peers, socialites, co-workers, church, or others. This self-evaluation leads to some *mindful* thinking and decision-making about her and her children's future; for *her*, it is a literal costs and benefits decision.

Like with *all* victims of spousal abuse, an upper-class victim's life is one of constantly feeling as if she's in quicksand and wiggling slowly in attempts to escape to safety. Professionals and society need to increase their training in upper-class economic abuse and their willingness to validate upper-income spousal abuse. More upper-income victims need to report their economic abuse. Reporting their economic and other abuse can give them and other economically-abused victims a *voice* that can lead to help them overcome their abusive lifestyle. Economic abuse *is* played out even more extensively if the victim decides to terminate the relationship through divorce. However, she faces the *same* economic burdens if she stays because he has her strapped into his economic regimen. If she leaves with the children, she fears that he may press charges of "abandonment." This can easily be taken care of in advance through legal representation. The abuser will always increase his rigidity with controlling the family finances if the victim initiates leaving him. In addition to his personal phone calls, texts, or emails, to devalue the victim and the children (after she has left him), the abuser proceeds to call the children's school and the victim's employer to demoralize her character and place her at a risk for losing her job and possibly her children. This is what a victim must be prepared for. She has to intentionally arm herself with the appropriate support to maintain the boundaries she has now set with him.

In today's society, more men are obtaining custody of their children. Parental alienation has always been one of the abuser's prime head games. For a lot of victims, this means being subjected to the abuser's name of the game: having his powerful job assets and reporting her as the unstable person and incompetent parent. Some abusers' approach to controlling the victim's financial mobility includes filing false charges with her employer, police, or child protective services. If he finds that, because of his exorbitant overspending, he's having financial difficulties, he will digress into his typical denial and blame defense mechanisms; he makes excuses for his inexcusable financial condition. Somehow, his financial difficulties are always the victim's fault. For a victim to overcome economic abuse, she must be willing to protect her most valuable assets—her life and her children's lives.

Using money as a form of control is a mark of the ultimate form of manipulation from an abuser. This is because economic abuse means the abuser has power over the entire victim's daily decisions through controlling the household's and her personal finances; it keeps her under constant stress and strips away her human right to use initiative or have any identity of her own. Economic abuse is seldom exercised in the early stages of the relationship; it's a gradual abuser's seemingly harmless balancing of household expenses, which has a grave effect over time. The abuser generally manipulates other areas of the victim's life first. Once he has those areas under his control and she is unable to make any decisions on her own, the financial abuse completes the entrapment. It is a sign that the abuser has total control over the victim and is now using money overall as his weapon. This is the final stage when the victim becomes aware of his financial control over her life, the deceitful aspects of their relationship, and how guileful he has been all along.

Most economic abusers keep the victim under the financial stress of thinking that there's never enough money to live on and maintain her debt by not paying off her medical bills or other necessary expenses in her name. This, in turn, degrades the victim to a level of shame when collectors call her. There are abusers that, while providing an affluent lifestyle, restrict the victim from all financial information and the use of his income as a shared income unless he decides on the purchases himself; the victim and children are expected to live within marginal means while the abuser is seen as providing a high socioeconomic lifestyle. In economic abuse, the abuser essentially disturbs the victim's reality about their finances and keeps her thinking that it's a struggle to pay their bills. This justifies why he's not willing to spend any money on major household purchases, recreational activities, hobbies, or vacations.

Meanwhile the double-standard of his being able to enjoy his expensive hobby is not seen as a recreational expense. It becomes a form of taking away the victim's right to relaxation or life interests outside of himself. The abuser does not see himself as being stingy with her and the family. If the victim shares her concern about not living life fully and just living to pay bills, he gets very upset and says in his escalated tone, "Don't start complaining again; why can't you just shut up and be DONE and be happy with the car you drive and the house you have to live in?!" Her abuser's financial control is very much hidden from her consciousness as he leads her to believe that she's ungrateful for what he provides and that she has no right to desire any more for her life (a life over which she has no control).

In summary, economic abuse takes many forms. Sometimes the abuser is well-employed but withholds or hides his assets from the victim. Then there are abusers who insist on the victim being the main source of finances in the household, and he becomes an economic leech to her. This type of abuser will steal money from the victim and even their children's lunch money. Such an abuser has a super sense of entitlement and will illegally fill out forms and get credit in the victim's name. There are cases of economic abuse whereby the abuser controls all the money with keeping his salary, investments, and savings a secret and separate from the victim's knowledge; all she knows is that he makes a substantial income yet he withholds funds from the victim by escalating if she makes any household purchases, saying that they're barely making ends meet. Some abusers provide a credit card for the victim so that she can leave an electronic paper trail for him to control and keep track of her whereabouts and her expenses.

It's easy for the victim to get distracted and busy with her own work and raising a family, to carry the stress of his maltreatment, and to overlook that there's not a long-term commitment to share finances in the relationship. The economic abuse may not be apparent until the victim becomes aware of the abuser's insidious ways with their finances. Most abusers will not share their tax information with their victim, let alone any retirement fund information. There are financial *yellow* (warning) and *red* (stop) *flag* signs all along, but the victim has justified, or rationalized, or put aside any concerns for later. A hallmark of economic abuse is that most victims protect themselves from the abuser's emotional and/or physical abuse by not bringing up the topic of finances. It may be past the *red flag* stage before the victim notices that her abuser has been monetarily behaving in highly inappropriate ways and now realizes that he has been in total control of their finances for decades. Victims of economic abuse can feel overwhelmed with confusion and traumatized with the thought that the relationship is supposed to be a lifetime commitment, yet the victim cannot trust if her abuser will deprive her financially in her later years of life when she's unable to work. She's ill-informed and is not allowed to ask if there's a retirement plan that includes provision for her as well.

Spiritual Abuse
A victim experiences spiritual abuse when the abuser manipulates her to serve *any* inanimate god, idol (including worldly things), prophet, saint, or religion that especially exalts the

abuser. Victims can also be subjected to a cult. A cult is an organization of people with a leader that teaches the precise words in the Bible (taken out of context) to control them as a structured religious group. A cult does not believe in the trinity (Father, Son, and Holy Spirit). A cult uses its people to further its own cause and has intentions and tactics similar to an abuser. A cult is attractive to the abuser because it does not have a personal relationship with Jesus Christ (God), a relationship which the abuser prefers her not to sustain. Some abusers partake in and encourage the victim to engage in satanic rituals which lead to a conglomeration of other abuses toward the victim. A victim may end up confused and unsure of what to believe. This state of confusion makes her walk around with numbed senses; she's unable to think clearly or make concise spiritual decisions. Her inability to discern what's true or not is influenced by the abuser's lies being offered as truth until the victim no longer knows what to believe.

Some abusers forbid the victim and their children to participate in any religious activities and become enraged if she speaks of God or of spiritual faith. For some victims that work outside of the home or are allowed to attend church, these places become a safe harbor from the cruelties of their abuser. Sometimes victims don't have a safe haven because they receive abuse every which way they turn (even through institutional abuse): by their bosses or spiritual abuse at their churches where they turn for help and are advised to suffer and to pray for their spouses.

Safety is always of utmost importance, especially when an abuser rejects God and forbids the victim to speak of God. It's imperative for the victim not to talk about God at this time. A victim can still maintain a quiet, private relationship with Christ in her heart; many terrorized prisoners have had to do the same. Do not allow your abuser to obstruct your friendship with Jesus. The good news is that no one can ever put a wedge between us and our Heavenly Father—none of His Creation can separate us from His love (Romans 8:35-39)! The abuser may refuse to acknowledge God, and just like God doesn't force Himself on us, the victim shouldn't force God on the abuser. God Himself would not approve of anyone doing anything under coercion.

The abuser may confiscate any spiritual literature or discard it in her presence to intimidate and deter her from bringing any of it into their home. There are some abusers that vacillate back and forth, allowing the victim to attend church and church-related activities but then suddenly and unexpectedly forbid her to participate. The abuser's goal with his spiritual abuse of the victim is to drive her away from experiencing a close relationship with God; he wants to alienate her from both God and her loved ones. Even employers and total strangers become spiritual contacts for him to target and monitor. Under his dominion, she lives distressed in spirit. This places the victim at risk for remaining confused about spiritual matters or to totally be removed from getting to grow and know the God that created her. In most cases when the abuser blocks God, the victim ends up blocking Him too. Because a victim's conscience, heart, and spirit have been penetrated and violated, the only way for a victim to recover from her spiritually-confused state is for her to find an opportunity to deprogram herself from the false doctrine.

It's not possible for the victim to heal and be made whole again when she remains entrapped within her spiritual abuse. Victims of spiritual abuse live with an incarcerated heart that thwarts their spiritual growth; they are restrained and not allowed to develop any faith or hope for their life. There are some abusers that use religion to cover up their abusive nature and make it a point to participate in church and church-related activities. Abusers sometimes even manipulate their way into leadership positions within the Church and live double lives as godly men in their church and community; they control, verbally abuse, and/or act violently at home with the victim and their children. This type of spiritual abuser believes that he is indeed the godly man that he personifies to others; he believes his own lie and convinces himself that no one would believe the victim's claims that he is otherwise. An abuser can turn into a wolf in sheep's clothing (Matthew 7:15).

In this case, the abuser is using the Church (in addition to the home) as an incarceration tactic to justify why the victim cannot have an identity that's not solely connected to him. This type of covert abuser uses his ministry schedule to restrict the victim from having close contact with others outside of his church and his church schedule. This spiritual abuser *must always be included* in or around her activities so he can keep her under his surveillance. The abuser uses gentle, emotionally-manipulative, loving ways to keep her under his dominion. She must always have his approval or permission to do any activity that doesn't include him. She cannot initiate, "I'm going to go visit my sister next weekend," because he will say, "let's go together," "you can't, I need you to be here," or "let's do something together." This is especially common if he did not have a good relationship with his parent(s) or sibling(s).

The abuser refuses to comprehend her need for close relationships outside of his person. The victim cannot have bonding relationships as she did before she met him; he controls the development of those relationships now. Generally, abusers that emotionally cut off their own families expect the victim to do the same with hers. These abusers will plant seeds of negativity about the relationship(s) that the victim once esteemed. She begins to forget what it was like to have those supportive relationships and now believes (as he does) that those relationships are unnecessary and that all she needs is *him* to maintain a harmonious home life. This is part of his manipulative way of breaking her spirit.

The abuser may use biblical Scriptural truths to twist Bible verses as he covers up his lies and selfish, abusive motives. She then regards the Scriptural references misquoted by the abuser as truth. That is the power of the abuser whereby she doesn't know she is being deceived. This distorted biblical view that the victim has now inherited from the abuser further entraps her in the bondage of the abusive relationship; she feels as if she's drowning and that there's no way out of her captivity because she would be spiritually in trouble if she attempted to leave. She is like a castaway.

When a victim *finally* meets an authentic Bible-teaching Christian mentor or reads the Truth and has a revelation on her own, it is as if an *Overcomer* life preserver has been tossed to her. Her saving grace is that if she stays consistent with the Truth, no one—not even the abuser's fictitious spiritual leadership—can take Christ's place. The victim has to believe that her Savior and Redeemer can raise her weak victim life to a new strong *Overcomer* level; she doesn't have to buckle down to abuse. Christ's presence *is* in the midst of your overflooding circumstances, and He *can* make you strong. He is your Defender!

> "The mouth of the righteous *is* a well of life,
> But violence covers the mouth of the wicked."
> **Proverbs 10:11**

PATTY'S STORY

I MET DAN IN Alaska the summer that I was a freshman in college. I was a mascot, and I was receiving a stipend from the college. I had gone to pick up my check; it was at that college office that I met Dan. Dan worked there, but I also saw him later on. Dan would flirt with me, saying things like, "Does your mother have any more like you at home?" I noticed he would hang out with the college trustees; he even did work for them in their homes. Dan had a super high I.Q. and would trade commodities in the stock market. Dan was actually genius level, and I was impressed with him! Even though he was going through college, he knew what he was doing and where he was going in life. That was exciting to me! One of the trustees would allow him to drive his car. Dan would go out to the country where some of the trustees lived, and he would attend their socials. Dan was not just a student leader, he was a part of a campus life ministry that evangelized. Dan had graduated from the local Seminary; he was this strong, Christian guy. Dan and I began to date, and I was *totally intrigued* with him!

Dan proposed my junior year, in October. We were going to get married in April, but I got pregnant, so we married quickly in February. Our wedding was at a little chapel, and only very close friends and family attended. My parents were separated at the time, due to my dad's alcoholism, and I'm not quite certain, but he may have been incestuous with me as a child. Dad would wake me up with a flashlight at night and ask me to come and dance with him. I remember him acting real weird with me. One evening we were sitting on the porch when I was about eighteen, and he was *real drunk*; I told him that I hoped that he would die. My dad came to give me away at my wedding. But, at the rehearsal right before the ceremony, a whiskey flask fell out of his socks. I got so mad at him—I told him that he was not going to give me away. My dad died early at age forty-five "from alcohol," and at the time they found stacks of pornography in a warehouse that he had.

The wedding was postponed that day because Dan's mother was at the hairdresser and was two hours late. I was so sick with my pregnancy, I was throwing up all over the place. It was *so very* disappointing (sobbing); it was *nothing* like what *you* would think *your* wedding would be like. At the same time, I felt like I had already messed up—so I kind of deserved it. We both did not finish college. We were really struggling for the first eight months of our marriage—we lived out of a suitcase. I lived with my mom for a while. Dan told my mom that he had an apartment for us, but then we found out that he didn't, and the baby was due any day now. She was very upset at him. Dan took me out of there. We left my mom's house without even saying goodbye to her. We stayed at one of his investor's homes. I remember the doctor telling us, "The baby is coming soon, so remain celibate for the next two weeks." Dan ignored the doctor's recommendation and that night demanded the opposite of the instructions. I said, "You know we shouldn't be doing this." Dan ignored me as well, and that night my water broke!

I had my first child. I had to stay in the hospital for several days because the social worker knew of our circumstances. We didn't have a place to live, no baby clothes or furnishings. But then Dan got a BIG deal to go through and he picked me up from the hospital with a car seat—he drove me to a beautiful, furnished condominium to live in! The doorman and butler opened the door for us and there was a baby room with a baby bed and a fully equipped kitchen.

I was WOWED on how God had provided! I was feeling God's grace because I knew premarital sex is wrong in His eyes—but I did it anyway. I was now living by my mom's adage that if you make your bed hard you have to lie on it—I hadn't expected God to come through for me. I was carrying a lot of guilt for having sex before marriage, so I just told myself, "You've gotten yourself in this situation so now you're married, and you just have to make the best of it."

You see, I have traumatic memories from my elementary *and* middle school years; there were things going on with me and my cousin, my two brothers, and neighborhood boys. There was a man down the street too. I was selling Christmas cards, and his family was even out there on the porch, and he molested me. I just said, "I have to go!" I did tell my parents, and they were *furious*; they told me *never* to go back there! My parents told me that that man went to our church and had been in trouble before for exposing himself. It was difficult to sleep at night; I couldn't relax because my cousin, brothers, or dad would stand by my bed. At the same time, I just moved on and rationalized it away, saying to myself, "It didn't happen, they really didn't do that to me."

One night, Mom and us kids we were walking home from church. My oldest brother said that he felt *much convicted*, and that he was going to tell Mom what we had done. I begged him not to; *we were just little kids.* I'll never forget how my brother walked ahead of me and how Mom walked real fast when he told her. I just lingered way back behind them, whimpering. She didn't talk to me about it; all I remember is her crying and being so mad and really getting on to my brothers. I walked in the house, and she yelled at me to never do that again! I begged of her not to tell Dad. My dad traveled a lot so he was only home on and off; I don't know for sure if my mom ever told him. The good part is that after my brother told my mother about us, all of the molestation stopped with my cousin who would take me into the barn.

There was *one time* after that, however. We were out playing on the field, and my cousin motioned that he wanted me to go to the barn with him. My eldest brother stepped in and said, "You're not taking her to the barn, we don't do that anymore!" My cousin's reaction was, "Make me!" and kept insisting. So my brother went over and told my grandpa on him, and I remember standing outside and my cousin got in *so much trouble* and got *spanked really hard.* I felt so *ashamed.* At dinner that evening—I remember sitting at the long, family table—nobody said anything throughout the entire meal. They never talked about it after that. But it's still there, because when I went to a family funeral as an adult, I saw my cousin there and *I felt such pain* and *such shame.*

I'm sad to say that my youngest brother, when we were teenagers, asked me to come into his bedroom. We were just lying there talking, and he also abused me. My brother had begun to come into my room when we were teenagers. My mom heard him one night and called out to him, "What are you doing? Go back to bed!" and he would pretend like he was sleep-walking. When my oldest brother became an adult and got married (I was already married), he called me to say that he wanted to talk to me. I told him that I didn't want to talk to him, but that I loved him. My brother said that he needed to talk to me to get something out in the open. We went to a mall and talked; he cried and said how sorry he was, and I told him that he was forgiven. My brother was very remorseful; he has become a wonderful, godly man—a changed man.

My husband, Dan, over the years of our marriage, would try to get me to reenact my past incest. Dan played mind games with me and wanted me to initiate what my dad had done to me and relive that in my mind. Dan would taunt me and try to get me to role play what my dad had done! Dan wrote out a report about me, as if he had done some case study on incest victims and said, "This is why your writing is all uneven, because of your molestations." I had opened my heart out to Dan, and had shared some of my pain with him, but he would always bring it up to my face *or* over and over again in counseling. When we went to counseling, he would use my past incest against me, identifying me as the one with the problems, saying that I had "repressed memories."

I had gotten to a point in my life where I could no longer deny that I was involved in an abusive relationship. So I ended up going to a safe house. We had gotten evicted, and I was living with family members. I only had two children at the time. I had attended an Adult Children of Alcoholics meeting and shared with them my situation with my husband; about thirty people gave me feedback that I was being abused with every type of abuse in the world! They told me that I needed to get away from the relatives that I was living with—and from my husband. My husband was heavily into pornography nightly now, which had been going on from the first months of our marriage; but back then, he would always deny it and say it was not his DVD. Then Dan would say that it was not bad—it was just pole dancing. I did kick him once during this period of time, and he hit me back! I flew across the room, past the king-sized bed, hit the wall, and landed on the floor. It knocked the air out of me! Dan got in my face and said, "Don't you ever do that again!" I swore that I would never hit him again—I said I was sorry. That was the first and last time that we were in a two-way physical fight.

While at the safe house, I had received some good counseling, but one of the therapists there began to come on to me, and I became very uncomfortable. That scared me so much that I began to want to be with my husband again. I was afraid. My family didn't want me to return to Dan. But I always felt that I was dumb, that I was stupid, couldn't get a job, that I didn't measure up, didn't have enough education, and that I wouldn't handle it well. I did make an arrangement with my husband that if he would get us an apartment, get a job, and go to counseling with me, then we could get back together.

My father had died at that time, and I remember saying in our counseling session, "I'm glad it's finally over with." The counselor thought this was an odd reaction, and Dan began to turn our session into explanations of what my dad had done to me. The counselor then began to worry about me. Our marriage counseling was turned around and I was told that I was the one that needed psychological help. We *never* focused on Dan's abuse of me or his contribution to our being evicted, his not managing our money appropriately, his lies, pornography, or why our marriage was a wreck! Dan's father had had serious problems himself: A distant relationship with his family, he had multiple affairs, he wanted to visit with the family only on his terms, he was standoffish, and left when Dan was in middle school.

Furthermore, Dan had a history of incest as well—which was never discussed. By the time Dan and I had four children, his two sisters had gone to his mother to self-disclose that Dan had molested them during their childhood. The problem with the confrontation was that his mother treated Dan like a god—like he could do no wrong! In her eyes, he was perfect. If I ever said anything negative about Dan, she would always take his side.

PATTY'S STORY

They would enable each other; when she needed money, he would give it to her, and vice versa. We needed to take care of our own family and our savings, yet he was always giving her money. I was very angry at Dan because one of our sons needed counseling, and he would not give him the money for counseling, but he would give money to his mother. I wanted them to stop, but neither would listen to me. They would keep secrets behind my back. I did not like her at all, but before she passed away, I did make peace with her.

Dan not only helped his mother out financially, but he suddenly began to help out a second cousin with money, who then began to live with us! We had five children at the time and Dan would say that this cousin could help me with them while he was out of town working. Dan would return from trips with gifts, flowers, and money, and we would go out on lots of dates. It was a life of having lots of money or no money; we had real highs and real lows in extremes. Sometimes for periods of time I hired nannies to help me out with the kids while Dan traveled—they would live with us for months. One time, one of our nannies wore a beautiful dress to one of our house parties. When I inquired about her dress, I found out that Dan had bought it for her at a very upscale store. Another time, I was out of town myself and I found out that one of the nannies that was helping out at his office had gone shopping with him and the children, for office clothes *for her*. This nanny was twenty-one years old, and Dan had an affair with her. I had trusted her; her mother was in Bible study with me. Dan had even helped her parents out with money to start a business!

Dan's justification for the affair was that she made him feel *good* and *like a man* and she wasn't "a nag." Dan had stared at other women even on our honeymoon; he always made me feel like I never measured up. Everyone else had always said how pretty I was, though; I just didn't feel that way with Dan. After he told me of the affair, he wouldn't let me out of his sight. Dan went everywhere with me, even to buy school clothes for the kids, which he never did before. During this time he was still viewing pornography, which he would deny. When I would confront him, he would say, "I'm not doing anything, what's wrong with you?" At this time Dan was very active at our church (he was an elder) and known for being generous; he had helped the nanny's parents, given money for missions, paid for people's honeymoons and Lasik eye surgery. Dan was listening to Christian music and reading Christian books written by top evangelical bestsellers.

The affair was brought out at church through the elders because the nanny's parents wanted to continue to receive Dan's monetary help. The head counselor at church stepped in to mediate couple's counseling for us. Because Dan is very intelligent and conniving, he could make you think or believe anything. One of the counselors at the church had said that he couldn't handle Dan! To make matters worse, at the time of this affair, I found out that one of my oldest sons had molested one of my daughters. So we also had to deal with that! We had to have family counseling. We got it worked out, but we had to keep it super quiet because of the social shame, the stigma, and how it would affect our entire family. In fact, until this day, my mom remains furious at my son (her grandson) for molesting my daughter, and she cannot understand that it is the *very same hurtful abuse* that happened to me with *my brothers* (her sons). She has totally absolved my brothers but is unforgiving toward my son.

One of my daughters, five years old at the time, suddenly went from being the sweetest little girl to having an explosive episode. We had gone to a restaurant, and while in the restroom there, she began to pull her beautifully French-braided hair loose, throw water all over, and pull out all the toilet paper rolls and paper towels. Another time, she did this again, only in her bedroom. We were getting ready to leave for the last day of Vacation Bible School, and I found her with her hair all pulled out and messed up; she was not ready to go, and there was pee on the floor. It was on that day that I started asking her questions about what could possibly be wrong. I asked if it was her brothers, or her dad. When I asked about the live-in cousin, she said yes. I told her that I would kill him, and she said, "No, Mom, that would be a worse sin than what I have done." I reassured her that she didn't do anything wrong—that it was *his* fault!

I filed a police report and got her in counseling. She was the only one out of all our kids that admitted to being abused by him—although I suspect the others were too. During a grand jury hearing, this cousin stated that he did not abuse our daughter. The sentence was for thirteen years but he got out early. Our daughter was very angry, and when she was in high school, she would inquire about his whereabouts; she said she hated him.

We have seven children; three boys and four girls. Throughout our marriage, I was a stay-at-home mom. Because we moved so frequently, I was pretty isolated from making any friends until the kids got older and we settled down in a house. The first years of our marriage, every Sunday I had to ask if we were going to go to church. It always depended on whether Dan wanted to go or not. Then if he did decide that he felt like going to church, I had to beg and nag for him to help me to change a diaper or to get the kids ready to go. I could never count on his help. The kids, now all grown-up, have told me that they are thankful that I never gave up and continued to take them to church as much as I could. They occasionally bring up the memory of my rejoicing when we were allowed to go to church and that I would say, "Okay! Get *in* the car, get *in* the car! We are going to *hear* Jesus' Word!"

After twenty-five years of marriage, I couldn't believe that we were in the process of breaking up! Dan said to go get a job because he was no longer going to support me. When I did get a job, he threatened me and wanted me to quit the job. Then when I enrolled in school, he wanted me to quit school because he wasn't going to pay for it. No *matter what*, I *knew* I had to prepare to support myself—so I went to a technical school. I got trained as a physician's administrative assistant. I found out that while I was out getting educated and working an internship, and Dan was home waiting for another "big deal" to come through, he was molesting one of our daughters; she was in ninth grade.

Dan was always threatening to sell our home. When he had the last affair, he pleaded for me not to leave him. Dan even bargained with me. Dan put some of his assets in my name and said that if I didn't like the way things were going, I could always kick him out, but he knew I wouldn't stand up to him. This offer didn't mean much to me because I knew that Dan could change the assets back into his name at any time—which he did when I filed for the divorce. Dan took back the house and land that he had gifted to me. Dan would ferociously run toward me, intimidate me, and throw the phone at me. If I got out of line (confronted him), I would be in BIG trouble. My daughter told my divorce attorney, "I didn't know that a grown woman could get in trouble, but it's sad because my mom gets in trouble."

During the divorce proceedings, I had decided that I was no longer going to be intimate with him, but he would come into the bedroom anyway and pull the covers off of me. So I decided to move into our guest house adjacent to our home. Dan was very upset. My thought was that since the kids were living in our home, he would not attack me with them being around. I would even sometimes have my kids at the guest house to sleep over as a means of protection. One night the kids notified me to lock my doors because Dan was headed my way.

About two-thirty in the morning, he banged on my door. I got scared, we had a huge fight, and I was *so frightened*. Dan had grabbed me before, straddled, and choked me to where I thought

PATTY'S STORY

I was going to suffocate and die—so I knew what he was capable of. One time he had held me down by the wrists and when I told him that he was hurting me he said, "You better thank God I didn't snap them!" I did open the door and let him in, and he said to get the "blank" back over to the house. When I told him that I was not moving back to the house, he moved toward me, turned the lights on in the bedroom, and sexually assaulted me in an unnatural way. I remember thinking afterward, "NEVER AGAIN!"

Some of my children didn't believe that their dad could be that dangerously abusive toward me, but one of my daughters heard her dad's yelling and my screams. She called the police that night. As the police arrested my husband, Dan yelled out to me, "I'm going to the judge tomorrow to get you committed!" My kids were looking so confused because Dan had been talking so badly about me to them over the years. I did not know that he had told them that I was a harlot, that *I* had other men, that *I* had affairs—and truthfully, I hadn't *ever* been unfaithful! My sons' views of women were very warped. The marital conflict in our home was so intense that my boys escaped by becoming addicted to computer games. One of my sons became engrossed with war games. All of them have been involved with pornography. One of my sons says that he got introduced to pornography by an older man at the library.

Dan had at one time begun a business in the States, mining precious metals; he would put big deals together with investors. We would live in high-rise condominiums in the States and fly back and forth to the mines. For many years I thought he was an entrepreneur, but during the divorce trial one of our nannies told one of our daughters that she had seen Dan one night with a lay-out of guns on the kitchen table. I have a protective order; I should have gotten one for the rest of my life! My attorney has asked me to continue to renew my protective order. During the divorce proceedings they suggested that I be escorted to the court house because they had asked Dan what kind of work he did, and he told them that he was an assassin for the government. After that, he told them that he worked for the CIA. When they asked him on the stand who he actually worked for, he took the fifth and said he was not at liberty to say.

Dan was not prosecuted with *any* assault or rape charges toward me during our divorce proceedings. The only reason Dan's in prison now is for molesting one of our daughters. Dan was only sentenced to seven years because at the time of the trial, only one daughter came forth. It didn't come out that he had also molested my sons—in fact, all of our children. The judicial system, I believe, did an injustice to me and my children by putting all my children on the stand—some of them were little bitty children—instead of taking them individually to question them in the judge's chambers. On the stand they could see their dad, the jurors, and others that intimidated them into silence.

Our daughter read her victim letter to her dad on the stand, and his response was just shaking his head *"no"* and whispering back and forth to his attorney while she read it. I stood by my daughter's side throughout the trial and continue to be supportive of her. While in prison, Dan wrote the kids a letter telling them that they're actually bastards, but he just felt sorry for them and took care of them anyway. Dan has to register as a sex offender for the remainder of his life, and he is banned from living in any of the surrounding counties where the kids and I live. Dan may be out in seven years, but he's not supposed to be let out until he completes the prison's sex offender program.

Throughout my abusive relationship and the divorce, my strongest supports were my girlfriends. Dan would try to control who I talked to, where I went—and *that* was scary. I felt like a bad wife because I was always in hiding. One night I was hiding behind a tree at home, whispering and talking to my friend on the phone and she said, "Patty, you can't continue to live like this—you have to do *something* about it!" I couldn't count on support through my church because when I secretly met with one of the church prayer group leaders, she betrayed my confidence and we soon got notice that we weren't qualified to serve at our church. She said that she was only trying to help. The church had no idea that they had not helped but made it worse for me; they had gotten me in trouble. Not only did Dan yell at me for talking to someone about him at the church, but I felt so much shame that I couldn't even sing in the choir anymore.

In total, I was married to Dan for twenty-eight years. We have been divorced for seven years. My husband was controlling, deceitful, manipulative—a liar. I should have listened to my gut, gotten out, and not shut my feelings off; I shouldn't have kept thinking it *would get better*. If I said that I should never have married him, that would be wrong, because then I would not have had the blessing of my beautiful and precious seven children. The only thing I would change is my wandering, the choices that I made, and having been separated from God.

Three months after our divorce, I met someone: Frank. Frank is several years older than I am, but we both fell in love. We ended up living together and got engaged. The problem was that we were going to get married, but we could never get a date set; he kept telling me that we were going to get married, but it just never happened. We got rings and I got a wedding dress—which remained in the closet. Frank and I broke up because he wasn't willing to make a commitment to set a wedding date. About that same time, a friend from my childhood, Ben, came back into my life. Ben said he loved me and had always loved me and wanted to marry me; I started seeing him and we got engaged. Ben had been married before; he divorced his wife because he had never been in love with her, according to him she had emotional problems. I broke it off with Ben because he would not get a job and he was financially dependent on me.

Then, Frank and I got back together. We had reconciled, but I wanted us to go to counseling to get help with our relationship. I told him that I was feeling *spiritually convicted* about us living together; he then said it was over between us. Frank owned a business, which I was helping him run. Throughout our relationship Frank had had a pattern of not answering my questions regarding the business; it just seemed like he could never come up with any IRS records. Since Frank and I were living together again, my oldest daughter asked me if I was a Christian. I said that I was but that I was beginning to feel a conviction about living with Frank. I had rationalized it before, as temporary, and had told myself that it was okay because we were older, and I knew the wedding was coming.

However, this time I felt like I was being a bad example to my children. My own mom was on my case about it too. I had a girlfriend say to me, "Patty, you need to walk the walk not just talk the walk." I couldn't sleep at night. Especially when I thought about my daughter's comment regarding my son (who was angry at me for being a hypocrite because I was sleeping with Frank). Ben had moved out, and now I was living with Frank again, and she said, "That's not what a Christian would do." I had been dealing with my son's anger already because of all of his hurt, our family's past abuse, his father going to prison, and me living this lifestyle; I wanted my son's relationship back! I decided: "I've got to get it right this time; I've got to make things right!" That was on a Saturday night—*I repented*. The next morning, I went to church and I was able to take the Lord's Supper with a clean heart. It's like I came home!

I sought Christian counseling, and I'm now in weekly sessions. I have made amends with my son who had not talked to me for two years. I have been transparent with him, and in return he has loved on me and said that he is proud of me. My son has returned to the Lord himself and has a strong walk with

PATTY'S STORY

Him. My son even invited me to meet his girlfriend whom he recently got engaged to. This morning he texted me and said, "Good morning sweet mom." Ultimately the only thing that has gotten me through *all* of this is *faith* in God and knowing that there is another purpose to all of this suffering! Leaving my abusive relationships has provided freedom for me that I've *never* experienced in my life—even the freedom to mess up—and to *partake* in decision-making. This has led me to realize that I am *not* dumb, that I'm *actually* a very smart woman, *and* I have gained the confidence that I don't have to depend on a man.

My kids gave me a book for Mother's Day about Jesus' love for me. Between *that book* and the breakup of the last of my abusive relationships, I have realized that Jesus wants to be the most important man in my life! In addition to that, it's liberating even in the midst of my pain and sadness, that there's also this sweet *peace* and *calm* that I can have *now*. It's like the strength *is* some kind of supernatural strength. My past life was a life of confusion and running away. Some people would say to me that I was going to end up in the looney bin with everything that I was dealing with, and it felt that way! But I don't feel like that anymore. I feel that as I trust Him, He takes care of me. I regret not opening up to my friends sooner. When my husband would call me a harlot in front of my friends, I would ask, "Does anyone want more tea?" My friends that know me from *that past* and know me *now*, tell me that I am *not* the same person as when I lived under my abusive husband's authority and control. I'm in the process of getting the training and license for a concealed handgun. I'm also having a security gate built and a video camera installed around my home and property.

The reason I changed is that I finally *tired out—I just wore out*; I was just *so tired*! I had had enough of it. I could only take so much pain. As I watched my children get hurt, I didn't want any more of it. As a mom, you feel so badly because you want to protect your children and you're *the only one* that can put an end to it. If I didn't start growing and making changes, the abuse wouldn't have ended. I don't want to *ever* again live with a man yelling at me, making me feel bad, or questioning me in controlling ways. I'm more than done with that! My life is full of revelation; things have been and are being revealed to me now. I continue to grow, and I like that!

PART II

THE ABUSER: EVERYTHING YOU EVER WANTED TO KNOW

Personality

I WOULD BE REMISS if I began a section on the abuser without first having a discussion on personality. So much of a person's life interaction is not just based on the particular gifts that an individual possesses but also on their unique personality type. Abusers, like all human beings, come in very different personality types. Therefore, even though the general characteristics that make up an abuser will always be the same, he will operate differently with those same characteristics based on his personality type.

I will briefly go over a basic personality inventory that is useful in order to obtain a quick evaluation of one's personality type, the DISC. The DISC is a set of psychological inventories created by John Geier and others. DISC is an acronym for Dominance, Influence, Steadiness, and Compliance.

The DISC proposes that people's characteristics of behavior can be found within those four dimensions of behavioral styles. All people possess the four behavioral styles but differ in the extent that each dimension is exhibited by each person. Most people have *two* of the four dimensions that are expressed *to a higher extent* in their personality style.

The following is a summary of what each of the four dimensions represents:

Dominance/Drive: "D" personality styles are described as determined, strong willed, ambitious, persevering, demanding, assertive/aggressive, forceful, and goal oriented.

Influence/Inducement: "I" personality styles are described as animated, demonstrative, enthusiastic, charismatic, emotional, communicative, trusting, and persuasive.

Steadiness/Submission: "S" personality styles are described as unemotional, easy going, calm, patient, preferring security, possessive, resistant to unexpected changes, thoughtful, consistent, and predictable.

Compliance/Caution: "C" personality styles are described as systematic, orderly, neat, preferring structure, compliant with rules and regulations, organized, precise, concerned with details, using tact and carefulness, and preferring to be diplomatic.

If you haven't figured out your abuser's personality type yet, hopefully using the DISC as a tool can help you become more aware of what personality traits influence his daily living. If you as a victim are uncertain about what your own personality profile is, this inventory would also be useful for you to use as a personal awareness guide. You can easily go to www.123test.com and take the free of charge, five-minute DISC test to determine your personality type. Understanding your own and other people's personality types is very helpful in developing social relationships with others because having this insight provides a guideline as to what the best approach is in relating to the person based on their personality style. For a more in-depth evaluation that can provide deeper insight about personality types and how people perceive their world and make their decisions, a counselor can administer and interpret the Myers-Briggs Type Indicator (MBTI), or you can go online and take the questionnaire.

Abuser Characteristics

The following characteristics may or may not apply to your abuser. Characteristics vary according to your abuser's family of origin's socialization process (how he was raised) and his individual personality profile. An abuser can have hours, days, even months whereby he behaves in thoughtful, kind, and even romantic ways. During these times, you may be convinced that his abusive nature has stopped and that he has returned to the loving relationship that you once shared. However, abuse just *doesn't* suddenly stop and disappear. Here are the dynamics and profile of an abuser:

1. Most everyone seems to see the abuser as a good person; only the victim experiences the bad person side of him. An abuser can convince your marriage counselor that he is *not* an abuser.
2. The abuser suffocates and paralyzes the victim with his controlling attitude and behaviors.

3. The abuser consistently tells the victim that he loves her, but his hateful words and actions do not demonstrate love.
4. An abuser manages to create confusion about most matters, especially about the abuse. One of the abuser's driving forces is to threaten the victim that he can convince loved ones, employers, or the legal system that she's the one that has a mental problem. Abusers concoct lies about their victim. An abuser does this through invariably twisting around what she has said or done—ultimately distorting what has occurred—twisting her words so that she now ends up on the defensive with his alleging that she is to blame and at fault.
5. The abuser's attitude is that the victim owes him something because he *chooses* not to understand give-and-take. In fact, he will at times demand back what he has given the victim as provision or gifts. Abusers brag about their contributions to the household and take the victim's contributions for granted. The abuser lets the victim know that she is ungrateful, that she does not realize how lucky she is to have him to meet the daily life responsibilities. If the victim does not give what the abuser feels she owes him, he is punitive toward her for letting him down.
6. When a victim disagrees with the abuser, no matter how respectful and humble her approach is, the abuser perceives the victim as mistreating him or as a form of attack on him. An abuser usually talks over her when she attempts to defend her position.
7. The abuser lives in his own reality and needs to control the victim's every decision and action, or she will not do *whatever* correctly.
8. An abuser may use psychological jargon or biblical Scripture to convince the victim or others that the victim is *not* being mistreated.

9. The abuser may attempt to control his victim by throwing out into the open her childhood issues with the focus or subject now changed to the victim rather than to his abusive nature.
10. Infidelity may be a part of the abuser's actions; if so, he is either profusely apologetic with promises not to do it again if forgiven (until the next time) or he usually justifies the infidelity by *blaming* it on the victim, the person with whom he had an affair, or his terrible childhood.
11. An abuser will very likely be loving, kind, and gentlemanly at the beginning stages of the relationship. Abusers make victims feel *s*ignificant, *s*afe, and *s*ecure (the three *s*'s that women like to feel in a relationship). These three *s*'s make a woman feel protected. However, although an abuser enjoys the role of a *protector*, his protection is not done in a cherishing way. It's done in a controlling and disrespectful way. Due to his emotionally and/or physically violent characteristics, it's only a question of time before the victim needs protection from the abuser.
12. An abuser will claim to be the victim himself. Abusers attempt to validate their abuse by stating that everyone (parents, family, church, boss, strangers, acquaintances, and friends) have done them wrong, especially women; therefore, they're not to be held responsible for their actions.
13. Mental health problems, drugs (prescription or otherwise), alcohol, gambling, sex, or other addiction(s) may be combined with the abusive behavior. Notice I say "combined" because it is important for the victim to be educated on the fact that mental illness or any form of addiction does not cause a man to be abusive to his spouse. Mental illness and addiction simply adds to the severity of

his abusiveness and contributes to the abuser's resistance to change.

14. The abuser has his own realm of thinking with a sense of entitlement—usually interlaced with double standards (he can do *whatever* he wants, but the victim *cannot* do the same). The abuser's lens of expectation is one of entitlement, even when the victim is unaware of his expectations. When these unspoken expectations are not met, he proceeds to communicate his disappointments through abusive rage.
15. The abuser's unpredictable mood swings are episodic; they may subside as a calming of the sea, then unexpectedly return like storm waves. Some abusers are intense daily (there's no break).
16. The abuser is pathologically controlling. An abuser's s ultimate goal is complete domination of the victim. Abusers accomplish this by isolating the victim from outside connections that would provide resources or emotional and spiritual support.
17. Abusers ignore and hide the obvious about their feelings or what their victim has undergone.
18. The abuser's objective is to confuse the victim during arguments.
19. An abuser takes it upon himself to control and decide on major purchases without consulting with the victim, including the purchase of a weapon(s).
20. The abuser is a proficient liar; he lies about his ulterior motives and intentions in order to manipulate the victim into doing what he wants.
21. The abuser intentionally misleads the victim into sympathy for him so that she will back off from her concerns about his abuse toward her. Abusers are experts at minimizing their abuse.

THE ABUSER: EVERYTHING YOU EVER WANTED TO KNOW

22. An abuser programs a victim's mind into thinking that his requests and what he wants the victim to do are all for her well-being.
23. The abuser brainwashes the victim into believing that the decisions that she has made in the relationship are her own.
24. Some abusers are carrying with them deeply hurtful parental/caretaker messages; they abuse the victim to make themselves appear stronger than their hurt.
25. An abuser lacks a morality alarm when relating to the victim and at times may expect her to engage in immoral behavior with him.

What Makes an Abuser Abusive?
Many have asked what would cause a man to become emotionally or physically abusive toward his spouse. There has been an attempt to put a closure on that question by blaming it on the abuser having come from an abusive childhood. However, there's more evidence that this is true for men that are bullies toward or violent against men *or* for men that relentlessly terrorize their spouse *and* are atrociously assaultive to them. An abusive childhood is not the reason a man is abusive, but an abusive childhood can influence a man into becoming a treacherous abuser. There are abuser profile reasons why childhood is not to blame for an abuser's behavior. An abuser may have a history or no history of abuse and still engage in the maltreatment of his spouse. If childhood abuse were the sole reason for the abuser's mistreatment of his spouse, then the problem could optimistically be resolved in therapy.

An abuser may (if he cooperates) self-reflect on his past childhood abuse and his current emotional and/or other types of abuse which he subjects his spouse to, but in spite of the insight he gains in therapy, he elects to continue his abusive behavior.

This is because abusers choose *not to* use their childhood abuse as a way of deciding that choice: "Being abused was devastating to me; I wouldn't want to put my spouse through the same pain." Instead, an abuser uses his abusive childhood information as an attention-getter and an excuse not to change. This is why individual therapy is *not* recommended for an abuser—and an abuser's program *is* (more about abuser's programs later). In most cases, abusers that participate in therapy use therapy sessions to their advantage in destructive ways. The abuser uses the therapeutic jargon he learns to manipulate the victim with new excuses for his behaviors; he tends to use his newly-acquired insight about his and his spouse's family dynamics as a way to obtain more sympathy from the victim and manipulates to gain pity and make her feel responsible for increasing his distress. Some abusers (once they find the theory of an abusive childhood as the reason for their remorseless abuse toward their spouse) begin to embellish what actually happened to them. The abuser rather enjoys finding someone to blame in addition to his spouse for his abusive behaviors; another woman (a mother or female figure that raised him) is a good target for him to justify his cruelty toward women.

This is not only a good rationalization for the abuser, but the victim also gets to excuse his heartless treatment in view of his sad childhood. Society plays a part in buying into the abusive childhood diagnosis as the reason for the man's actions and then both the victim and society don't have to look deep into the true reasons for his inhumane treatment of his spouse. If you can blame the abuser's childhood, then you don't have to look further to explain his sadistic behaviors toward his spouse and children. This acceptance of an explanation for his brutish ways toward his spouse only helps him to escape his responsibility for his criminal act because he can go around stating, "I abused my spouse because I was abused myself."

THE ABUSER: EVERYTHING YOU EVER WANTED TO KNOW

The truth, and only truth, is that the abuser abuses his spouse because he has an abuse problem—he is an abuser. A man that is abusive who has experienced abuse as a child has two separate problems to work on: his childhood abuse *and* being abusive to his spouse. This is not to infer that the victim or society should not have compassion toward an abuser who suffered abuse as a child; it is to say that there are many non-abusive men that have experienced traumatic abusive childhoods who don't use this as an excuse to abuse their spouse. It is important for both the victim and society to recognize that a lot of abusers misuse their childhood abuse to induce guilt on behalf of the victim and the judicial system for confronting him on his abusiveness.

Now, there are the abusers who temporarily let their guard down while in therapy when they process their childhood abuse or other difficult periods of their past. When this occurs, the abuser leads the therapist and victim on as if he's ready to make some changes and heal. At this point, the abuser appears to have softened his heart and the victim feels tender toward him; she can't imagine that he would ever return to spew out offensive words in a volatile tone toward her or frighten her with threats of assault. Some time goes by whereby the abuser stays in this harmless state, but suddenly it's as if the nucleus of his abusive nature was dormant during that quiet phase and now he's back alive and kicking with his intimidating, moody insults, and the victim is placed back on that abusive wheel of fortune—what's it going to be today?

She's back to square one, wondering *what* went wrong as there's no evidence of *anything* going bad since the last therapy session. The abuser leads her back to spinning her wheels, wondering if she's the one who caused things to go so wrong because she's being punished with this offensive treatment. When she inquires as to what set him off, he does his usual twisting of her words (even though she used choice words to gently approach him). Now he has her back on the defensive! The reason given for his explosion is that *she* said something during the inquiry. The abuser's version of his mood change is worlds apart from hers. The *thinking* of abusers is the answer to the victim's inquiry, a dynamic that will be discussed further in this book. The true etiology of his abusiveness lies in how he thinks! Neither a victim's or therapist's inquiry of his escalating moods is appreciated by the abuser.

An abuser doesn't want to be found out; his ploy is to be able to get away with his abusive behavior. If the victim were to clear out all of the cobwebs of confusion that the abuser creates to keep her from figuring out the way his abusive thinking works, his power and control would be overcome. So, in order for his abusive nature not to be challenged, he has to convince himself and others not to focus on the way he thinks and the real causes of his behavior. However, the way that he thinks in his mind is the key to predicting how he sees himself, others, and life. It is indeed the way he thinks (before he acts abusively) where he first forms thoughts of who he thinks he is in relation to others, and it is in his selective mind that both his abusive thoughts and actions are conceived. There is a consciousness to keeping the victim and others in a state of confusion. The abuser can't maintain his status of a loving spouse if he doesn't throw the victim off track—or anyone else that interferes with this image of himself (the image of an innocent spouse being wrongly accused of abuse).

The Abuser's Self-View

Unfortunately, this distorted view of himself as being the victim works itself into the real victim's mind, and she replays his excuses to a point of self-doubt and self-blame. This creates a vicious circle when society gets involved because the abuser then acquires these allies to support his distorted excuses, which

THE ABUSER: EVERYTHING YOU EVER WANTED TO KNOW

further aggravates his denial of his problem and increases the victim's and society's blindside to abuse. Whether the abuser presents himself as being a victim of his abusive childhood, previous romantic or other relationships, his *underlying intent* is to play on the victim's mercy and sympathy.

The first duty for a victim and her support system is to be aware that in order for an abuser's denial to stay intact, he is counting on his own distorted role as a victim and his excuses. Just know that he does leave a trail of pathological lying. Be warned. This is useful to monitor and to record because it sets the precedence for the victim and her support system to be watchful and consistently document the exact details of what he is really doing. By the time you finish reading this book, you will have figured out the abuser and you will never be set up to be confused again; this abusive relationship that you're in will come to light in a way that you have not had an opportunity to see before.

The abuser prides himself on his ability to successfully argue that it *is* the victim's instability that needs to be evaluated—not his. Abusers are masters at crafting any *excuse* to fit their ways of thinking or any controlling behaviors that they may be exhibiting. An abuser's goal is to keep his real self from being discovered. If he hides his true self from the victim, he can play up the part that the victim is the real cause of his behavior or that she's partially responsible because if it wasn't for what she said or did, he would not have abused her. Abuse is the abuser's problem; it is a problem *within the abuser*. A victim cannot assume and accept that his abuse is a product or byproduct of the bad relationship that they share; she absolutely cannot improve the relationship by managing herself or him better. The abuser is the one that has to choose to entirely manage his person and *his* abusive behavior. Our feelings are powerful, and they can affect how we act, but ultimately how we choose to behave is determined by how we think, our personal values, and our attitudes.

A significant time when feelings play a part in an abuser's interaction is when his feelings overrule any decision-making or disagreement that takes place. Abusers are not the typical men that are stereotyped as being men of little words; they're known for expressing their feelings in exaggerated ways compared to non-abusive men. This is because most abusers have inflated, insecure ideas about how important their feelings are, and they act out those feelings, eventually leading the victim to dread inquiring about his feelings or being around him when he dumps on her aggressively. Her abuser can come on strong with his feelings like a machine gun or sulk like a moping child, ultimately creating an ambiance in the home that life is at risk until the victim or someone else rescues his misery.

It's unimportant to him if there are special occasions, activities, holiday plans, or significant events to look forward to; he makes it known that nothing matters except his feelings. It's obvious that the abuser *does not* have a problem with his feelings. Feelings *do not* cause his abusive ways; it's his lack of respect for the victim's feelings that he has a problem with. The abuser's self-focus and attitude that nothing else matters *except his own feelings* and his lack of consideration for the victim and their children's feelings is actually one of the driving forces of his abusiveness. A common indicator of an abuser's lack of empathy for a victim's feelings is his pattern of being insensitive toward the care of the victim's property.

Most abusers take care of their own personal belongings, but when it comes to the victim's possessions, they are insensitive and either "accidently," out of carelessness, lose, damage, or break the victim's property or purposely threaten and at times deliberately hurt or ruin their belongings. The abuser sometimes may lend or sell a victim's property without first consulting with her. If he breaks some of her belongings, it's normally something that she has sentimental value for, and he neither offers to pick it up after he throws it across the room nor replace it after he breaks it. Sometimes he will apologize by saying he will replace the item—just to quiet her about the loss and to portray himself as good—but he never does.

The Abuser's Profile
Many have asked: "What makes a boy grow up to become an abuser?" "What does an abuser look like?" Abusers are not distinguishable. Part of the answer therein lies in the evidence that abusers are outwardly non-distinguishable during boyhood or manhood. The only distinguishing factors are his family values, social upbringing, and peer and adult role models. Whenever I have led an abuser's group, I have always selected a male for a co-leader so that we can work the group together as a united front. This is important because if the making of an abuser is influenced by significant female and male role models, then the group leaders have to represent role models that will not tolerate or endorse abuse. It's a given that when a professional confronts an abuser's *mindset,* he will become unglued, and his inner debasing and defaming tactics, which he normally reveals only to the victim, will eventually leak.

An abuser may try to conceal his contempt toward his victim while in group, but over time he will either attempt to intimidate with his tone or use profanity to any group member or therapist that challenges how he thinks about being abusive. An abuser becomes insolent when the group therapist and group members want to focus on how he thinks because the abuser wants to process how he feels. The abuser prefers to derail from answering questions about his abusive mentality because he's afraid to lose his desired dominion over his victim.

The abuser is a deceiver who is a tyrant. Abusers are secretive about their cruel and arbitrary ways of abusing their victim. Abusers are well versed on the expected social norms and the powers of the legal system. An abuser is quite the maestro when a police car pulls up to the driveway of his home. By the time the police officer rings the doorbell, he has a calm and smooth quality about him; after all, who would suspect he just slapped his spouse around? Most abusers are able to manipulate officers into leaving without any charges because they are eloquently reporting all that the victim has done. When the officer sees the victim, he sees her in a disarrayed state as if she's the one out of control and the abuser just pleads self-defense. An abuser's thinking about himself is grandiose, and he portrays himself as a conformist in appearance so that the public can't possibly believe that he would act out such deviant and criminal behavior. The abuser's normal comportment is one of the ways that he circumvents the law.

An abuser has a home and a public profile. At home, the abuser is flagrant and outspoken in his daily tsunami of complaints. The abuser entrenches upon the victim's right to peace of mind; she's flooded with his habitual grumblings and warnings with frightening threats. In public, an abuser is known for being friendly in their community, which is in direct contrast to the way he conducts himself at home with the victim and children. An abuser's family may even receive compliments on the abuser based on his public image. It's not uncommon for the abuser's family to observe or experience one or more of the following when around him in private:

1. A pattern of intimate relationship conflicts with women.
2. Critical views of women when around victim but openly supportive of women when in public.
3. Intimidating, combative, and/or assaultive, yet non-threatening to others.

THE ABUSER: EVERYTHING YOU EVER WANTED TO KNOW

4. Controlling at home but makes concessions with others.
5. Furious at home but has a smile for everyone else.
6. Very selfish with victim but selfless around others.
7. Attends religious activities but doesn't allow victim and children religious freedom at home.
8. Economically flexible and even generous with others but tight with victim.
9. Lazy/wanting to be catered to at home but industrious hard worker at his place of employment.
10. Offensive toward the victim and children but does not use foul language around others.
11. Ruthlessly rude with the victim and genteel with total strangers.
12. Forgets important communication from the victim/family celebrations/events but never misses information pertaining to his recreation and commitments with others.

The abuser relentlessly silences the victim and does not allow her to recount her abusive experiences with him (which she gives as examples and proof of his abuse). In order to silence her and to keep her from confronting his history of abusive episodes, he accuses her of keeping a list of his wrongs. This then reverses the focus and makes it seem like something is wrong with *her*. In his opinion, she's the one with the problem; after all, no one else in the community has a problem with him! An abuser plays the "Mr. Charming" role to assist him in feeling good about himself when indeed *he knows* the abuse he has committed. The abuser is a bully to the victim and children, but popular and a charming friend to everyone he meets.

Keeping the "Mr. Charming" image helps the abuser feel good about himself when the victim confronts his abuse. The abuser lives with belying behaviors about being an abuser. Being "Mr. Charming" for others benefits him as it serves as a cover-up from himself. There are "Mr. Charming" abusers in every socioeconomic class, ethnic group, or race group. The hurt that a victim endures while living with the contradistinction that the abuser lives out, treating *others* with respect and mistreating *her*, gnaws at her soul. Sometimes she feels as if he has a split personality, but she knows better; she knows deep down in her soul that she has indeed experienced his abuse, which he denies. This *other* "Mr. Charming" personality that the abuser projects is just one of his mechanics in managing his need for total power and control over the victim. An abuser is cavalier; he believes that if he "looks good" in public, who is going to believe or give any support to the victim?

Also, abusers do the groundwork with a good public image as a part of their scheme; if she does indeed report him or if he gets caught, others will rescue him as a can-do-no wrong neighbor. The abuser is confident that they will wonder what *she* did to try to control *him* and cause him to get into trouble. When abusers are caught engaging in immoral behavior, they readily attempt to manipulate law enforcement and the judicial system by asking their allies (friends, family, co-workers, and neighbors) to send letters of reference, alibis, or testify on their defense regarding their history of remarkable conduct. This is a manipulative tactic to evade full responsibility and the consequence of their choice to abuse their wife and children. This is evidence of the abuser's outright denial of the severity of his crime undermining that he has charges against him for the abusive crime(s) he committed against his victim(s). The abuser refuses to acknowledge that it is *not* about his conduct in the community—but about his role as an abuser.

Normality in demeanor is one of the abuser's most perplexing idiosyncrasies that the victim, professionals, and society experience. This presentation of his *self* is what has created the dilemma of diagnosing an abuser. Professionals concur that it would make their diagnostic assessment process less cryptic if

THE ABUSER: EVERYTHING YOU EVER WANTED TO KNOW

the abuser's composure were more uncooperative or exemplifying some type of mental disorder. An abuser is a closed book except when he is bamboozling the victim. Usually, the abuser is a fairly calm and reasonable individual while interacting with others—except when it relates to the victim. Abusers can easily get into a fall-out with anyone if they feel threatened by or jealous of the individual's interactions with the victim. For the most part, anyone else that has dealings with the victim is treated nicely by the abuser. A victim is always taken aback as to how her abuser can treat other people with respect while starting a brawl with her in his two-sided nature.

One reason *why* abusers are able to treat others cordially is because they're not in an intimate relationship with them of which they feel jealous and possessive. Abusers notoriously attempt to control the victim as a possession that they can take for granted and coerce into staying in the relationship (despite their mistreatment of the victim). There's also a chronic rage that an abuser displays around the victim which escalates into destructive actions whenever she mentions that she wants to terminate the relationship. Ending the relationship means abandonment to an abuser. Unlike the grief experience that an ordinary relationship break-up or the end of a relationship through separation, divorce, or death brings on, an abuser's desperation levels of abandonment increase. The abuser's phone calls or other forms of technical contact, threats, stalking, and attacks may end in the death of the victim or her loved ones.

This extreme reaction is a part of his obsessive, possessive, jealous framework which cannot (or won't) deal with the idea that someone else can have his victim; she is his possession. The same mindset that he operates with whereby he believes he has a right to treat his spouse however he wants is the same mind-messing that he uses with the victim, seducing her mind to return to him. In his thinking, he owns her, regardless of how he treats her. The abuser does have an ego problem; his self-importance overrides the victim's self-worth. This self-importance is not formulated based on his self-esteem but more on his underlying need for power. An abused victim expends a lot of her zeal and energy lubricating and re-applying WD-40 to the abuser's loud ego (praising him even when he blows his nose), wishfully thinking that if she keeps him well-oiled, he may tone it down and refrain from blowing up at her. Trying to build an abuser's ego is an eternal task. You might temporarily reduce the squeaking, but sooner or later he'll sound off louder than ever (without any provocation), and no amount of WD-40 will keep him from blaring at you. The outcome when a victim attempts to build his ego into a positive self-image is the opposite—the abuser becomes *more* abusive.

When an abusive relationship progresses, the abuser becomes more apathetic about his abusiveness; he has had a lot of time to justify his maltreatment of the victim. By now, he believes he *is* entitled to abusing his spouse. The abuser's thinking is that it is her fault; he tells her that there's no use in trying to work out the relationship because she's "Mrs. Know-it-all" (referring to her concerns about the abuse and suggesting counseling). The abuser gives himself the authority to take abusive action on the basis of his belief system. It's not about the low self-esteem in his ego; if that were the case, then the victim who suffers from his constant bullying and own shattered self-esteem would be transformed to be as cruel as he is to her. The overall profile of an abuser is that he indulges in the basking of being served on demand. Abusers thoroughly enjoy having their victim at their beck and call. Abusers expect to be taken care of and get used to the victim's constant giving. Regrettably, her efforts to build him up so that he will feel better and not be so mean do not work because he is never satisfied with all that she does for him—his ego neediness is never satiated.

THE ABUSER: EVERYTHING YOU EVER WANTED TO KNOW

This is one of the reasons why neither the victim nor the professional can change the abuser's abusive mentality by improving the couple's dynamics in the relationship. No amount of building the abuser's self-esteem, role-modeling respect, or teaching him impulse control, conflict resolution, or anger management can change the driving force of his abusive behavior. It's not that an abuser is unable to resolve problems in a non-abusive way, it's that he's *unwilling* to participate in conflict-resolution. Studies show that abusers have the ability to communicate assertively and participate in conflict resolution in other arenas of their life. For example, at work they use self-control, but they choose not to manage themselves around their victim. A therapist can provide an abuser with state-of-the-art therapy that equips him with skills for active listening (instead of selective listening), mediation, and communication skills, and he just goes home and continues to abuse his victim. The abuser, once home, tells the victim that the therapy didn't work because of her, or the therapist, or both of them.

Most abusers believe that it's their privilege and right to control everything their victim does. As his spouse, she is to keep him informed at all times of her whereabouts (she's not to engage in lunch-time office runs or personal errands). She's to report those with whom she is associating, and he pretty much tells her what time she's allowed to leave and return home by his reactions to her comings and goings of ordinary life. An abuser's response to her feelings of oppression is that she ought to be grateful that he cares enough to take care of her. The opposite, of course, is true; he wants to manipulate her into staying home all of the time to take care of him. The abuser expects her to honor and respect him and not to disagree with him on his dictatorship.

The abuser's control tactics are all wrapped up in his **manipulation, denial, love-bombing, gaslighting, mood swings, lying, sympathy, selfishness,** *and his* **decision-making.**

Manipulation—Abusers are masterful at *manipulating* the victim. They use manipulation frequently while interacting with the victim. Manipulation is used by the abuser when he is not verbally or physically intimidating her in order to still get his way. The abuser's lack of empathy for her feelings fuels his need to manipulate her into being distressed and keeping her confused about her unsettling feelings regarding the abuse. Manipulation as an underlying tactic helps the abuser to refrain from the constant verbal and/or physical attacks, which gets the victim on his good side and keeps her from identifying him as an abuser.

Manipulation is a form of mental abuse because it is not as obvious as the abusive actions that the victim can witness. Manipulation places the victim in a compromised, traumatized position where she's constantly wondering, *what just happened to me?* When verbal and physical assaulting occur, she can readily identify what the abuser has just done to her, but with manipulation, she is left sad or exasperated, not able to identify what exactly went down to cause her to feel so awful. She finds herself with a feeling of impending blame. The mental abuse intensifies when the abuser combines outright abusive behavior with manipulation, and at that point, the victim is manipulated into thinking that she's either the culprit or losing her mind!

Denial—An abuser can turn all red, yell profusely, pout, stonewall, or point his finger at the victim and deny his abusive demeanor blatantly. An abuser's middle name is "denial." Invariably, abuser group members would tell their story of a recent explosive episode they had had, and they would admit that their hostility levels and abusive acts toward the victim were wrong, *but* in the same breath, they would interject minimization of the incident and reverse it back to blaming the victim—or something outside of themselves. If the group member was confronted on his denial, he would revert back to other stressors at work, social upbringing, drinking, financial difficulties,

THE ABUSER: EVERYTHING YOU EVER WANTED TO KNOW

having worries, or blaming the children. Usually he will blame the victim for the incident that evolved out of his own behavior. Ultimately, he manipulates his way out of the incident and scolds the victim for confronting his denial.

Abusers even feel that they can blame the victim for their life disappointments. Their sense of entitlement takes over, and they regress from admitting that their abusiveness is unacceptable to feeling justified for what they said or did. When abusers are confronted with the idea that everyone has life disappointments but it's not their spouse's fault (and not everyone that has life disappointments goes home to assault their spouse and/or children), they become enraged. They become irate to this observation because they realize that when they are at work or at another life activity, they don't become explosive if they face a disappointment; they simply deal with it! This denial takes over because they know that it is their sense of entitlement around the victim that makes a difference in whether they choose to become explosive or not.

Denial is a form of silent lying. It makes a victim feel like she's on a terrifying roller coaster ride when the abuser has just had an ugly verbally-explosive episode and she asks him for an apology, and he says, "What do you mean? I don't know what you're talking about?!" An abuser lies as his defense mechanism; he's proficient at fabricating denial stories. An abuser can either deny with a straight face while eye-balling her, laughing at her encounter, or repeatedly saying, "You're ridiculous; I don't remember any of that." Many victims feel like their heads are spinning when the abuser reacts with such lying. After repeatedly hearing the abuser's denial of every disturbing fight and altercation, a victim can feel symptoms of anxiety and depression or that she's starting to slip her mind.

The abuser welcomes these symptoms in the victim because it strengthens his case that she's the one that is the real unstable person in the relationship. Abusers are powerful guilt-inducers; they make the victim feel wrong about bringing up the examples of disrespect and hurt which they have caused. After lying so many times when the victim confronts him, he really believes that he wasn't abusive and that it's a figment of her imagination. Why does he use such a strong defensive denial (silent lying)? An abuser lies about his abusive behavior because he takes pleasure in making the victim feel like she's going insane (bullying) and because he doesn't want to be held responsible and accountable for what he has done (abuse her).

Love-Bombing—Love-bombing is the classic way that abusers seize their victim by stealth. Love-bombing can mean excessive compliments, romantic advances, public or private displays of affection, unexpected gifts, or his sudden attentiveness to being very helpful around the house or involved with the children.

Gaslighting/Confusion—Abusers have finesse about changing the subject during an intense discussion—which then leads into an argument—because they turn the focus on the victim. An abuser manipulates his way into accusing her of things that she has *not* said or done. The victim falls into the trap of feeling confused about the point(s) she wanted to make as he twists her words and leaves her feeling as if she's going crazy! This tactic to confuse her is called gaslighting. Gaslighting is one of the abuser's favorite argument tactics through which he has his own version of what happened, and re-scripts and denies what occurred with the victim. Then, she questions herself as to what actually took place. The abuser lulls her into admitting that she's responsible for something she didn't do. (The term gaslighting comes from the 1944 film *Gaslight* whereby the husband plays tricks on and controls his wife's mind by convincing her that she's losing her mind; her possessions are missing, she hears sounds coming from the attic, and she sees the gaslights brighten and dim.) This tactic warrants having a full discussion because it is the abuser's most frequently used strategy in order to keep the victim confused and entrapped in the relationship.

Gaslighting is the formal term for: *deliberately* distorting or twisting another person's reality to manipulate and control them, causing the person to distrust their self and trust them instead. Have you ever been in a discussion with someone, and their version of the conversation or order of events that took place seems totally different than yours? This difference of perspective happens frequently, mostly because our human memory is not always precise, but also because we come from various backgrounds and that affects how we perceive people and situations. It's not uncommon to remember things from a different perspective than others.

However, in unhealthy circumstances, when a person manipulates someone else's memories and attempts to make them feel like they're going out of their mind because their memories are completely different than the other person's, it's called gaslighting. Gaslighting is never about someone having a variant opinion than the other person. Gaslighting is a manipulative tool that abusers use to cause the victim to question her reality (her version of what really happened) and therefore make her become more submissive to her abuser. Gaslighting is a tactic progressively employed by the abuser, and even though the victim sees what has happened once she has been gaslighted, most of the time she doesn't even notice his subtle brainwashing techniques which accumulate over time in her mind.

How does a victim determine if she's being gaslighted? Look for feelings of confusion whenever you have a disagreement with the abuser; his main goal in gaslighting you is to keep you in a confused state. The confusion pattern persists because abusers lie, and they lie with a straight face and will not change their mind even if the victim has evidence of the truth. Watch for the abuser's pattern of thinking and behaviors: his mind and actions are repeatedly assailed by either covert or overt defaming, slanderous accusations. Gaslighting serves the abuser's purpose to keep the victim unbalanced and believing that everything the abuser says is the true reality of what occurred. The more certain that the victim is that the abuser is in error, and the more she pursues the truth, the more he will persevere with his lie of what "truly" happened.

The victim can know she's being gaslighted if she suddenly finds herself being isolated from her friends and family. Abusers don't want their victim to compare information (others' version) of what really happened or to share what the abuser has been telling her (his version). The abuser lies about her friends and family—that they don't love her as he does—and she begins to believe him because he has lied to them as well. This further isolates her, and she lands under his control (the only relationship to which she can turn). The gaslighting abuser will use the victim's loved ones as weapons against her, and this fulfills his goal to make the victim believe that others' relationships with her are insignificant compared to the special relationship she has with him. When she consistently hears only the abuser's perspective, she begins to believe him. Having already either put the victim on a pedestal of love-bombing or belittled her as worthless, the abuser manipulates the victim into seeing the gaslighter as her only relationship on which she can count.

Another sign that the victim is being gaslighted is if the abuser appears to be a different person within the same moment, hour, or day; at one point he is kind, and so the victim is unsure if the insane negativity that transpired really happened because he was so remorseful and gentle afterward or the next day. However, that idealization of the victim after his episode will be followed by another round of devaluation, and the insults just bring the victim right back to asking, *what on Earth went wrong?* The abuser's ploy is to put her back in that place of

THE ABUSER: EVERYTHING YOU EVER WANTED TO KNOW

chasing him for the display of kindness he showed her before, to bring her back to blaming herself for the way he treated her, and to compromise her request for respect. The abuser interjects affection in between his abuse because he knows if anyone receives insults or shouting every day, the relationship could be at risk; he wants to lead the victim to believe that their relationship is valuable and worth saving because of the good times. The abuser counts on the victim working very hard to restore their harmony. Abusers lead victims to believe that they have said or done something wrong and it's the victim that has to behave well to get the abuser back on his good side. This then reinforces the abuser's belief that if the victim hadn't done something wrong, he would not have escalated.

A typical gaslighting abuser will do a lot of projective identification; he will accuse the victim of doing the very same things that he does. If he's being explosive, mentally or physically abusive, unfaithful, or using vices or any other immoral illegal behavior, he will say that she is doing the same. Of course, none of the allegations are true, but it's a distraction tactic to keep the victim off-kilter and on the defense. In the meantime, the victim is expending her focus and time defending herself while he gets away with all of the behaviors he accused her of.

The most obvious behavioral tactic exhibited by an abuser who is gaslighting is insisting that the victim is "crazy." It raises his ego to minimize and dismiss her interaction with him and to totally ignore her feelings. It is, of course, beyond condescending to call her "crazy," and that definitely confirms that he's done listening to her and that she will not be heard. The more the victim hears that she's crazy, the more she believes and sees herself as crazy. The victim is now under the abuser's power to make her believe that she's unstable around him, and he extends it further into what others will think of her if they know that she's not mentally stable. This is where the abuser wants her to be—under his abusive spell. She will no longer trust her judgment and will submit to everything he says and decides. Questioning his lies or behavior is no longer an option because she's disoriented, confused, and under his total control.

The key to preventing or getting out of a gaslighting relationship is education on the signs, traits, and techniques the abuser uses so as to be prepared to avoid falling into the abuser's captivity. The way out is by becoming completely aware of the dynamics of gaslighting, then stepping back and asking yourself this question: Does being in the relationship mean constantly having to compromise my mental well-being by having to defend myself all the time on my thoughts, ideas, opinions, and requests for boundaries? Ending an abusive relationship is possible, and every victim that overcomes her abuse reports that she finally understands how inhumanely she was treated once the relationship has been terminated. Every victim that reaches the end state of her abuse vows never again to be pulled into a relationship with an abuser. A victim can heal from the abuser's mental bashing and control, but she is unable to do so in his presence and while under his spell, not while ignorant of his love-bombing, gaslighting, and the truth that all he has promised will not come true due to *his* choice actions.

Mood Swings—It's the abuser's unprovoked constant mood changes that keep the victim hopping. One moment he looks approachable and like he's feeling friendly toward her, but it turns out to be his way to manipulate her into always keeping her compliant and on-guard.

Lying—One of the first lessons that a victim needs to learn is that her abuser feeds on her ignorance to his lies. Abusers operate under falsehood and know their victim can be easily deceived. Abusers are deceitful in their conversations and their actions when interacting with the victim, the community, or the authorities. This tendency to be untruthful is a way to manipulate the victim and others into not knowing the abuser's true desires and purposes in the relationship. An abuser uses lying to manipulate the victim into accepting him or doing the things he prefers for her to do. If an abuser is confronted by the victim about a weapon that she finds in their home, he says he purchased it to protect her and the family (from burglars) or he announces that he's going to begin taking up hunting. If that's the case, then why didn't she know about the weapon? An abuser lies his way out of anything that's found in his possession that she doesn't know about—he says that it belongs to someone else or has another reason for being there. The only way out of the abuser's lying trap is for the victim and others to be alert and discern between truths about abusers, and their lies.

Sympathy—Abusers are attention hungry and will manipulate the victim into reversing the empathy in his direction so that he is the focus and the one that's a "victim." This aids the abuser in keeping the victim from verbalizing her concerns over his abusiveness toward her.

Selfishness—An abuser is an accomplished manipulator just being himself—selfish. The abuser coerces the victim into thinking that his desires are solely for her interest, making it seem as if he's being giving by doing something good for the victim. An abuser is always on the lookout for his personal well-being at the neglectful expense of the victim or children—it is all about him.

Decision-Making—Abusers prevail upon the victim by manipulating her inner desires. The abuser's ulterior motive for getting the victim to make a decision about something is hidden from her. The abuser manipulates her into believing that the decisions that she has made within the abusive relationship are her own. It may take a victim quite some time before she catches on to his past intentions and the fact that his motives were not pure (or even to realize that he made the decision). One of the abuser's claims to fame (in keeping his incognito role as an abuser) is his excuse that he loses control of himself when the victim supposedly instigates him; that's why she should know better than to mess with his feelings. Abusers claim that they lose control of themselves; this is reversing the problem once again. The abuser does not have a problem losing his self-control—his problem is that he controls his spouse.

This is the very reason an abuser exasperates the victim with his unyielding abusiveness. An abuser dares to mercilessly trifle with his victim; she becomes his footstool. The abuser's blame on the victim for his agitated abuse is a form of punishment: to retaliate against the victim's resistance to his controlling behavior. An abuser demands adherence to his rules, and his word is to be respected by the victim as law. An abuser rejects the victim's feedback and treats her like a child as if she is back-talking when she attempts to interject a question or thought. Abusers believe that it is appropriate for them to withdraw privileges from their victim whenever their mood strikes. The victim cannot count on what he has offered her or future promises because whenever she forgets her "victim composure" and resists his controlling behavior, he uses vengeful tactics like changing things up and taking away what he had previously allowed or decided to give her.

What's it Like to Live with an Abuser?
Typically, when a functional person hears that their friend, co-worker, or family member is in a relationship with an abuser, their advice is to leave them. However, for a victim of abuse, this may feel impossible because her life is entirely centered on her abuser. Usually the victim asks for advice on how she can improve their marriage to make it better and to work things out. Sometimes, there are children involved and the victim doesn't view disrupting the children's lives as an option. At times, a victim feels forced to stay in an abusive relationship because she

fears parental or community disapproval if she were to break her vows.

The alternative is to continue her relationship with her abuser, but she needs to be made aware that there is nothing that she herself can do to improve her relationship with her abuser. Living with an abuser is an arduous undertaking for the victim; he will gradually and ultimately wear her down to the point of draining the life out of her spiritually, emotionally, and physically. The abuser's focus is to enervate the victim. A victim who chooses to live with an abuser subjects herself to his treating her derisively and only intermittently offering her loving acts of kindness. Most victims see a good person within the abuser, and they live to relish the abuser's goodness through his periods of love, romance, affection, and generosity. Sometimes the abuser will come around and act genuinely apologetic; he may not verbally apologize but will instead offer gifts and treats—he thinks it's all good and that's the whole nature of his love-bombing tactic (to make *her* come around). Over time, the gifts are either to make up after his meanness or are self-focused gifts to brag on what he gave her; sometimes they're gifts that are for him to share with her.

The abuser does periodically reveal his true cruel self to her, but he only lets his guard down when he's certain that the victim is sure to stay; he randomly breaks up the emotionally-abusive episodes with periods of affection, which are the better moments that the victim lives for! Abusers aren't abusive all the time; there are cycles, patterns, and modes of control that the abuser engages in throughout the relationship. Sometimes the abuser is irresistibly romantic, bearing gifts and tenderheartedness, but suddenly an unprovoked side of him is displayed as he turns to the victim with revulsion. Even if the victim becomes aware of this love-bombing pattern, she chooses to stay and instead lives a silent life of abuse or seeks guidance from a counselor as to how to work on her part of the relationship. Most functional counselors will advise that the abuser is the only one that can work out the relationship. A wise counselor tells the victim the truth; that he's unable to tell her how she can live a healthy life with an abuser.

A victim lives an intermittent life of affection, arguments, and insults with her abuser; the victim has to sacrifice her values and most of who she is as a person. She has to accept a life of unreality because she's lied to all the time. An abuser basically sabotages the victim's reality, and he believes what he says stands because he knows he has been stripping her of her humanity and her independent thought. If the victim disagrees with him, he attempts to make her feel guilty for even bringing up the subject and for being ungrateful for the material or family life they have together (even though she has no control over her own life). The abuser denies it and is very prideful, hypersensitive, easily offended, quickly defensive, and infallible when the victim brings something to his attention. It can be as simple as her saying, "I smell something burning; do you?" The abuser responds with a tone, "I don't smell anything." The next day, she notices a burnt dripping on the stove where he warmed up his dinner.

Or, they could be at a restaurant and she notices his flirting with the server and comments on his friendliness toward her; he responds defensively with, "I don't know what you're talking about. I was just joking around with her." For an abuser to be content, the victim has to accept his take on what happened during his high tone argument as nothing but the truth. Or she'll end up receiving his wrath, which could lead him into a rage episode. Even if the victim complies with *all* of the abuser's requests, he will attempt to invalidate, undermine, or minimize every chance he gets. A victim gets used to not receiving *any* recognition for her attempts to please him—it's expected of her. She has to be prepared at all times that, even when she has pleased him and all is going well, he will create an argument over a trifling matter, especially during an event that's supposed to be a joyous, significant, or celebratory occasion.

An abuser overtly or passive-aggressively hooks the victim into believing that he values her thoughts and will invariably ask for her ideas or her opinion on a project or work situation. When she has thoughtfully come up with suggestions, the abuser will say he would rather not do the project anymore, and it wasn't such a big deal at work anyway. If she notices him undermining her suggestions, he makes it obvious that he's in charge of his own decisions and that she's ridiculous and demanding in suggesting her ideas and giving him feedback on any of his business, that she should be grateful to him for even sharing anything with her.

Abusers *always* seek to blame something or someone. Usually they say that everything is the victim's fault, and she begins to accept self-blame. This blame-shifting game that the abuser favors generally accompanies most arguments. The abuser will say or do whatever it takes to justify that he's not responsible for the conflict; he will lie or even be disloyal and violate the victim's trust so as to come out on top (to appear flawless). The abuser is by no means the victim's confidant because he will betray her confidence in exchange for maintaining his admiration from family, friends, and even strangers.

An abuser will blackmail his victim into believing that if she complains about him to her friends and family, he will make it known to all of her kith and kin that she's unstable. So if the victim wants to make the relationship work, she has to be quiet and not respond or react to his lying or devaluing remarks; she has to accept his offensive accusations that she's crazy, just a baby, and supersensitive. If she reacts to his cruelty, she will pay for every thought and feeling that she shares. A victim has to live with the abuser's unspoken or spoken rules, intimidation, sarcasm, denigrating comments about her, and she has to tolerate restriction or isolation from her interests, job, career, hobby, talents, friends, or family. The abuser overtly voices or covertly, via actions, lets the victim know that her interests or loved ones are insignificant as he gradually, over time, works on changing her into somebody else.

Some abusers lead victims to believe that it was *her* idea to put her education, career, or other interest aside in order to spend most of her free time cleaning, cooking, or running household errands and assisting him in building his career, even if she has never voiced seeing herself in that sole capacity. Essentially, the abuser's happiness becomes the victim's goal to keep the peace as she lays low, avoiding being his emotional punching bag. Then, he turns that around and says she's become someone boring and needs to perk up and be livelier.

Whether the abuser is gainfully employed as a high-empowered career man or has difficulty deciding on a career or maintaining a job, the abuse extends to the victim becoming part of his financial well-being. The abuser is not embarrassed to take income or financial benefits which she has earned and leave her without incidental spending money. She either works to help out with household bills on top of her household duties (even when there's a substantial income through his employment), or she makes herself indispensably available to build his career nonstop at his beck and call, sacrificing her identity in the process, or she ends up supporting the household because of his unstable income. The abuser's expectation of the victim is rationalized as "we are a team," even if there's only one calling the shots in the team. Consequently, the victim is weary and constantly running on empty. Her life energy and vitality are expended on and revolve around trying to make the abusive relationship work.

No matter how powerful a job position he holds, the abuser is insecure and might even stalk the victim. Even if the victim has given no reason to be distrusted, an abuser's self-entitled nature and lack of respect won't give the victim the right to lead a separate life apart from being conjoined with him; he prefers to and actually enjoys monitoring her whereabouts. Some abusers electronically track their victims and maintain surveillance with or without the victim's consent.

Abusers groom their future victim spouses by making love-bombing statements like, "you're so beautiful," "you're the love of my life, and I adore you," "I'm so in love with you; I've never felt this way before," "we were born to meet and live our lives together" and "you're the most beautiful woman in this room!" Think about that last compliment; how would he know if you're the most beautiful woman in the room unless he has been looking at other women in the room? These abusers are very attentive to the victim's needs while courting and offer to assist her in any way they can with tasks, chores, projects, even cooking. Helpful, attentive abusers stop their kindhearted nature once the marriage license is in their possession. Naturally, the victim enters into the false sense of security that it will be a team effort marriage because she is so special to him. In reality, this is how the victim becomes captured and isolated from everything and everyone who wants to have a relationship with her—even employers.

When the truth is revealed that she is not his special love after all unless he can control every part of her life and identity, she has to be prepared to keep his possessive, hurtful expectations a secret or pay the price dearly for telling on him. The abuser's pride and exterior reputation are everything to him; whether it's his family, friends, or employer, the victim must not confide in them or he will follow through with his threats to harm her and/or her loved ones. Most of his family members or buddies would not believe the victim and would defend him anyway because he's such a "good guy" around them.

Love-bombing is always a temporary, manipulative, intermittent maneuver. As soon as the victim displays any form of attachment to anything or anyone other than the abuser, the abuser will then get enraged and allege that she's selfish in her pursuits (projecting what he is doing to her). The victim can now see the results of the booby trap as his true character comes out—he's unable to comprehend how she can have interests outside of him, and he turns on her as an unreasonable and mean abuser. The abuser is only kind toward the victim if she does whatever he wants. If she doesn't comply, then he continues devaluing her and withdraws his kindness and approval, raises his voice, or stonewalls her; sometimes he's physically punitive. Since the abuser is always straddling between abusive and non-abusive days, living with an abuser means that on the good days it's like the sound of a clock ticking, waiting for the next calamity to happen.

An abuser never takes responsibility for his bullying behaviors. Whether the abuser overtly or covertly abuses her, she remains frightened by her abuser; this is a fear with which she lives every day. The abuser only apologizes so that the victim won't leave; he offers her the moon on a silver platter if she will just stay. Abusers have an intense fear of abandonment, and that's the only fear they express. The abuser will have an explosive episode if she reacts to his emotional, physical, or sexual harassment. An abuser will use excuse after excuse and rationalize why he was abusive toward the victim and expect her to respond with compassion and understanding. An abuser is notorious for bragging about his ability to forgive and forget as if nothing ever happened; he asserts that he isn't holding a grudge and letting everything roll off his shoulders while all along disguising the fact that if he blows off the inappropriate episode, he doesn't have to admit to his abuse. Recognizing the incident and episode would mean apologizing; ignoring and forgetting the incident

THE ABUSER: EVERYTHING YOU EVER WANTED TO KNOW

is an indication of his lack of remorse or conviction about his behaviors. The abuser can become volatile if the victim does not forgive and forget everything he has done to her; an abuser wants everything to be glossed over—and to have total absolution of his abuse.

An abuser knows beforehand whom he can and cannot prey on; he always seeks someone who appears to be kind and compassionate. The abuser knows all of her buttons, the positive, kind, compassionate button as well as the negative, reactive ones; he can obtain the result he seeks by pushing her likes and dislikes buttons (her emotional triggers) because he's keenly aware of them. The abuser takes advantage of her positive traits; he's quite certain that someone that's kind and compassionate will be empathic toward him and may explain away his swinging moods. Are you emotionally and compassionately drawn to your abuser? If so, that may be one of your triggers which may keep you in the abusive relationship. There's a myth that victims are weak individuals, but the abuser is manipulative with all types of victims from gentle to strong-willed and high-achieving women. The truth is that victims come in all personalities and all walks of life. They stop caring about themselves, are unaware of their emotional triggers, and explain away all of the abuser's behaviors. Do you know your emotional triggers which he can manipulate to keep you in the relationship?

When a victim learns her emotional triggers, she discovers the truth about her abuser, and she becomes aware of their nonexistent healthy relationship. The victim is now devastated and traumatized by the onslaught of the devaluation and dissolving of her person. She gives it all she's got to improve her living conditions with him and tries to restore him to the charming, wonderful person she has seen he can be, but that person never existed; it was just to make an amorous impression. An abuser only gives his love in arrogance as if he's bestowing an honor on the victim. All of his love gestures were calculated, as with any transaction in the abuser's life—to gain something in return. All the victim's kindness and compassionate forgiveness will not bring his loving personality back; it may come back sporadically on a temporal level, but not on a long-term level. The victim has been hearing empty promises of sharing dreams together, but they were only to be used to serve his purposes, so now the victim is always vigilant as to what his next move will be. If she does anything he considers wrong, it gives him leverage not to fulfill what he has offered for their life together. Living with an abuser means the victim loses her own sense of self, identity, purpose, and future goals.

Former victims compare living with an abuser to hell on Earth. It means living in an unsafe world within their own home and having to sacrifice their lives for the abuser. Happy times living with an abuser are few and far between. Those victims that choose to stay in an abusive relationship choose to live in a chaotic, unpredictable relationship. The victim's expectations from a relationship have to be compromised to meet the needs of her abuser; that's the type of lifestyle that a victim can expect to live when she chooses an abuser for the rest of her life. It's *all* about his needs. The abuser pretends to be interested in listening to the victim's dreams and aspirations, but should she decide to strive toward her goals, he will balk at her hopes and make comments to induce guilt for even thinking about proceeding. If he's a covert abuser, he will verbalize support of her goals but indirectly sabotage her progress in reaching any objectives by prioritizing his career goals over hers, involving her as a supportive spouse (she spends more time on his vision rather than hers). If she addresses the imbalance in the pursuit of their ambitions, his justification is that he's the head of household and his career as the main provider must come first.

THE ABUSER: EVERYTHING YOU EVER WANTED TO KNOW

For the most part, the abuser will talk badly about the victim with a critical, sarcastic, or mocking spirit or just report negative things about her behind her back to friends, family, co-workers, employers, or anyone they both have a relationship with so as to divide them, to separate them from her so he can have the better relationship with them to which he feels entitled. An abuser is very self-centered and experiences no true remorse, so the victim can't expect sincere empathy from him when she approaches him about her pain. The abuser might put on a front of caring about her, but usually that's because he wants to silence her from telling anyone about his apathy toward her feelings, goals, or about his lashing out at her. Living with an abuser means electing a turbulent lifestyle by choosing the abuser because you don't believe you're worthy of a non-abusive relationship.

To live with an abuser is to live with a thief of joy who's incessantly needy for attention and lonely without the victim; it's a relationship gone wrong because initially there were two individuals (the prerequisite of a relationship), and in the end, the victim's individuality has been extinguished. A victim has to get used to living with her abuser as his emotional and/or physical speed bag, and eventually she has to ask herself: "Is it worth my life?" Living with an abuser is a choice—not making a choice is a choice. Sometimes it's most helpful for the victim to ask herself if she would prefer to live as a victim or as an *Overcomer* (See Part V: *Overcomer* Defined). The reality is that when living with an abuser, she only has two choices.

The Abuser-Parent Profile
With respect to parenting styles, the abuser's attitude is one of superiority in his belief system. In his view, he is the better parent, and his authority rules even if he doesn't spiritually, emotionally, physically, and/or financially contribute to the raising of the children. The abuser seldom compliments the victim as a

mother except for empty praises or when he's in public and the compliment is made to build her up; however, he does this only to impress others. Sometimes he tells of his children's accomplishments, but he rarely tells his children how proud he is of their achievements; again, he elevates himself as to what a great father he must be. Some abusers are absent parents (they may or may not financially provide). They're only heard when they inflate their egos by bragging about their children or when they make it known to the entire household that they're dissatisfied and unhappy. When an abuser declares that he's unhappy, there isn't anyone in the household that dares to be happy! Most abusers don't admit that they are too selfish to raise children, but they see themselves as good and smart parents (knowing truthfully that they are only watching passively from the sidelines as the victim rolls up her sleeves daily to pour out her blood, sweat, and tears over her children).

Generally, abusers have delusions of grandeur as being an authority on parenting and will step in to discipline the children when it's uncalled for as if the victim is not doing a good enough job. When the abuser has been passive in helping her to correct the children appropriately, she assigns consequences to them, but at that point, he elects to interject his own consequences or sabotages the consequences she assigns. Abusers complain about the victim's parenting style, even though they are not doing the actual work (meals, laundry, disciplining, driving to activities, helping with homework, tending to children when they're ill, taking them to the doctor, running errands, and spiritually encouraging them). Usually they are not around during the children's schedules, so they lack comprehension about their children's needs. If they are around, they entertain themselves and do leisurely activities while the mother does the child-rearing role.

THE ABUSER: EVERYTHING YOU EVER WANTED TO KNOW

An abuser's vision that he's a good parent is far from the truth. It does not matter if the victim is a good mother and has wonderful qualities; he believes that he knows best about parenting. In most cases, the abuser's thinking and beliefs about his parenting will pull the children into his belief system, and they begin to reflect his view and become "Daddy's buddy," or "Daddy's boy/girl." Whether the victim leaves their abuser or not, the children begin to form the same disrespectful opinion that the abuser has about their mother. The abuser prides himself on building a wedge between his children and their mother; his thinking is that if he can't have their mother submit to his control and abuse, then he can still have control and continue to abuse her through the children.

What mother's heart doesn't break when her children disrespect her? Not only does the abuser continue to control and break the victim's heart through her children, but if this disrespect remains, then the next generations (her grandchildren) learn to disrespect her. This keeps the abuser in control of the victim. Many former victims live geographically miles apart from their past abuser but continue to experience his control whenever they interact with their children or grandchildren. An abuser has a hero complex, and in the same way that the victim believed he was a good guy at the onset of their relationship, the children see him as their hero even when he loses his guard and they see the real bad side of him. They, like the victim, believe the *real* him is the good guy (who doesn't exist). Naturally, an abuser doesn't volunteer openly that he controls the victim through their offspring. If the victim confronts him about poisoning their children's or grandchildren's mind with negative talk about her, he either denies his actions or states, "I can't help what I say, and I can't help it if they don't like you" while swelling with pride because of how much they prefer him over her.

The abuser may even attempt to maintain this dual world he creates by hiding his abuse of the victim from the children. Some abusers reserve their most disrespectful attacks on the victim for when they are at home—alone. This way, the children are not exposed to the abuse; they only see him as a good husband and father; they only see him as respectful toward their mother. If the abuser succeeds in keeping his mistreatment of their mother in solitude, eventually his maligned, abusive mentality is exhibited in his parenting. The majority of abusers are not able to keep this dual world long-term or keep the children from being involved. Life for the children ultimately becomes just as overwhelming and confusing as it is for their victimized mother.

Most children in abusive homes are under constant anxiety as they listen and watch the abuser verbally and/or physically attack their mother. They fear the splitting up of their family and losing their father. The children hear the shouting out of foul names and/or the throwing of things which scares them even on calm days for fear this can unpredictably happen any time. Children, like the victim, begin to have recollections of each episode and worry at home or at school and are always on guard, like the victim. They also start to think that it's their fault and that something is wrong with them. Children that experience their father abusing their mother wonder if they have caused the abuser to abuse their mother; they worry about not having been able to find a way to stop him from abusing her.

Be that as it may, they find themselves torn between loving their father, the abuser, and hating their mother for all of the arguments. Other times, the children uphold their mother who takes care of them 'round the clock. Victimized mothers have a huge challenge: to maintain a bond with their children due to the abuser creating so many hostilities in front of *or* while alone with the children. Children are one of the most destructive tools that an abuser uses against the victim. An abuser is well aware that there's nothing more devastating to the victim than hurting one of the children (or having her listen to his threats and watch his attempts to hurt the children's relationship with her). When abusers play out the dual role of good father and husband in public and abuser in private, this juxtaposition can manifest itself into years of emotional separation between the victim and her children. Particularly as the children age, the abuser uses conversational strategies to tell them devaluing untruths that develop in their heart and mind, resulting in the children associating a negative reputation with their mother.

Unlike the abuser, the victim stays neutral on her opinions of the children's abusive father. If the abuser has kept their mother's abuse isolated from them, most victims stay loyal to the abuser's dark character and do not verbalize to the children his true entity. Even over twenty years after escaping from her assaultive relationship, one of my patients said that her adult children (who were still in diapers when she escaped) asked why she had divorced their father. She relayed this response: "Because he said he no longer wanted to be married," and left it at that. This patient knew full well that in addition to his private assaults with her that he was also an emotionally-absent parent. Victims do want to protect their children from the abuser's true uncouth, abusive nature, but most of the time the abuser makes this impossible. Furthermore, the victim fears that if she reveals the abuser's volatile behaviors toward her (which she is silenced from telling the children), he will increase his assaults and then start abusing the children.

Some abusers build a wedge between the victim and her children by forcing her to work inside and outside of the home, not allowing her time to bond with the children. This, in turn, interferes with proper attachment to her children and vice versa. Remember that this is only one tactic and level of abuse which, combined with multiple tactics, forms an abusive relationship.

Not every two-income family makes for an abusive spouse with the victim as a workhorse while the abuser relishes in recreation, being the only one privileged to hang out and bond with the children. She becomes a workhorse because the abuser does not offer to help with household or child-related responsibilities. That is not the case in most two-income homes; the parents balance work, child-rearing, chores, recreation, and play. When asked to share in household work, an abuser balks, and if he does comply, he does it in a poor mood or "forgets" and procrastinates so that the victim eventually stops asking for his help and just does it herself to avoid conflict.

If the abuser initiates helping out with chores or any project, he wants recognition for anything he does; if he is not complimented, he subtly makes it known that he's connected or attached to that action. Sometimes he makes it known in his tone that he's offended because his efforts were not immediately recognized. There is no selfless giving on his behalf without expecting some form of return from the victim, and sometimes if she watches carefully, this behavior extends itself unto others; but, because he's so swift, it's normalized and overlooked. The abuser prefers for her to work both outside the home and in the home as he says she must contribute to the household (even when his salary can be budgeted so she can stay home with the children).

You've heard of the abuser pounding on the children to inappropriately discipline them even when they're not in need of any discipline. There's also the passive abuser who never exerts any appropriate discipline of the children and is able to win over the children as the "good parent," and the victim is then forcefully placed in a position of being the only parental discipline to guide the children. This therefore labels her as the "bad parent" in the eyes of the children. This is an abuser's triumph over the victim as he controls the bond between mother and child, while he's looked up to as the children's friend. This also fulfills the abuser's neediness for love, affirmation, affection, and admiration. The abuser's desire to monopolize all positive attention to him is achieved as he passive-aggressively abuses the victim (through the children) by allowing the children to talk back to, be sarcastic, scold, mock, correct, or insult their mother when she appropriately disciplines them. Abusers use this disrespect tactic with children and continue the pattern into their adulthood.

This is a progressive underlying tactic which is cumulative in developing the abuser's ego as he gorges and derives prideful pleasure from hoarding the relationship with the children—instead of sharing a balanced, responsible relationship as a parent. The abuser is built up while the children uphold him as a nice guy! The abuser is not only a thief of the victim's dignity, but he also steals the mother-child bond. This enables others in his life to engage in stealing her children as well. In some cases, the abuser extends the wedge between the victim and the children by giving them the spin-off message that his family is also the better family. Therefore, the children must look up to his family as more special, and neither the victim nor her family can offer the same kind of loving bond as he or his family can.

The children grow up idolizing the abuser's family, as he has ensured that they have more contact with his family who, in turn, undermine the children's relationship with their mother. They prioritize their family narcissistically as "the good one" to visit and bond with. There are children brainwashed by the abuser who echo his voice: "Anyone would kill to be a part of Dad's family!"

It is the nature of an overt abuser to openly defame the mother or for a covert abuser to passively devalue the mother or to overvalue his family. If the victim confronts him on his lack of involvement in appropriately disciplining the children, rescuing them when they are in need of parental discipline, being unfair in sharing parental workload, not allowing connection with her family, or splitting and building a wedge between she and the children, he denies his irresponsible position and reacts in a defensive tone. The passive abuser's tactic is similar to that of a covert narcissist, who, of course, sees himself through his inflated ego as the better parent (even though he has minimally helped in raising the children). To the children and others, he appears as the more loving parent, never questioning his selfishness or lack of empathy for the mother-child bond which he has destroyed.

If the abuser and victim divorce and she remarries, most abusers want the last word with their children. Even if an abuser has stated that he has no desire for the children and has to be forced by the court to pay child support, he usually refuses to allow the children to be adopted by the victim's new spouse. This keeps the abuser thinking that he's entitled to control his victim and children's future. All of my group member patients have stated that they knew they could always count on using the children as a weapon. Some of my patients would use their children to terrorize the victim whenever they wanted to swing back and forth from verbal assaults to hurting the children. The only time that abusers are cautious about not threatening or abusing the children is when they worry about the children telling someone. An abuser knows that abused children can risk his good public reputation. This is when the abuser steps back in his destructive mindset and renders the abuse to the children through torturing their mother in front of them.

An abuser may resort to punishing the children, but not by assault; instead, he uses unjust punishments. The abuser favors this indirect and unjust form of punishment toward the children because it accomplishes his need for total dominion over his home. The children are under his control, and he knows that it's very painful for the victim to watch her children being unduly punished. It also fulfills his need to bully her parental decisions and undermines her authority as a parent in front of their eyes.

Abusers feel justified to delve out unfair, harmful punishment on both the children and the victim because they are used to externalizing any responsibility for their abuse. Abusers ignore the subject of mistreating their family because they feel entitled to treat the victim and children however they want, justifying the idea that they provide an income and don't have to do anything else in the home. If challenged by this idea, they escalate. An abuser sincerely believes in his abusive mind that it's the victim and/or children that make him act abusively.

The Abuser and Anger
When it comes to abusers that are having verbal and/or physical, out-of-control anger outbursts, abusers have self-reported to myself and other professionals that they are adequately able to maintain control of their thinking and awareness while being abusive. In the middle of their rage, they ask themselves questions such as, "Will this incident be found out?" "Will this incident affect my reputation?" "Can I get hurt in the middle of this altercation?" "Could I be legally charged, and would it affect my job?" "Will this really affect my kids, or will they just bounce back since they're just kids?" "Am I going too far this time?" The abuser constantly asks himself questions of this sort during his blowups because an abuser's mind thinks differently about right and wrong. If he can quickly answer his questions with denial, rationalizations, or excuses that he can justifiably use, then he can proceed without regret or remorse because he can explain that he just lost control when *she* pushed his out-of-control button. An abuser's anger is not what leads him to lose control; the abuse is *not* about losing control but about taking control. In the abuser's conscience, right and wrong are interchangeable.

There is a serious degree of premeditated consciousness that's infiltrated into an abuser's angry, malicious actions. At the same time, there are many occasions where the coast is totally clear, and the abuser doesn't have to be concerned about thinking and answering his questions to cover himself. Most abusers are competent about bringing themselves under control, even though they don't like to admit it. They would rather blame their out-of-control actions on their inability to recoup after the victim, someone, or a circumstance made them angry.

It's not to say that they plan every explosive episode that they have, but abusers themselves will self-disclose that they could have stopped their escalation but didn't because someone or something made them mad. This reveals that there's forethought into their level of escalation. Most abusers usually map out the direction that they are heading with their abusive relationship pretty well. It's as if they're driving and are quite familiar with the direction they're traveling; they know their limits and realize when they are traveling on a one-way street and when to anticipate a dead end (limit to their outburst). Against this background, they also are very observant of the limits of the victim, and they use this awareness to their advantage in order to create a number of concurrent misconceptions so as to confuse the victim and set her up to doubt herself, trip over her words, or block her thinking. This empowers the abuser to steer her down a dead end. Most abusers are quite aware of the tactics that they use to manipulate the continuation of their abuse.

Blaming his actions on "anger" is one of the abuser's tactics to manipulate others into giving him a break from his inappropriate behaviors; after all, he says that he was just angry, and everyone gets angry every now and then. Yes, everyone experiences anger; it's a part of being human and daily living. We have all been disappointed and angry at a person(s) whom we believe has done us wrong in some form or another. But we don't proceed to emotionally or physically attack them just because we're angry. It's not the same as what the abuser states; he is saying that anger causes him to be abusive. The truth is that he's angry because he knows he has been abusive, and he's being confronted about it. An abuser's furious attitude has a lot to do with the way that he processes and thinks about his spouse, others, and life circumstances; he is angry because he expects his every need—as an entitled being—to be met.

I've worked at several hospitals (military, veterans, public, private) where I conducted "anger" groups, which were appropriate for the diagnosis of the patients involved. I have led outpatient anger groups for mandatory probation clients that were useful for them in order to gain insight and to have as an accountability support system. However, these patients and clients were not in treatment due to having a history of being abusive. They had varied diagnoses, and the anger management groups were used as a tool to assist them in managing their feelings and pain (anger is generally a cover-up for pain). The group served them well through the learning of self-control and self-management and by gaining productive communication patterns.

While working with couples dealing with the deaths of their teen children due to drunk drivers, I learned that these parents were angry when they entered therapy (even after attending a grief group). These parents were livid! Some of these couples were referred to an anger group because of how their unresolved anger was affecting their relationships and daily responsibilities. Did they go home and verbally and/or physically abuse one another? No. But their anger symptoms came out indirectly through depression, hypertension, sleep disorders, or decreased libido, and relationships at work were less than amiable. In cases such as these, the foundation of their behaviors *was* anger. Anger management individual and group therapy was the appropriate referral for them.

When working with inmates, I came across an anger group that was not being used effectively. The daily afternoon anger group had already been established when I began to work with these inmates. The blunder I had to work with was that there were inmates in the anger group with various diagnoses. I saw some of the inmates in individual therapy, and in working with these inmates that had a history of being abusive, I noticed they were assigned to this anger group. These abusive inmates were being done a disservice because they were convinced and had convinced other inmates that it was their anger that caused them to be abusive. I had to undo their abusive thinking by telling them a realistic statement after they said they were in prison due to an anger problem. "No, you're in prison because of your history of abuse toward your wife, for shooting and attempting to kill her (or whatever the abusive crime was)." Inmates in my individual sessions were brought back to the reality that all humans experience anger and sometimes even lose control of their emotions with respect to the issue at hand, but they don't react by verbally and/or physically attacking their spouse.

An abuser is a con man, whether he's in prison or not. An abuser will use his violent anger to distract the victim and divert any others involved from attention to the severity of his disrespect, profuse denying lies, or other irresponsible controlling behaviors. The abuser chooses not to admit that he has explosive episodes, even on days when he's not angry about anything in particular. Granted, on days when the abuser is especially upset about his expectations not having been met, he gets angry over that; anger does add to an abuser's meltdown, and he may act fierier and more dangerous. Other than that, he knows that most of the time he creates situations about which to become angry. One inmate that was imprisoned for cutting up his wife and putting her in the trunk of his car felt very justified in his behavior because he said to me that he grew angry and tired of his wife questioning him about the women that would call their home asking for him. This abuser was saying that anger, in his perspective, is the cause of his abuse, and that inquiries by the victim on infidelity also cause abuse. These are the types of irresponsible, controlling behaviors that an abuser wants everyone to redirect their focus from; he would rather be looked upon as needing to learn "anger-management skills."

The Abuser and Mental Illness
In addition to using anger as the cause of his abusiveness, an abuser and society will also blame mental illness for his behaviors. When the abuser has bouts of depression or cycles of volatile combative behaviors, it's sometimes misunderstood as being a mental disorder diagnosis (as the person experiences remission periods). Sure, there are abusers (just like in the general population) that have a diagnosis of bipolar or a personality disorder such as borderline narcissistic or antisocial, but these are secondary diagnoses to the diagnoses of Adult Maltreatment and Neglect Problems cited in the Diagnostic and Statistical Manual of Mental Disorders (DSM-5).

A mental disorder is characterized by major impairment in the person's cognitive processing, emotional regulation, and behavior. A mental disorder is a disability of the person's mental functioning in social, occupational, or other activity participation. Most abusers are not mentally disabled; they are able to function in their day-to-day activities. Yes, it is quite a sight to watch an angered abuser in action; he does look and act a bit like an insane person. Abusers do get agitated and scary-looking when they get in a victim's face. However, psychological testing and research does not indicate that abusers are mentally ill. They may appear like they are decompensating with swinging moods that range and change rather instantly from a jovial mood to a verbally or physically assaultive state, but the underlying cause is not a mental disorder.

Admittedly, it is true that an abuser tends to exhibit paranoid tendencies when he randomly and frantically accuses his spouse of behaviors aimed at hurting him, including infidelity in which she wouldn't even dare to engage. In whatever way, abusers' testing and evaluations in a clinic, at work, or at school are always average or even above average in functioning (I.Q. scores, logic, cause and effect). An abuser is alert and oriented times four; he knows who he is, where he is, what date/time it is, and recent events. An abuser is conscious before and after an abusive episode. Reports from peers, employers, and co-workers are clean; no one except the victim and children think that he appears as if he's mentally unstable. It's his thinking that's wrong—he's not mentally ill—he has an abusive mentality.

Another reason victims and others are quick to assume that the abuser has mental issues is because his bitter and hateful facial expressions are enough to frighten someone into thinking they just saw a deranged look on his face. Especially when he's throwing out all the remarkably distorted information he retrieved from unfounded sources, and when his views of his spouse are so demonizing, this in and of itself can make him look crazy. There is *no* substantial research that concludes in even the most assaultive cases that abusers have a high rate of mental illness. The research simply states that the most violent abusers do have an increased rate of mental illness. Basically, that means that these extremely violent abusers, in addition to having an abusive profile, also have a diagnosis of a mental disorder.

Mental illness diagnoses do not cause abuse any more than using drugs does. The abusive behavioral patterns, in conjunction with an abuser's psychiatric diagnosis, make for a lethal combination. Abuse and mental illness are two separate problems to be treated, just like spouse abuse and drug abuse are. The same applies to alcohol; it's a distinct problem by itself, but it does not cause a man to become an abuser. Neither does sobriety cause a man to heal from being an abuser; he's just a dry abuser. An abuser is a coherent individual, whether under the influence of drugs, alcohol, or other forms of addiction. The abuser is responsible for his abusive behavior. If he's a drug or porn addict, a gambler, or an alcoholic, then that's what he is—an abuser who also has an addiction. If he's an abuser, he is just that—an abuser. Abusers with explosive lunatic behaviors toward their victims are not mentally deranged—they are just *abusive.*

The Abuser as a VIP & VEP
Another strong dynamic that is at the center of an abuser's behavior is his belief that he is a *very important person* (VIP), unlike his victim. An abuser believes that he is entitled to unique rights in the relationship with his wife; whereas she is excluded from these privileges (double standard). In other words, he sees his status as *a very entitled person* (VEP) in comparison to her. All of the excuses that abusers use to deny their abusiveness are based on this extra edge and sense of entitlement; they view themselves as a VIP and a VEP. When abusers are confronted with the reality that most human beings suffer the same disappointments and life tragedies on which they blame their victim's assault, they become enraged. The think, "How dare someone expect me not to be explosive when undergoing such life pressures and stress!" They view themselves as too important and too entitled to bear all of the stress imposed on them.

The abuser's VIP and VEP status plays a strong role in his justifying his abusive acts as related to his childhood upbringing and his rationalization and excuse for extramarital affairs, along with other forms of abuse. An abuser will blame his life circumstances, and will not take responsibility for choosing the temptation to abuse and acting upon that choice (sin) over fidelity and respect. The abuser learns to entitle his sin as an "addiction," "stress," or "anger" problem instead of calling it what it is—his abuse of her. There's pride, privilege, a lack of empathy, immunity, and a double standard regarding respect, when the abuser justifies his abuse as resulting from his dysfunctional family background and past abuse from others. Yet the victim coming from a dysfunctional family upbringing or past abusive relationships herself has made the choice not to engage in infidelity or other forms of disrespect toward him. The abuser *expects* the victim to submit to his abuse and to accept a relationship with him because of his believed VIP and VEP position. The underlying message is that he is more important and valuable than she is, and she's not worthy of a respectful relationship; and she believes him. A VIP and VEP abuser can easily manipulate his victim. She endorses his VIP and VEP status by loyally returning to him after he abuses her multiple times and says he is sorry.

An abuser expects the victim to honor his views and demands because he considers himself to be above criticism; he feels entitled to her support at all times, and she is not to disagree with him in private and especially in public. The abuser feels entitled to the victim deferring to him unquestioningly. If she voices her opinion, he accuses her of trying to outsmart him and makes it known that she is to be invisible with her thoughts and ideas. She is to remain silent about the abuse, and if she brings it up, then she is told that she is antagonizing him and needs to change the subject or else! An abuser believes *he* is entitled not to be accountable for any harm that she wants to discuss; he is quick to stifle her inquiry.

An abuser makes it clear to the victim that she is to pay homage to him; he feels unquestionably entitled to her devotion, and if she fails to anticipate his every need (even the ones he hasn't expressed), then she is to blame for their relationship not going well. The victim is to have a total focus on his needs. She's not to ever get angry at him for being so demanding of her, no matter how abusive he gets. An abuser's thinking is that *he* is entitled to being verbally and/or physically assaultive and that the privilege of getting angry is reserved entirely for his discretion. If the victim gets angry at his abuse, he uses her anger against her, accusing her of being irrational and trying to control him.

The abuser has a presumptive entitlement; he considers himself fully entitled to abusing his wife and feels as if the victim is attacking his status of being above reproach whenever she objects to his abuse. The abuser doesn't want to hear the victim's feelings of hurt and resentment or any powerful words when she's feeling angry at his control of her; he fears that he's losing ground if she defends herself because it shows that she has an identity of her own. In an abuser's timeline, it is never the right time to bring up the abuse, and besides that, he lets her know that she never brings up the subject of abuse correctly. The abuser wants to be the sole authority on the relationship. The victim is not allowed to express her anger to which he believes she has no right, and she is not entitled to challenge his authority. This is where the victim either gets silent or attempts to talk over his voice, to which he reacts by overpowering her anger to prove to her that *he* is the only one entitled to show anger. An abuser has an inveterate lens of entitlement.

When a victim attempts to defend herself against the abuser's verbal and/or physical attacks, he defines her actions as aggressive and/or violence toward him. The abuser turns her behavior 180 degrees by saying that she is doing what he is essentially doing to her. The abuser's reflexive defensive system, combined with his deep sense of entitlement, causes him to reverse the victim's words and actions. In his mind, the victim is to remain silent during an argument. She is not supposed to stand up for herself; if she does, she is complaining, nagging, or bringing up the past. The abuser can berate her all day or all week intermittently, but if she expresses her feelings—that's too much. If she speaks up, the abuser proceeds to accuse her of having said things that have little connection with her actual words or happenings.

An abuser prefers to avoid taking her seriously, thinking about what she is saying, and then actually processing it and possibly owning it at all costs. The abuser feels entitled to ignoring her, treating her like an annoying gnat, and getting rid of her with his increased tone and verbiage. The abuser's accusatory perceptual system escalates when she confronts him with his disrespect, lack of genuine love, or other misdeeds. This can lead him to graduate from verbal abuse reversal to reversal of violence as he manages to reverse aggressive confrontation in the same way. The abuser sees her confrontation as his self-defense for her aggressive (self-defensive) attack on him. The abuser's reversal tactic keeps him believing that she, the victim, is the one controlling him. According to his belief system, he doesn't believe that the victim should set any limits on his behavior toward her or request that he take any responsibility for his actions, either.

The abuser's massive view of his entitlement(s) in the relationship leads him to have unrealistic and unreasonable demands of the victim. An abuser's expectations generate his attitude of "I deserve everything, and you're only entitled to what I say you can have." An abuser consistently wants recognition whenever he decides to be kind or does some good gesture. Abusers ask for recognition of their positive actions before a victim can even notice or initiate a thank-you or a compliment. Whenever he gives, he expects double in return through recognition or actions. An abuser's sense of entitlement oozes of wanting total devotion from the victim—even at the expense of hers or the children's own needs. Sadly, because of his *mindset,* he will always expect more and more from the victim and will never be satisfied with what she puts into the relationship. This sense of entitlement contributes to most abusers' thinking—they are entitled to using violence in their relationship with their victim.

One of the items on an abuser's long list of entitlements is his opinion on anger management. We all have the basic human right to feel angry; however, this is a right that the abuser fights to take away from the victim. The abuser denies her the right to be angry with him, no matter how disrespectful he is to her. The abuser believes that the victim's tone shouldn't ever rise and that she shouldn't get angry about the abuse. The abuser immediately escalates in his tone if her voice level increases—and asserts that the victim is the one being loud, making it known that being angry is an entitlement reserved for him alone. The abuser quickly redirects the victim's anger back to her strong, unresolved feelings, silences her, or goes a step further and actually puts his hand over her mouth.

Over time, victims who are forced to bottle up their anger about their abuse usually begin to suffer from symptoms of withdrawal and apathy, which can lead to numbness, sleeping and/or eating disorder, nightmares, and sadness that can convert into depression. Depression depletes self-esteem and motivation and increases apathy which then leads to a loss of sense of purpose. Unfortunately, the abuser uses the victim's abuse symptoms as another reason to put her down and make her feel as if she's losing her mind. Whether the abuser is calm or if his anger is out of control, the abuser resents the victim's powerful words which describe his pattern of abuse toward her. The abuser's greatest fear is that he will lose ground, so he exerts his authority with his tone of voice over hers so that his escalated, angry tone overpowers the victim's voice. This assures him of his importance and believed entitlement and privilege. The unjust rule and other unspoken expectations assure him that the victim will never be able to have a precise ability to follow his rules and demands. This guarantees his importance and frequent entitlement to become suddenly enraged at her consistent lack of following his expectations or rules.

The Abuser and Disrespect
If mental illness is not one of the core reasons for an abuser's emotional or physical assault—what is? Disrespect. One of the equally important abuser behaviors which he exhibits, in addition to an attitude of importance and entitlement, is disrespect. The definition of abuse would include to oppress, disparage, persecute, and desecrate the victim. Whereas the antonyms for abuse would include words such as: approve, protect, cherish, and respect. When a victim stands up for herself, she is seeking to be cherished and respected. An abuser's thinking does not choose to comprehend the use of respect in a relationship with his victimized wife. The abuser insists that he does respect the victim and that her claims are invalid and allegations of her imagination.

It's unfortunate, but an abuser actually believes and is able to convince others that the victim is being respected and that the victim is the one who is being demanding of him. The abuser exhorts that it is her judgment of him that is in error and that he must protect her from this irrational claim that he's disrespectful of her. Only an abuser and the mentally ill think and believe in this way; when she insists on being respected, he sees her as out-of-control and says that he has to be aggressive because he has to protect his spouse for her own good. This is a lie about the definition of respect and the victim's ability to function. Abuse and respect are not just antonyms; they are absolute opposites. It's not possible to respect someone and abuse them at the same time. If you respect someone, you do not abuse them.

An abusive man usually confines his abusiveness to the interrogation of his victim. But, it's also typical among abusive men to have supremacy attitudes of contempt toward women in general,

THE ABUSER: EVERYTHING YOU EVER WANTED TO KNOW

which then manifest into destructive behaviors toward their victim once they become intimate with her. This condescending approach to their view of women can include women in their family with no regard to authority, wisdom in age, or dependent age (grandmother, mother, daughter, and granddaughter). The attitude of irreverence that an abuser has for women in addition to the victim is the impiety that he lives with—it is sole disrespect. There's a tendency for the abuser to use the excuse that his disdain for the victim and his impertinence toward other women is because he was abused by a woman in the past; this is just another manipulative tactic to share his hard-luck story and to portray women as being responsible for men being abused. There again, he reverses into his victim-of-abuse role, though he has just abused the victim himself.

Studies show that the disregard and disrespect with which abusers treat their victims is generally born out of the abuser's socialization process; this includes behavioral conditioning and transmitted family cultural values. The data does *not* stipulate that abusers learn to disrespect women because they were victimized by a woman. Contrariwise, research does indicate that abusers who have abusive mothers *do not* necessarily develop ultra-negative views of women—abusers who have abusive fathers do. This is because the disrespect with which abusers treat their victims and female family members has usually been observed in action, played out by their father and now being acted out by the son—the current abuser.

Abusers don't always keep their disrespectful comments between the victim and themselves. I have observed many abusers in group comparing stories with roaring laughter at the degrading words that they used; they actually upheld the bullying of their victims. Every group member spoke about his victim as if she were just another one of his conquests. They voiced that they were correct to have put their women in their rightful place; there was no empathy, just a lot of schadenfreude. It was noticeably evident that when speaking of God or the victim they were actually proud of their heathenism. My colleagues and I have listened as abusers chuckle over their victim's response or reaction to their abuser's indecent bullying. The facial expressions of these abusers in group were ones of taking pleasure in the bashing of their victims. They did not recognize their disrespect of the women in their lives—they chose not to know the antithesis of right and wrong.

Depersonalizing the victim is a crucial ingredient as to why an abuser's prognosis is so poor. An abuser's tendency to debase the victim continually increases while his conscience adapts to higher levels of objectifying the victim; the brutish words and violence that once sufficed no longer satisfy him, so he moves up to higher levels of brutality. Since he has succeeded in depersonalizing the victim, he doesn't have to feel guilt or remorse for hurting her feelings. This is similar to an addict that has to get higher doses of a drug to feel its effects. This is why an abusive relationship may begin with offenses that are overlooked by the victim and then, over time, exploit the victim to a level of being totally controlled.

The Abuser—The Controller
Abusers tend to be control machines; however, all abusers vary from one end of the controlling behavior spectrum to another. Some abusers turn their victim into a prisoner of home (POH). I have worked with many POH victims who have been living with a fear, as evidenced in their obviously dilated pupils similar to prisoners' eyes when they come for their parole hearing; the difference is that victims' eyes are like glazed steel bars from their heart. The abuser holds the victim's soul hostage. The victim lives in an invisible prison cell; comparable to wearing an invisible fence collar and receiving painful shocks (that only she

THE ABUSER: EVERYTHING YOU EVER WANTED TO KNOW

can feel and experience) if she attempts to cross the fence. A victim with such an abuser becomes an emotional slave to him as she withdraws her right to have feelings and shuts down her humanity.

Some abusers, like non-abusive spouses, choose their battles, and they control what they want to be obsessive-compulsive about. The distinction is that the battles in an abusive relationship are *real* war zone battles. A number of abusers allow their victims to come in and out of the home freely as long as they take care of their abusers, the household, and the children. This is convenient for the abuser because he is a slave driver; he thrives on sitting back and watching TV sports, news, entertainment, and napping while the victim does all the household work and caring for the children on top of her outside home job.

A victim that is allowed to interact with her abuser about their plans or the children can do so with limitations; if she interrupts his internet surfing, ballgame, or favorite TV program, watch out! The front end of the battle zone is usually reached whenever four of the common areas on which the abuser has a monopoly are *not* in line with his prescription (her freedom to be her own self, decision-making, money, and parental style). An abuser's tenet is, "I'm the only one in the relationship that knows what's best for us; I know what is in *your* best interest and the interest of this family. If you continue to argue in opposition, I will have to become forceful, so back off!" An abuser must win every explosive argument, and his violence is to be accepted without complaints (this is to keep her in her place).

Regarding her freedom to be herself, decision-making, and money, the abuser puts his foot down and sets his limits with threats and blackmail if she doesn't comply with his requests of reporting to him the "who, what, when, where, why, and how," as if he's not her spouse but a private investigator. Other times, whenever it is in his interest, he acts as if he has parental control over her. These control rules make sense to him, and he will become combative if she is objectionable. There is no negotiating or compromising with an abuser as to *who* is to do *what* inside *or* outside of the household. The abuser uses a systematic approach of repetitive infliction of emotional and/or physical pain in order to establish control over her. This is a method that he uses to wear the victim down to a submissive state of cooperation.

Sometimes the abuser makes plans to hang out with buddies or to partake in a hobby. This is a relief to the victim for some alone time without his controlling presence, but it's not always reliable because he changes his mind frequently and stays home instead. The victim has to change her personal self-time and is now underwhelmed by his presence. The abuser is the victim's kryptonite.

Some abusers, instead of yelling their threats, exhibit a horrendous, ongoing low-level of petty or major complaints that wear the victim out to a frazzle; this is how they passive-aggressively inflict their abusive control over the victim. After a while, the victim makes some decisions about her personal freedom that she begins to believe were her own choices (school, work, money, children, recreation, friends, and family). Having normalized the pressure of the abuser, she has tuned out the fact (to spare herself the agony of losing her freedom) that he has actually pressured her into her decisions. The abuser's control barometer pressure goes unnoticed by the victim because she has all but relinquished her role as an equal in the marriage and is essentially operating as if she's a child and he is the parent that grants her privileges. This is the phase where she is at risk for becoming a POH.

This is the stage whereby the victim has begun to lose sight of what a normal, healthy marriage is supposed to be like. She vaguely remembers that a husband's rights are the same as a wife's rights; they are to mutually respect one another. The

THE ABUSER: EVERYTHING YOU EVER WANTED TO KNOW

victim has forgotten (in order to stay safe) that her opinions, her desire to be respected and to be included in decision-making, and her desire for her and the children to live free from verbal and physical abuse are not privileges but are her rights as a human being. An important goal for the abuser is to have the victim become totally devoted to him as a willing sufferer, and he succeeds in reaching his goal by controlling every facet of the victim's life. The abuser becomes her master as he enslaves her into complying with his commands and demands. Along with his selfish and cruel demands, he expects her to love and respect him in return. Even after an abusive episode, he seeks her admiration and romance. This is how he justifies his abuse through converting the victim's inner mind so that she surrenders her will over to him with her grateful attitude and affirmations. The abuser wants to intimidate her and paralyze her with fear, but at the same time, he infuses loyalty and gratitude in her for allowing her to live.

One typical intimidating tactic that an abuser uses is pointing the finger at her; it's accusatory, communicates an ultimatum, and signals to her the stage of rage he's in. Eventually, through his controlling intimidations, the victim feels disempowered and disconnected to anything or anyone else except her abuser. All of his painful attacks on the victim are aimed at ultimately terrorizing her in order to deplete her of her sense of self in relation to others. Not all abusers use physical pain to frighten their victims. An abuser has the control to keep his victim in constant fear without physically torturing her; usually, he reserves violence as an ultimatum. Many victims live under the threat that if they don't meet the abuser's demands, he will physically hurt her, the children, her friends, family, or pets. Some abusers threaten to kill their wife and/or children if she does not comply with his requests or makes any attempt to leave him.

A lot of the abuser's requests are unreasonable and unpredictable. This keeps the victim on guard for his inconsistent expectations and erratic temper outbursts when his unspoken or nonsensical rules are not followed. The end result of his short-fused temper is to bring the victim to a level in which she experiences him as her god and thinks that her life depends on him.. The abuser is able to increase his controlling demands over time; at first, the expectations may be camouflaged with normal requests, but as his victim becomes more amenable, he is able to gradually insult her spirit, mind, body, and *all* of its bodily functions. Sometimes abusers even decide how the victim will dress or do her hair. Some abusers exploit their victim by purchasing seductive clothes for her to wear for him, and for him to sensualize her as his display that belongs to him. If he has seen a certain hairstyle in women that he favors, he will ask her to cut and style her hair that way. Once the abuser oversees and presides over the victim's waking and sleeping hours, observing what she eats, wears, drives, buys, gives away or keeps, who she associates with, and when she uses the restroom, exercises, rests, or works, he is able to micromanage *every* move she makes. The abuser is like a hovering helicopter indoors or outdoors with an invisible "control" panel that's always on autopilot!

The abuser uses the knowledge that he gains regarding her day-to-day living to subject her to ongoing questioning about her actions and scolding her for deviating from his rules about her activities. The victim eventually becomes desensitized to his scrutiny and ends up apologizing for her unruliness over normal day-to-day activities. This desensitization is fueled by the victim's need for his approval; she detests his disapproval and longs for a kind word as opposed to words of humiliation and interrogation. When a victim is deprived of positive affirmation, she becomes willing to submit to her abuser's unsound restrictions in order to receive some comfort or favors from her abuser.

Victims are at times sedated by the abuser through drugs and/or alcohol; this maintains a level of lower resistance. Some abusers find that they can control their victim better by occasionally rewarding the victim with provisions. Some victims have been deprived of basic living needs; others have all of their provision met, including an allowance. Regardless, the abuser's controlling programming of her mindset achieves the same outcome no matter what level of debilitating deprivation or generous provision she has. She experiences his relentless control and overruling of her right to self-determination as he disgraces and demoralizes her personal being. She's now passive: half dead while alive.

The Abuser—The Silencer
When a victim approaches the abuser to talk about his pattern of abusive ways, he resorts to his classic defensive reaction which is to quiet the victim with his accusation that she has been storing grudges and only wants to bring up the past to start an argument. The abuser very creatively twists the truth from her experiences to his distortion. She is not allowed to articulate the reasons for her hurt and angry feelings by giving examples of past incidents because he alleges that that's all in the past; she is expected to forgive and forget without his apologies *or* accept his recurring apologies as he continues to repeat the same abusive behaviors. The abuser's apologies with indignation focus on the victim and not on him—the one that emotionally/physically attacked the victim. A victim, over time, learns to permit and tolerate his abuse by generally just being quiet when he's disrespectful and rude toward her. This inadvertently gives her abuser support and approval, which encourages him to leave her abashed and disconcerted as if this is the norm without a need for an apology. It doesn't ever occur to him that intimidating or frightening his spouse is unacceptable, no matter how upset he

is over some unmet expectation. "Why can't she just get over it?" This is his thinking.

The reason she can't just suck it up and get over it is obvious to the average person—because his verbal and physical abuse is stored in her memory! The victim is unable to reason with the abuser that she just wants to process the incidents and come to an understanding as to what each expects in the relationship. She's unable to verbalize her expectations and set limits with the abuser because the abuser does not allow her to verbalize examples of where he overstepped her boundaries. In his mind, hearing her examples of incidents where he has been abusive interferes with his unfair rules and treatment of her in the relationship. This is one of the reasons that abusers don't do well in counseling: they either keep the victim silent, or if she tells of his abusive patterns, his gross sense of entitlement and justification for his behaviors keeps producing more and more reasons to continue to be abusive toward the victim. With this chronic sense of entitlement, his attitude about his abusive ways remains intact. The abuser's attitude about these entitlements and respect for the victim would have to change. But in order for him to even know what the victim needs in the relationship, he would have to listen—which he's unwilling to compromise and do.

An area that some victims typically want to address with the abuser is his tendency to humiliate and put her down in person or in public. Some abusers make devaluing remarks about the victim in order to exert their superiority over her and to keep her in her place. This further enhances their power and control over the victim. Other abusers, in addition to devaluing remarks, use foul language to refer to the victim, deliberately call her names when she fails to meet an expectation, or when she confronts him about his abusiveness. Abusers that I have worked with in therapy will flaunt their name-calling of the victim and express that they call her these names because the victim made them mad! And, besides, they call all of their women friends by these same "ninny" names, so what's the problem? The list of ways that abusers belittle and undervalue their spouses is endless. A small sample would include comments or words of contempt in either a calm or escalated tone such as "tramp," "female dog," "female sexual body part," or "her ugly bodily figure." The abuser's tactic is to reduce her to a devalued, inanimate being whose safety is always at risk. This tendency to dehumanize her is known as *objectification* or depersonalization. There is *power* in the abuser's aim to make the victim vulnerable, and to intimidate, oppress, defame, control, and silence her.

To Love and Control—'Til Death do us Part
Most abusers that I have worked with are convinced that they love and respect their victim. The abuser uses his own belief system about love to persuade the victim and set her mind at rest that he loves her deeply. The abuser's claim, "I adore you," does not match up to the truth that abuse is the reverse of love. This way of thinking about love for the abuser is not surprising since he is a genius at reversing reality. The reality which is most painful for the victim to accept is that if the abuser truly loved her, he would be considerate and respect her needs instead of focusing only on his needs.

The love that an abuser offers his victim is not unconditional, sacrificial love. An abuser is unwilling to sacrifice his abusive nature toward her. If he gives up any abusive act toward her, he substitutes it for a new abusive tactic. The victim has become so mesmerized by his prophesied love that she is unable to recognize that love *is* the fuel that drives true sacrifice. The abuser may make efforts to demonstrate love-like behaviors, but over time, a victim finds that he is more of a taker of her love and care; he gives love out in rations, as it's convenient for his needs. Some abusers do express an intense sensation which they call love for their victim. However, most of them don't have any other intimate and powerful relationship to compare it to (other than the media), so they have no evidence of what true love is. When an abuser declares that he is "in love" with the victim, he also has feelings of apathy for being vulnerable to intimacy, obsession in possessing the victim, an interest in the victim taking care of him for life, having the victim all to himself without others intruding, sexual gratification, and impressing others as if the victim is a trophy.

If the abuser were willing and capable of seeing the victim as an important entity worthy of love and respect, then the romantic love that the abuser expresses could be a genuine love. That can only occur if the abuser decides to change his way of thinking about her. An abuser's confusion about what it means to love and respect a spouse is the force that drives many abusers to conclude that it is because of their devout love for their spouse that they assaulted or murdered her. The abuser's mindset is not able to recognize that true love means respecting his spouse's dignity—that dehumanizing her does not even come into the picture when it comes to love. The abuser's way of thinking does not want her to grow as an individual; it doesn't allow for the boosting of her self-image and does not think about doing what is in her best interest.

Verbally and/or physically assaulting or killing her is not in her best interest—and it's certainly not love. An abuser's "I love you" is not followed by loving actions. "I love you" is an action sentence because love in such a declaration statement is a verb; therefore, it requires activity and is more than three mere words. An abuser's love is not kind; it is prideful and expects and demands that the victim accept his disrespect. An abuser refuses to humble himself and prefers to feel proud of his inaccurate self-image. The abuser believes he's doing the victim a favor simply by existing in her life and stating that he loves her.

THE ABUSER: EVERYTHING YOU EVER WANTED TO KNOW

The abuser's pride refuses to take responsibility for his abuse and demands her acceptance of it; love is not demanding. True love knows how to genuinely apologize; it does not fumble nor avoid an apology only to repeat the same or increased severity of past abusive offenses. The abuser's declaration of love is just an emotional gimmick. Love is a constructive action. The destructive evidence of absence of love manifests itself by the abuser's behaviors. An abuser's love is a conditional, sentimental, varying love that is dependent on the mood that he's in.

A way of differentiating an abuser's love from genuine love is to consider *agape* love as the type of love with which a spouse is to cherish his wife. *Agape* love is an unconditional love that a spouse demonstrates to his wife—no conditions are attached. The spouse will love her whether either of them are having a good or a bad day—she does not have to be perfect to earn his love. Agape love is a thoughtful, considerate, and intentional type of love that actively displays affection for the other. It promotes the well-being of a loved one. It is not opposed to selfless giving (considering the other's needs and not just one's own) when compromising in problem-solving. The abusers that I worked with described their feelings of love toward their victim with *Eros* undertones; their affections were of a sexually-driven attraction. It was never surprising to me to hear uncountable love stories from victims that, through processing, realized the reality that their abuser's love was not genuine; they were devastated to finally admit that all of that rejection and control was not love.

An abuser's possessive love toward the victim involves sexual jealousy, which leads the abuser to monitor all of her acquaintances whether she's alone or in his presence. Studies indicate that most post-separation murders are committed by abusive men. The mindset of an abuser who claims to be in love with the victim is all about ownership of the victim. Abusers have an extremely high rate of jealousy accusations toward their victims;

ironically, it's the abusers who have a high level of infidelity. The abuser's double standards in the marriage, his sense of entitlement, and jealous possessiveness of the victim give him the freedom to be unfaithful and to demand fidelity from her.

This obsessive-possessive love is also a part of his scheme to isolate her from all relationships. In turn, this places him at the center of her life so that she can fulfill his needs with which her social contacts interfere. The abuser is fearful that if she develops social contacts, she could stop being dependent on him, become independent, and escape his control. A victim can meticulously work on reassuring the abuser that she will not be unfaithful or disloyal through her social contacts, but his power and control are not reduced. The reason for this is because his fear of her infidelity is secondary to his fear of losing her as his possession. A possessively jealous abuser can escalate to dangerous levels when a victim attempts to break up their relationship; he will not only threaten to hurt her, but he may even pitifully cry and state that he will commit suicide or hurt her friends or family if she leaves him.

The abuser's use of alternating rage and loving is the glue that keeps the victim and the abuser bound. During his explosive episodes, the victim may attempt to leave him. Most of the time the abuser is able to persuade the victim to return through his profuse apologies, verbal love commitment, and promises to be more sensitive and tender toward her needs. The abuser is now reversing in his role as the one in desperation and verbally submits to her beck and call just to have her back. This melodramatic plead for reconciliation is just another controlling tactic to break down the victim's resistance. When the abuser begs and appears genuine, the victim is further entrapped because she temporarily forgets about his history of outbursts and her pain, and she is now smothered with the way things could be good in the relationship; it's all in her hands to make things right. The

THE ABUSER: EVERYTHING YOU EVER WANTED TO KNOW

abuser leads her to believe that if she would only return to him, things would get better, and the fate of their marital relationship is in her decision not to leave him.

There's only one problem with the abuser's declaration that things would get better if only the victim would stay in the relationship with him. The problem is that his sense of entitlement and disrespect are still a part of him. The problem of always wanting to be in control of the victim and their relationship is still one of his top priorities. Take a moment right now to digress from reading. Reflect back into the pattern of communication and interaction that you as a victim have experienced with your abuser. As you drifted back into the numerous discussions that you attempted to have with your abuser, did you notice that those attempts were controlled and ultimately sabotaged by your abuser?

A typical communication bid for positive interaction by a victim can quickly and consistently turn into a heated argument that is no longer anything close to the topic that she initiated. The abuser usually dominates the subject and controls the direction that the discussion takes. For example, the victim wants to talk about making plans for an upcoming event. She has carefully made sure that the day and time is just right to approach him in discussing details of the event. The abuser's tone in response is one of escalated frustration, and when she asks if everything is alright and states that he sounds angry, he denies any anger (although he's very obviously furious). The abuser then proceeds to what he would rather talk about—the victim's negligence or fault in something that has not met his expectations. During this diversion from discussing what the victim has initiated, the abuser then begins to insult and offend the victim with belittling remarks about her or loved ones. The abuser may even add that he's *not* being critical but that others also see her in this way. The abuser raises his voice and overrides her attempts to get a word in on her defense and then accuses *her* of shouting and mistreating him—and of *her* being the one that's yelling. After he has focused on her faults and made her doubt her self-confidence, he both pouts and sulks silently or walks away, leaving her without any information on the upcoming event she wanted to discuss. The victim is left dejected.

The victim's focus is now on thinking: "What just happened here?" She may wonder if she's to blame or if something happened to the abuser that led him to be angry—which may have some truth in it, but in actuality, that has little to do with it. So, what happened? The same as what has happened before, and the topic the victim brought up would not have mattered. The abuser's arguments always aim to impugn the victim's knowledge of what just happened and cause her to doubt her own comprehension of the incident. What happened is not the victim's problem—it is the abuser's problem: the problem of control. An abuser reacts to the victim out of his need for control. The abuser replies resistively and inappropriately to discussions initiated by the victim because he doesn't choose to respond to her appropriately. If he responded to her appropriately, then he would no longer feel like he's in control of her conversations and her being. If the abuser responds with respectful selflessness when the victim initiates discussion, then he's not able to use his conversational control tactics. Even if he responds politely, it will always have a self-aggrandizing view. The abuser has a heightened focus on himself with no empathy for the victim when he naturally engages in his unprovoked, derogatory diatribe toward her.

There is no win-win situation when a victim enters a discussion with an abuser. Most discussions the victim has with her abuser are infested with his core values and abusive outlook, so a discussion can either proceed to fulfill his desires or lead to nowhere. The reason for highlighting the aforementioned discussion on outcomes is because it's important to note that for

THE ABUSER: EVERYTHING YOU EVER WANTED TO KNOW

the abuser, it's all about winning the discussion; it's about *who* controls the decisions in the household. In a victim-abuser discussion, there is no room for thinking about the other's desires, exchanging information to understand one another, or thinking *together* on a beneficial idea that would bring mutual satisfaction (love). An abuser just wants total control that brings him victory in all discussions. Basically, this means that he believes that she is wrong and he has to *always* be correct, so where can the discussion lead to with this *mindset*? The abuser is proficient at reversing reality to himself, the victim, and others. An abuser is *not* going to be a realist and admit his wrongs, even if he noticed that the victim is correct at something. The abuser's message is that her opinion doesn't count; he makes it clear that he doesn't want to be influenced by her way of thinking because she's always wrong, except for when he catches himself off-guard and adopts some of her ideas and then claims that they were *his* ideas to begin with (this way he's still in control).

Each abuser's profile is different other than his belief in being entitled to disrespect and control his victim. Control tactics that abusers use may vary depending on their personality, additional diagnosis, and the victim of their choice. The most commonly distorted love and control tactics, which victims may experience, are as follows:

1. Making recurrent, undeserved, heartless criticism.
2. Scolding vindictively in a lower tone, sarcastically making faces while muttering under his breath, or outright unprovoked yelling.
3. Outshouting when an attempt is made to talk.
4. Raising the music or TV volume while victim attempts to talk. Lowering tone of voice when asked but mocks victim's request.
5. Refusing to look at victim or listen when she's talking and focusing on electronics instead.

6. Rolling eyes, smirking, ridiculing, intimidating glances, mimicking, or looking at her with contempt.
7. Replying with sarcasm; pretending he didn't hear her.
8. Interrupting her frame of thought.
9. Swearing, insulting offensively, or name-calling.
10. Stonewalling or ignoring.
11. Laughing at her after she has spoken.
12. Walking away or slamming the door while she's still talking.
13. Twisting the words that she said.
14. Distorting reality for her; exaggerating what happened.
15. Insisting with a tone that *what he* says is *really* what has happened in previous interactions with him.
16. Turning her concerns around and using them against her.
17. Changing the topic and focusing on his concerns.
18. Accusing her of thinking and doing the same as he does.
19. Inducing guilt; reversing as if she's controlling *him*.
20. Towering over her or walking aggressively toward her.
21. Threatening to leave her and the children.
22. Leaving angrily without saying where he is going.
23. Threatening to harm her, loved ones, or pets.
24. Getting in her face while talking to her.
25. Blocking her path; getting *agitated* and interrupting her.
26. Disconnecting the phone landline, taking her cellphone, keys, or purse.
27. Moping and playing as if he's the victim; turning loved ones against her.
28. Demanding for and taking back gifts he has given her or rejecting gifts she gives him.
29. Frequently arguing about *anything* and *everything*; pointing his finger at her when arguing.
30. Only hearing the negative and omitting the positive, leading the discussion to arguing.

THE ABUSER: EVERYTHING YOU EVER WANTED TO KNOW

31. Using a tone indicating that he's the final authority on *everything* including *her* and the relationship.
32. Gunning the car to frighten her.
33. Gaslighting and/or love-bombing her.
34. Blaming her for the relationship problems.
35. Comparing her to and telling her she's acting like a low-life or crazy person.

Fill in your abuser's favorite distorted love and control tactic(s):

_____

An abuser's main emotional and physical intimidation ammunition is control. One measure to decipher how deep a spouse's power and control problem is, is to observe his behavior when the victim begins to request respect. Controlling spouses have a range of behavioral responses to the victim's confrontation—from those spouses who insist the confrontation is preposterous, to those who are willing to admit to their disrespectful attitude and make the effort to change, to those spouses who won't accept the victim's feelings and believe their disrespectful behavior is justified, to those who retaliate when confronted by the victim.

The abuser's daily goal is to discredit the victim's perspective on his abuse toward her. If he can get full control of the victim, then he can get her to stop thinking on her own and can keep her silent about the abuse. Ultimately, the abuser wants the victim and others to believe that she is to blame for any grievances that she may have about him or their relationship. The abuser makes it known to the victim that she is "ridiculous" in her allegations of his (controlling) abuse—that she's analyzing too much, misinterpreting him, and is simply too sensitive. The abuser accuses her of not having any endurance, and therefore she's weak and a failure at dealing with her concerns. An abuser insists that the victim is being selfish for voicing her concerns about her person and how she's being treated; he does not see himself as the selfish one that controls the victim's self. The abuser is quick to also blame the victim's past that she has vulnerably shared with him and accuses her of projecting her past onto him.

All of his rationalizations and "poor me" attitudes are a part of his controlling nature, which he's *again* using to tell the victim how *she* thinks; he is using it as a way of avoiding having to look at the how *he* thinks in controlling ways. Even when an abuser goes through a period where he behaves in kind and loving ways, he uses it as another avenue to control and manipulate by leading the victim to a calm state, leaving her open and vulnerable, as he gradually or suddenly goes back to overtly being abusive toward her.

There must be a way for an abuser to stop being abusive, you say; all he has to do is stop feeling self-entitled and stop being disrespectful and controlling. First off, abusers deny being abusive. If an abuser admits to being an abuser, then he would lose his privilege to blame the victim and others for his abusive acts. To an abuser who enjoys the benefits, amenities, and rewards he gets from being self-entitled, disrespectful, and controlling, stopping his abusive thinking and nature is not an option.

Secondly, abusers become attached to the self-entitled privileges they receive. Abusers are haughty about being disrespectful; it gives them deep satisfaction to have full power and control over the victim. An abuser's de-stressor from daily living is to feel important and to know that he rules. In a healthy marital relationship, there's a balance in negotiating between each individual and in getting their needs met. The abuser always gets his needs met. The victim usually sacrifices her personal and family needs to maintain harmony in the relationship. Contrastingly, the abuser partakes in the luxury of never having to compromise

THE ABUSER: EVERYTHING YOU EVER WANTED TO KNOW

and getting to do the things he likes to do. Getting his wants and his way is essentially what matters to him. It's all for him. If an abuser were to give up his abusive thinking and behaviors, he would have to give up someone (the victim) to take care of him and the children. An abuser thrives on his right to come and go as he pleases, his right to contribute or not contribute to the household—whatever *he* wishes.

Thirdly, abusers take pleasure in always being in the victim's limelight. An abuser is enthralled with being the center of the victim's world in meeting all of her needs and wants—which are wrapped around his whims. Likewise, with the children, he is the focus of their attention. The abuser manages to have the children's undivided attention by manipulating the household with his unpredictable mood swings. Abusers keep their victims on their toes so that they are thinking fast about how they will improve themselves in the abuser's eyes. Victims think at length about how to approach the abuser and about what to do to calm him down if he gets mean. Abusers prefer their victims to have little time to think about their own lives. This magnifies the abuser's position and makes it difficult for him to give up being abusive because he does want total control of his victim's thinking and every aspect of her life.

Why Abusers Won't Change
Some may ask, "Does the abuser ever genuinely *want* to give up his benefits from being abusive?" "Does the abuser not value the benefit of having a wife and children—a family?" Even though the abuser *does* lose the prospect of having an intimate relationship with his wife and children if he doesn't give up his abusive ways, he is *not* all about giving up being a leech in his victim's life and keeping her on a leash. The abuser operates from self-centered feelings. Genuine intimacy, compassion, selflessness, and empathy are necessary feelings for maintaining a commitment to

the victim and his children; these are not feelings that are at the forefront of what the abuser values. The absences of these types of feelings are not characteristics that are noticed or missed by him. Being abusive is his choice. An abuser would have to be willing to change in order to stop being an abuser. It's about his thinking—plus his will. Abuse is an act of the will. An abuser's will functions regardless of his heart. An abuser does not generally engage in intimacy; intimacy requires dialogue transparency and vulnerability, to which he's unwilling to submit. That is one of the main reasons abusers say no to counseling when the victim suggests it. An abuser refuses to problem-solve; his way is to buffet the victim and anyone who opposes his way of thinking. Usually an abuser craves increased intimacy, but this craving is outweighed by his intrinsic attachment to the benefits, rewards, and privileges that he gains from being abusive.

Furthermore, it's not just about the abuser's mind impressing upon him to stay the same, but it's also about the culture in our society and where he may find support not to change. An abuser is created through a socialization process that allows him to maintain an attitude of disrespect, self-entitlement, exploitation, power, and control. Historical, familial, judicial, and societal messages about the exploitation of women have an impact on the abuser. A victim who sustains oppression and does not seek help to overcome her abuse influences her abuser in *not* giving up his abusive behavior. To end his abuse of the victim would require the abuser to quit creating turbulence and to stop exploiting her; most abusers are not willing to give up this recurring behavior. For an abuser, remaining abusive is easier than changing his pattern of controlling intimidation.

An abuser is *not* interested in admitting to abusing because that would mean giving up the admiration of others who see him as a good citizen. The abuser's main interest is to justify himself in the sight of others. To admit to the abuse of his wife

THE ABUSER: EVERYTHING YOU EVER WANTED TO KNOW

would mean that he would lose the esteem of others whom he has conned into seeing him as a good man. Or, it can be, to him, a huge risk to be seen by some of his male peers as a wimp; after all, some males may condemn him for hitting a defenseless woman. In other cases, his male peers may rise to protect him from coming forward and admitting as a weak male that he assaulted women and children. If he caved in to his wife's pleas for change of his abusive nature, he would have to admit to her that he was abusive, and he is unwilling to do this because it would mean relinquishing his control over her and others. Abusers seize any opportunity they can grasp to excuse their abusive actions so that they can elicit sympathy from the victim and others (if confronted) in order to absolve themselves of any responsibility for their abusive acts.

The goal of the abuser is to silence the victim from speaking out about his abuse. If he were to consider stopping his abusiveness, he would have to be willing to *hear* her perspective. Instead, an abuser *chooses* to devalue and discredit her, avoiding her position on his abusiveness. An abuser is the happiest when everything in the marital relationship is harmoniously working out on his terms. Changing his terms creates a disruption in the way he wants the relationship to proceed. No one can persuade an abuser to let go of his insatiable need to control his victim. The abuser's unquenchable need to be in charge of the victim *and* their relationship is not one that can be easily dissuaded through coaxing. The victim has to have a support system, including society as a whole, if she is to stand up to her abuser. I'm sorry to say that even when an abuser enters an abuser men's program, most abusers do not generally make lasting changes. The main reason for this is that most abusers enter the program with external motives (ultimatum given by victim and/or legal system). Even if the abuser develops internal motivations to change his abusive patterns through the educational aspects of the abuser's program, most abusers in the program learn to make amends and apologize.

But, since they are adept at their manipulative skills, it's fairly simple for them to create an appearance of sorrow and change while they offer up their "I'm sorry." This is where he dramatizes his compassion and sympathy for his wife and family. The abuser's thinking is that if he *says* that he is *sorry*, she will stop her efforts to discuss her feelings about his abuse, and she will stop getting on his back about changing his ways! There are various high-quality abuser programs in the United States. All around the country, the prognosis for these abusers is the same. I have colleagues that lead abuser programs who refer to themselves as a stepping stone for the abuser because it's only a matter of time until the abuser goes back to the thinking and privileges that drive his behavior. These abuser program leaders are eyewitnesses, as victims and their children stand by, and the leaders play the role of umpire.

An abuser's program is intense, and the list of what the abuser would have to accomplish in order to stop being abusive is extensive. Here is a list of a dozen prerequisites for most abuser programs just so you can get an idea of what the abuser is unwilling to do:

1. The abuser would have to stop using denial as a defense mechanism when the victim discloses her grief over her abuse; he would have to stop discrediting the victim's recollections of his mental, physical, spiritual, economic, and/or sexual abuse. Instead, he would have admit fully to *all* of his abuse toward the victim and others; he would have to accept constructive criticism and feedback, and he would have to stop trying to change the focus of the discussion from his own behaviors to the behaviors of the person confronting him.

2. The abuser would have to stop making excuses for his abusive behaviors (due to others provoking/hurting

him). An abuser would have to become honest about his motives for being abusive; he would have to stop engaging the victim on guilt trips whenever she discusses his abuse; he would have to stop complaining about the problems that are a direct result of his abuse (victim's lack of libido, his having to be in an abuser program, the children's withdrawal from him).
3. The abuser would have to stop minimizing the traumatic effects his abuse has had on the victim and others; he would have to demonstrate remorse and compassion selflessly without focusing on himself; he would have to come to terms with the fact that the victim will feel the effects of his abuse for years to come; he must be willing to accept accountability and responsibility for his past, present, and future actions; he would have to truthfully report any backsliding.
4. The abuser has to admit to his false allegations and accusations of the victim and replace them with the realistic view of recognizing her positive attributes rather than looking down on her.
5. The abuser has to accept that he has had a negative impact on others in addition to the victim and acknowledge their right to be hurt and upset while accepting the consequences of his behavior; he has to develop a sense of empathy and consideration for others' feelings; he has to learn to stop attempting to reverse and twist the victim's and others' mistreatment while making himself the victim; he has to stop interrupting grievances and playing mind games to confuse the victim and others when they are angry at him.
6. The abuser has to evaluate and admit to his self-entitlement mentality and chronic disrespectful control tactics.

7. The abuser has to acknowledge that his abusive behavior is unacceptable and is a criminal act.
8. The abuser has to surrender the privileges that he gains by being an abuser and do so without reservation; this includes letting go of the rewards he previously obtained with the double-standard relationship (infidelity, time spent with family/friends/hobbies).
9. The abuser has to give up being taken care of by the victim and commit to consistently listen to and act upon the victim's' request for help with childcare and/or household responsibilities.
10. The abuser has to commit to treating the victim, friends, co-workers, and family with respect; he has to learn to value the victim's personal growth and allow her freedom of individuality; he has to accept that everyone has unconditional rights when in a relationship.
11. The abuser has to completely stop his cyclical periods of non-abusive behaviors followed by unpredictable abusive episodes; he is to never *ever* intimidate or threaten the victim and others.
12. The abuser has to make a lifetime commitment to relinquish his hostility toward the victim and her loved ones; he has to accept that his ability to stop being an abuser is dependent upon his willingness to make a life-long, unconditional commitment to not repeat his abusiveness even under any unexpected circumstances. To stop abusing, an abuser would have to come to terms with the fact that he has to work on stopping the abuse daily—for good.

Abuser programs are especially designed to confront the abuser's dynamics. The focus of most abuser programs is on the abuser's way of thinking. The abuser is encouraged to develop empathy for the victim(s) in his life. Abuser programs don't allow the abuser to stay in the program if he continues to act out violently. Most abuser programs make it a point to obtain released permission to stay in contact with the victim so as to follow up on the abuser's progress during treatment. An abuser program confronts, addresses, and educates the abuser on his characteristics, core values, and attitudes as an abuser.

It's *very easy* for most abusers to make apologies when they think they've gone too far in their abuse of the victim and could potentially lose her loyalty to him. The abuser then feels that the apology should suffice to make the relationship reconciled. The problem with this arrogant abuser misconception is that in his thinking, he has the privilege of satisfying the victim's need for an apology and a way to silence the victim from ever discussing her feelings about the abuse she experienced or what needs to change. In other words, the abuser prefers to make a pact with the victim (a pact which he either manipulates underhandedly or outright proposes to her) that he won't mistreat her *if* she would just *do* as he says and not talk about the abuse anymore.

To the abuser, this appears to be a good deal, but truthfully this requires the victim to give up her right to be heard and be validated; it suppresses her freedom from doing unwanted, unconsented behaviors the abuser requires of her. This is purely just another form of his abusive bargaining. It does not matter how kind he is whenever he apologizes and offers the pact, since all abusers have periods when they are kind.

The important factor in discerning his apologies is *you*; you must discern how genuinely he admits to his mistreatment of you and how disrespectful and controlling he has been toward you. Being afraid of the pain involved in confronting his abuse is a deep, temporary feeling; regretting that you didn't say or do anything about your abuse is permanent. God has spelled it out for us in His Word: "Do not be afraid." Being afraid is like a virus; that fear spreads quickly into our spirits, minds, and bodies and then moves on to infect others. All of the victims that I have worked with who have elected not to be upfront and honest about their pain and have accepted their abuser's lack of change (pact) have deep, sorrowful regret for the way they wasted their and their children's lives away while waiting for him to stop his abuse.

Be honest with yourself about your abuser; don't over-compromise yourself and your children and make concessions of a lifetime. If he's appealing for you to stop asking to be respected, and he doesn't agree with your request, are you a willing participant in this relationship? Be wise in your judgment about his deceiving ways and beware of your own self-deception. Spare your life and the lives of your children (and future grandchildren) by accepting nothing less than his total respect. As with all of the abusers that my colleagues and I have worked with (and all of the abusers that have been researched), any abuser who does not take full responsibility for his abusive behaviors will not remain non-abusive.

When abusers hold on tight to their rewards and privileges and learn of the prospect of losing their power and control, they do not greet the equal rights and responsibilities in a marital relationship with open arms. The abuser generally can't fathom living on the same plane of respect as their victim; it's almost intolerable. The abuser resents the victim for requiring him to respect her; he feels he's being unfairly treated by the victim and is petrified of losing his off-kilter, controlling belief system. Unless the abuser is willing to loosen his white-knuckle grip on the rewards and privileges of being an abuser, he will always favor his warped sense of special VEP status as an abuser. This is where it's most important for the victim to be honest with herself about the realistic possibilities for her abuser to stop abusing her. In the heat of an argument whereby you're requesting to be respected or you will have to end the relationship, he can make numerous promises to stop being abusive, but it never materializes; to him, they're just promises. These fictitious promises are just another downward spiral in the cycle of abuse for the victim and her family.

Some victims do compromise their expectations of their abuser. They settle for the abuser's promises to attend individual therapy, which does not specialize in providing the contents and structure of an abuser program. Even with very highly-skilled individual therapists, the abuser is a charmer and is known to outsmart and manipulate the therapist as he does the victim. The abuser can be superficial and appear sincere to the therapist, and through this external appearance, he can get away with continuing to be abusive because most individual therapists do not follow-up with the abuser's victim. A victim who settles for her abuser's claim of attending counseling sessions to deal with his abuse wastes her life away accepting minor improvements from her abuser instead of total respect and a permanent stop to the abuse. A victim has to come to terms with the truth that she can never have a positive communication experience with her abuser if he doesn't respect her. She has to accept that no one can ever experience feeling safe and at peace in a relationship that doesn't give each person equal value. A victim that accepts the abuser's lack of respect and controlling attitude is setting herself up to walk through a menacing, abuse yellow warning flashing light every day (leading to a red light).

Neither individual therapy nor the highly-recommended abuser programs are the cure-all for an abuser. It has been mine and my colleagues' experience, and the experience of research findings, that most abusers choose *not* to work the requirements of an abuser program. This isn't because an abuser can't change (any person who doesn't have a major mental disorder can change), but most abusers *choose* not to change. They don't want to change. They do a cost-benefit analysis in their way of thinking, and they choose the privileges they receive from being in control of the victim and the relationship, and this outweighs the costs for them. Abusers believe that it's awkward and too difficult for them to learn to totally respect the victim. Frankly, in their prideful voice, abusers state that they are rather offended that their genuineness and certainty about the details of their relationship with their spouse is being questioned!

A lot of abusers fail to complete the abuser program because they enter the program with their sense of entitlement at full-blast, thinking that the program is designed to serve them as abusers. When an abuser discovers that the program is supportive of the victim and actually holds *him* accountable for the damage he has done to her, he walks out believing that they are servicing the wrong person! The abuser wants to continue steamrolling the victim, and the abuser program won't allow it. Some abusers even get worse while participating or after having been in an abuser program. Just like when the victim challenges him about his abusive attitudes and behaviors, most abusers are not able to accept the program's confrontation or requests for responsibility and accountability.

Some abusers can come in and walk right out of an abuser program. Most abuser programs recommend that the abuser attend the program for a period of eighteen to twenty-four months. Some of my colleagues even suggest thirty-six months in view of the substantial rate of recidivism. There are currently no sufficient reliable studies which conclude that abusers who complete an abuser program do make the changes that stop them from returning to abuse women. It's all dependent on the abuser's willingness to work the program. Most abusers prefer to stay in their old abusive rut or get worse; this is more common than the decision to change. The main reason abusers are unable to complete the abuser program is because if they exhibit a reasonable effort to make any changes to their abusive nature, the changes are superficial. An abuser has a condition of the heart—he's heartless.

THE ABUSER: EVERYTHING YOU EVER WANTED TO KNOW

Abusers become accustomed to tearing apart the victim's heart. They believe they have a right to her heart and to her complete devotion. When they learn in an abuser's program that the victim actually has a right to share her heart with other people, they can't deal with this reality. Anyone in the normal realm of human experience would view the abuser's perspective on the ownership of the victim's heart as egotistical. Abusers demand their victim's total heart and self.

Through this same lens, an average person would view his attitude as vanity and that no one deserves that amount of total self-sacrifice. An abuser program will address what is in his heart that is precipitating all of his relationship problems with the victim and his family. The abuser program is designed to help him deal with his issues of the heart as a way of conquering his abusive character. Since the victim has allowed the abuser to be the only central owner of her heart, she is unable, under his dominion, to understand the perversion of his heart. The abuser needs the abuser program because the victim is not able to bring to his senses that the reasons he is failing as a husband and father is because he has a heart-based problem.

Completely working the abuser program means getting to the bottom of the abusive behavior, not just managing the symptoms. If the abuser is simply managing the symptoms but not touching on the root of the problem (heart), that abusive character will resurface. Working on the abuse symptoms may temporarily subdue abusive behaviors, but the deep-seated heart problems will remain unresolved in the recesses of his soul. A renewing of the mind goes hand-in-hand with a renewing of the heart, which then brings on healing from all manner of hurts. An abuser who has a change of heart is much better equipped to combat his abusive mentality with the cure being in his heart and *not* just to demonstrate superficial behavior modification.

So, in order to complete the abuser program with lasting effects, the abuser would have to have a heart for the victim and others. As has already been discussed, the abuser is not very interested in infiltrating the principles of the abuser program in his heart. The abuser could choose to, by grace, change his heart, but he doesn't usually elect that option. That's incredibly important information when a victim is working on deciding whether her abuser will change his abusive ways. If an abuser is not going to battle his abusive character with his heart, then it's essential to know this, because the heart is where his abusive behavior originates. Wherever his heart is, his actions will follow. No abuser program's textual positive results research or success case calculations will change the abuser. There may be some improvements, but in the final analysis he has to change his heart. The abuser can work the abuser program until the cows come home yet never change his heart. It's not chipper news, huh?

Regarding the children, abuser programs seek a heart change there too, not just conformity to a pattern of expected husband and father behaviors. If his heart is going to be addressed in an abuser program, he has to be confronted and come face to face with the fact that when he enters the abuser program, he is on the blacklist as a husband *and* father—on the very worst of humanity list. Some abuser programs have abusers sign commitment contracts to abstain from the abusive tactics they've disclosed. On paper, it all sounds good, but even though they may be staunchly committed to follow through on this homework to abstain, they invariably go home and align themselves with what is true in their heart and lose their commitment. This is because they embrace the idea of refraining from their abusive tactics, but it's with a rationalized state of mind and not with their heart. Their ideas about abstaining from abusive tactics are in the right place, but their hearts don't follow suit.

THE ABUSER: EVERYTHING YOU EVER WANTED TO KNOW

These abusers give the appearance of being committed to restrain themselves, but the limits of their heart do not allow for a total radical change in their behavior. It's a radical change of heart that is needed if the abuse is to stop. Their prideful heart denies them the ability to push out those abusive traits from within the soul, even after remembering all that they have learned in their abuser program. The abuser program experience doesn't become a frame of reference for awareness or a developed burden in their heart for the victim and the children; for them, it's just a collection of new knowledge.

The best way and only way to help an abuser is to demand that he stop his abuse and not to settle for anything less. Abusers don't change their abusive patterns because they suddenly feel empathy, compassion, or give up drugs/alcohol or accept "salvation." In order for an abuser to feel genuine love and compassion, he would have to change his heart. An abuser is not able to manufacture unconditional love, which demonstrates caring and compassion, without a changed heart. The same goes for salvation: An abuser can go through the motions of accepting salvation, but without a change in his heart, he is *unable* to experience and demonstrate God's unconditional love, which is the root of compassion. I'm not saying the abuser should not be offered the gospel and the plan of salvation; I'm saying salvation doesn't work in a person's life if his heart remains the same, because then it's a false conversion. Making the abuser hopeful by only offering salvation without stipulating a need for a changed heart and without discussing his current status of sin when he spends his eternity experiencing the consequences of his abusive acts is tragic. The boundary line must be kept clear between the meaning of salvation and the implications of true salvation. Evidence that salvation has gone beyond taking root is when it sprouts in his heart and drives out all temptation to abuse, and he does not act out anything but his newfound respectful acts of love. Salvation must penetrate his heart: "For with the heart one believes unto righteousness" (Romans 10:10).

The abuser must be able to realize and comprehend that there's a difference between going through the motions of the gospel's plan of salvation and God's plan for us to resurrect into a new life with Him (just as His Son had to die to self and resurrect into a new life and relationship with His Father). The abuser must recognize that this expectation of resurrecting into a new relationship with God was actually there from the beginning of time with the first marriage of Adam and Eve. Their broken union in marriage presented the gospel to us, symbolizing Christ's resurrection; Adam and Eve had to die to their sinful, selfish nature, resurrect, and reconcile their relationship with God. That is the gospel—salvation. The abuser has to exemplify this type of transformation. A new life with God has evidence of bringing resurrection into that person's new characteristics: a rededication to loving unconditionally, safe companionship, inexplicable peace in spite of suffering, and joyfully accepting the shared mission as a couple.

This kind of new life perspective can only be acquired by the divine life that enters our hearts through Jesus and the Holy Spirit's presence. It is not sufficient for the abuser to accept salvation when his salvation stays put by just calling himself a Christian but living on the periphery of his commitment as a surface Christian, not allowing the Holy Spirit to form and reform him. Most abusers want the salvation or do the salvation act but refuse to allow the life of Christ into their hearts and therefore are unable to resurrect into a new life with God. These abusers have yet to find out that salvation is not a ritual or religious masquerade; they must be willing to surrender their complete hearts to God.

Abusers don't want to change for God, the victim, or their children. When it comes to their children, they don't even

THE ABUSER: EVERYTHING YOU EVER WANTED TO KNOW

experience their children being frightened by them or notice that they're not bonding with them. Abusers don't suddenly have an insightful revelation that the victim deserves to be treated with respect. Because of an abuser's self-centeredness and the various privileges and gains he indulges in from controlling the victim, he changes only when he feels he has to. Therefore, as it turns out, the victim is one of the most important elements in creating an environment that's conducive for the abuser to be forced to change. A victim can put the abuser in a position whereby he has no other choice but to attend an abuser program and take the steps to change.

Obviously, a victim cannot *force* an abuser to change. All she can do is make the request to be respected, and the rest is up to him. Most of the time, this is usually only possible when the victim leaves the abuser as a result of the abuse. A victim *cannot* work on the abuser's root of his problem (disrespect, self-entitlement, control, and his heart). In some cases, the court gets involved and demands the change or sets him up for probation or jail time. My colleagues and I have yet to come across an abuser that initiated signing himself up into an abuser program unless somebody referred him or required him to do so *or* as a manipulative tactic to pull the victim or a job back into his life. Most abusers are unwilling to care enough about the victim to seek help on their own; they don't usually have the sentiment and empathy for their victim or family.

The Abuser, Judicial System, & Society
Yes, generally, abusers don't seek help—unless they get into legal problems. For the most part, the abuser succeeds in closing the abusive case through his intense and intentional denial. The abuser usually reports that the victim has done the same type of abuse to him and that his assaults were in self-defense, so the case is dropped as a cross-allegation. In some cases, the legal

system does not take the time to investigate the abuser's actions and presumes him to be a responsible citizen, not acknowledging, of course, that if he were a responsible spouse, he wouldn't have been served papers that report his abuse. The legal system's task of exposing the abuser's cover-up act is the same task that the victim faces at home.

In order to conceal his criminal activity against the victim, the abuser practices intentional forgetfulness. To silence the victim and keep the abuse a secret is the abuser's barricade. If the victim asserts herself, the abuser does everything in his power to distress and distract her and works to ascertain that she is not heard. The abuser is an expert and a mastermind at minimizing and covering up any truths that would reveal his abuse of the victim. The abuser not only silences the victim about his abuse, but he also manages to silence her friends and family with the plagued fear of sharing the secret which the abuser has indirectly and/or directly said is a "private family matter." An abuser's denial is so credible that he begins to believe his own lies as he is proficient at rationalizing every abusive incident. An abuser is able to impress the legal system and society with his eloquent words.

The abuser has formulated his defense in such a way that in many cases, the justice system will allow him to be his own defense. The abuser's alibi is that he apologizes, that the abuse never happened, and that it's time to note that these are all false, exaggerated accusations; he deems the victim a liar, and in any case, he says that it's time to realize that the victim has brought this terrible misunderstanding upon herself. This defensible attitude is fortified by a legal system in a society that gives the abuser the power to define the reality of the abuse and for his arguments to prevail. The abuser not only wins his case in spousal and/or family abuse, but he can usually get the courts

THE ABUSER: EVERYTHING YOU EVER WANTED TO KNOW

to continue to victimize his wife long after they have separated and/or divorced.

If the abuser can't win by controlling his victim in his home, he finds ways to continue tormenting her life by using new avenues which include litigation for baseless allegations as a way of furthering his abuse. The abuser extends his manipulation via the judicial system. Most of the time, the judicial system justifies affording the accused abuser all of his rights which ends up permitting excessive harassment of the victim in the process. It is not unusual for victims to incur astronomical legal fees after the abuser gets through with his legal demands; he purportedly claims financial hardship, and the judicial system does not oversee or protect victims from the legal costs of defending themselves from the abuser. The outcome is that the abuser comes out winning whether the victim stays in the abusive relationship or not. Generally, abusers partake in preferential treatment within the judicial system and use this to their controlling advantage. When a judicial system takes on a prejudicial stance against a victim of spousal abuse, it compounds the victim's suffering and entrapment.

Yes, there are cases whereby a highly-disturbed person alleges abuse that never happened, but that's a problem that can happen with any type of alleged crime. Such cases with false allegations can ruin the true testimony of a victim of abuse. The judge and jury base their decision to believe the victim on whether her detailed testimony is credible or unreliable. Her testimony consists of multiple counts of abusive actions by her abuser. The victim presents her evidence to the court as she is cross-examined; all the factors are there, and she presents details that could have only been experienced by herself as an eyewitness—she was there. The abuser testifies for himself and will sometimes bring in his allies (even his employer) to testify on his good character. Of course, they're good witnesses—they weren't there. The abuser vehemently denies his abuse. She's deemed as not trustworthy, and her testimony is deemed as unreliable. Such details of inhumane maltreatment with cruel facts simply cannot be made up. No victim takes pride in shaming herself before the court, telling her testimony before total strangers with whom she does not have a relationship. She has already been shamed by her abuser; she's re-victimized by deeming the abuser as a credible witness without any evidence other than the manner in which he tells his own version of what happened—his story.

In some very rare cases, an abuser may not deny the abuse but instead eloquently apologizes to the court and the victim so as to prevent any further discussion of his hideous abuse toward her; he makes the appropriate comments that the victim and judge want to hear, including offering to attend an abuser's program so that the charges will be dismissed (yet all the while taunting the victim, the previous day or day of the hearing). I have witnessed abusers frighten their victims by a look or gesture during the court hearing (while verbally impressing the legal system). The abuser or his attorney present a long list of his accolades or good citizen contributions, but the truth is that a list of rightful behaviors does not make the wrongfulness of abuse any less wrong. Some abusers make redemptive promises or claim that they have sought counseling or are already enrolled in an abuser's recovery program. However, this presentation in the court room does not nullify the abuse that has been inflicted upon the victim; yet, the abuser is released for good behaviors with no penalty for his crime.

Abusers that are ignored or released without any criminal implications are basically being given walking papers to propagate abuse in our communities. Abusers have no respect for both the institution of marriage and the judicial system. Unsanctioned abuse gives the abuser permission to be a part of his informal nonprofit organization of abuse; which then becomes the

THE ABUSER: EVERYTHING YOU EVER WANTED TO KNOW

abuser's unofficial institution of family abuse. Justice, if it's going to be productive, must always be tempered by mercy for abuse trauma to ensure that the abuser's injustice is not repeated by re-victimizing the victim on the stand. Otherwise, she is relegated to second class citizenship as the abuser has already done. Most courts are not teaching abusers that they are to be responsible (response-able) for the crime of abuse; they're not requiring the abuser to be able to make the right response to his crime. It is usually the military court that holds the abuser responsible for his crime. When abusers are released to think that they themselves are the victims by being brought to court, they're unable to see that they have made a choice as to how to respond by continuing their abusive, wrongful behavior—a crime.

In court, most abusers only admit to abuse if there is some form of evidence such as photos, voice or video recordings, DNA, or other incriminating evidence. Most victims don't have the financial means to hire an attorney to present such exhibits in the court room. Most attorneys want an advance in legal fees and will not agree for the victim to hire their legal services on contingency. Even when there's evidence of abuse, the majority of abusers have the means to post bail and do not do any jail time. My colleagues and I have watched many an abuser offer to pursue counseling as a tool to escape legal consequences and even plea bargain jail sentences. Some abusers are ordered community service or offered military duty as opposed to a jail term, relocating their abusive behaviors to community grounds or military bases. Abusers usually deny their abuse and plead "not guilty," no matter how grave their acts of abuse have been. Some of these abusers have tied up their victims (using rags, belts, or chains) and/or have attacked their victim with every type of abuse that exists. Some inmates I have worked with that had tortured or murdered their victim would negotiate to plead "guilty" if talk of capital punishment could be taken off the table. Some abusers that had been bailed out of jail and were in my probation group attempted to negotiate visitation with their children when it had been previously denied by the judge.

Once in a while, a group member would confront such an abuser and ask, "Man, what makes you think that a judge would let you see your kid when you beat up her mother in front of her?" An abuser's manipulation tactics aren't ingenious—they're maneuver-devious. I have heard abusers proudly announce in group that their attorney supports their "not guilty" plea. When I have asked my attorney friends how they can represent an abuser and advocate for his *not guilty* plea, even when there is substantial evidence against him for his horrific acts against the victim, the reply is the same across the board. These attorneys are like-minded and state that their job is to defend their client because that is how they make their living; besides, they say, their client is actually a "nice guy, and he loves his family, it's just that affirmations are not his love language."

When a legal system elects not to hear the claims of a victim who has been exploited and violated in more ways than one, it is traumatic for the victim to face the abuser's arguments in solitude. The victim has taken a gigantic leap to set a boundary with the abuser. A negative, lackluster response from the legal system places her back in her victim role of a boundary-less position; it places our communities as very willing to RSVP along with the victim to the societal invitation to *not* establish boundaries. She feels no sense of social support because society, as a bystander, looks the other way as the legal system has done. This neglect of the victim's claims and siding with the abuser can happen to *any* victim, including prominent women in the community. The message to the victim is that in spite of being a valued community member and an outstanding citizen who notably always participates in her civic duties with honor, the abuse *cannot* be validated and is *not* to enter into any further discussion. Our nation

THE ABUSER: EVERYTHING YOU EVER WANTED TO KNOW

must awaken to the need for justice when it comes to spouse and family abuse.

Irrespective of the extensive investigative studies that have been done and the medical research and literature that has been made available on the trauma of abuse, there still exists a lingering question by society and our legal system as to whether the phenomenon of marital abuse trauma exists. This type of questioning, way of thinking, denial, and lack of action in the dismissal of the subject of marital abuse as a human concern has to change in order for the trauma of abuse to be resolved. A victim is coerced into ongoing exasperation by the community and the legal system as they discredit and expect her to disappear with her abuse allegations. Ironically, it's the same secrecy and invisibility that the abuser wants for his victim. Must victims continue to be stigmatized and re-traumatized for seeking legal assistance for their abuse? There needs to be statutory reform in the way both abusers *and* victims are treated within society and the judicial system.

Up until today, the majority of abuse cases are still being perceived and approached with the same interventions. An adult school bus driver raped an adolescent this week and was given less than a year of probation. When the judge was asked why the abuser did not get any prison time, the judge responded that the abuser had never done this before. If we truly face the daily acute distress of victims of abuse trauma, much of the recurring abuse in our society can be ascribed to the lack of legislature and community involvement. A government's and society's concern or the lack thereof for the victims of abuse are a barometer to the outcome of abuse cases. When abuse (of any type) criminal laws are not enacted, justice is not served. The government has a responsibility—justice. Sadly, bystanders of victim abuse (officials and lay people) are suspicious of investigators of abuse and challenge research credibility with allegations of, "anything can be proven in a study." These bystanders are *not* eyewitnesses to the realities of abuse, and they have not had firsthand opportunities to work with abusers and victims of abusive relationships. If they're not able to justify questioning the victim's reality, they question the integrity of the investigators and those that treat the victims of abuse, inferring that abuse trauma is contagious and can infect investigators and clinicians.

This is ludicrous because it's like saying that missionaries who dedicate their work and lives to the oppressed will get contaminated with oppression. The truth is that generally investigators of abuse and clinicians basically give a voice to disempowered victims. But, in order for abuse within relationships to be recognized as a serious reality, which brings on the onset of trauma, there needs to be validation and affirmation for the victim and her professional advocates. The legal system, the community, and the larger society have to have an alliance treaty that joins together in a common goal: to recognize and acknowledge abusive relationships as real, refrain from silencing, and politically move legislation for justice to be served. There may not be justice found in some of the states of the U.S. Criminal Justice System for victims of abuse, but nevertheless, we are called as a people, as humankind, as professionals, as Christians, as *Overcomers* to never cease to give it. We must be faithful, fair dispensers of justice.

> **"Learn to do good; Seek justice, Rebuke the oppressor; Defend the fatherless, Plead for the widow."**
> **Isaiah 1:17**

MARY'S STORY

I MOVED OUT OF my parent's home right out of high school. I had just completed my associate's degree, and was working in civil engineering, when I met my husband, Zack. In total, I had been living on my own for four years. I met him through a group of mutual friends that we both had grown up around. Occasionally, I would go out with these friends after work to a bar or out on the town. One day he was *just there* with the group, and we began to visit. A few days later we began to date; that was the beginning of our relationship. Zack proposed five months later after I learned that I was pregnant. We had already discussed marriage before that.

Even though the engagement evolved rapidly it *just seemed like a good idea* because we both had good jobs. Zack was a respiratory therapist; we were both *done* with school. Even though he wasn't *perfect* from the beginning, we both had never been married. I had been working all of that time and I was just *ready* for a relationship, ready for a companion, it seemed like a good-fit. We were both Protestant, professed believers; so we had a church wedding. As far as Zack...*well...everybody where we were raised* claimed to be a professed believer! I'm by no means the judge of his salvation, but looking back—basing it on being a *believer* by *relationship* to the Lord—I would say Zack's not a believer. Our son born out of this marriage is now seven years old. Zack and I divorced after four years of marriage; he continues to have joint custodial visitation rights.

I had already noticed Zack's very emotional and controlling ways while we were dating, even *before* I got pregnant. Although it seemed like he was acting jealous, he always said it was because he *loved me so much*. As it turns out *he* was unfaithful throughout our entire marriage; which explains to me a lot of his erratic behaviors. When we were living together, and I had an hour and a half commute to and from work, this in itself was very unsettling for him because that was time that I was unaccounted for every day.

The very first time that he did anything out of the ordinary was involving a couple (that were friends of mine). I was more friends with the wife, but her husband was a friend as well. Zack had noticed that my friend had texted me, and Zack asked who he was. When I responded, it didn't seem to bother him in any way; but later he made it a point to tell me about a girl that had called him a few times. At the time it didn't affect me since I just wasn't a jealous type. I did think it was weird that he had brought this up, but I didn't put it together until afterward when he mentioned an additional gal that had been talking to him. When I didn't take the bait (because I didn't know what on Earth was happening) he *out of nowhere* proceeded to say, "I don't think it's fair that *you* can get jealous about me talking to other girls, but *I* can't get jealous about you talking to other guys." I was just totally blown away and said, "I didn't know I was *being jealous* about you and other girls? I didn't realize I had done anything?!"

Then he just lost it and got *uncontrollably mad*; he said he didn't want me talking to other guys, that it was just so disrespectful to him. It was early enough in the relationship that I was just going to leave, but that made it even worse; he started to throw things, punched a hole in the wall, began to cuss and said that if I left to never come back! I was shocked because I had not grown up with cussing or any form of profanity—it was just disgraceful to me. The angrier he got the more that I wanted to leave; and the more I wanted to leave, the more uncontrollable he got. I don't know what he was thinking; maybe he thought that if he freaked out I would stay? I was living in his home so he began to throw my things out in his yard, yelling out, "If you leave, take *everything* with you!" Then when I finally got into my car and was ready to leave, he was holding on to my door pleading with me, "Don't leave, *I'm sorry*, don't leave." I *did leave* and went to a friend's house. Of course, the next day he apologized *again*, he cried, and said that he was sorry—he said he just had never felt this way about a girl before. So I believed him; and we went back to dating and I moved back in.

I had not completely moved out of my apartment while living with him (and that was another discontent with him) because he thought I kept my own place so that at any time I could leave. Zack always thought I was going to leave him. The truth was that it was my commitment to my roommates; I continued to pay my share of the rent and had planned to do so until I was legally married. The next big incident was when I came home from work one day and he was *very in the mood;* I was in the kitchen cooking dinner and it just wasn't a good time for me. I was exhausted, plus, that morning I had woken up late and I hadn't showered; I just wasn't feeling romantic. I had managed to brush him off. Later that night, however, I had gotten cleaned up, changed clothes, and changed underwear. When I got into bed, he made advances again and when he realized that I had changed my underwear, to *him,* that meant that I had had sex with someone during the day and that was *why* I had changed my underwear. This accusation was just disgusting to me because I knew that I was not that type of person and how could he think that way of me? I felt so offended. It was so irrational, but he didn't see it that way at all, he saw it as: *Okay, I caught you, and you should be bowing to my feet for forgiveness now.*

Something that I found out along the way (after we were married and doing our own finances) was that Zack had an oddly close relationship with his parents. Zack's house was actually owned by his parents, and apparently he didn't have very many adult life skills because his dad took care of depositing Zack's paycheck, paid Zack's bills, and left the remainder in Zack's account. This explained why Zack's initial reaction to my pregnancy was one of being unhappy and so terrified of disappointing his parents; as they had been taking care of him. Zack didn't want us to go together to tell our parents that I was pregnant. We had to go separately; he said he would tell his parents and that I should go to tell mine.

As it turns out, he *never* told his parents. I got sick and threw up while visiting his parents, and his mom asked, "What if she's pregnant?" Zack's response was, "I don't know, she could be." So his mom went out and purchased a pregnancy test and I was stuck in the middle of this lie, so I had to go along as if we were *just now* finding out! They were not very upset: Zack's two sisters had had children out of wedlock, married, and divorced, so it didn't seem out of the ordinary for them. Even Zack's parents had been married, divorced, and re-married each other three times. *So*, his parents weren't *really happy* together, but they just decided to maintain their relationship to stick it out and stay together. Zack's mother has the same temper issues as Zack.

The issue with the parents being involved in Zack's finances continued throughout our marriage, even though I had taken over bill paying (because when Zack did it for a few months the bills were being paid late). It seemed like he liked his parents paying his bills. Zack didn't want that responsibility; all he wanted was to have spending money so he could say, "This is the pocket money I have and I can spend it any way I want." Zack continued to rely on his parents for financial support—he was very impulsive. If he wanted a new car, he could count on his mother to co-sign his loan for a better interest rate. I would come home from work and he would have a new truck that he had financed during the day through the help of his mother. Whatever he decided that he wanted to buy, he used his parents and borrowed to pay them later.

I of all people surprised myself as one who would put up with abuse, because I was always the friend that would encourage a friend not to put up with abuse. I even knew from my childhood that my dad had divorced my mom (when I was four) because of infidelity. Mom had been self-sufficient, and she independently did well. Even though Mom came from a good family that could have helped her out, she survived all on her own. Sure, we lived in the projects, but Mom was strong and decided to move on and raise my brother and me as a single parent. So I had grown up with that attitude: *Never let a man get you down.* Mom didn't remarry until I was in college.

I definitely knew early on that I was in an abusive relationship with Zack, but a combination of things kept me there. One thing was the fact that I didn't tell people the really bad parts. However, about a year before the divorce, I started to confront him in front of others (family and friends) when he was being disrespectful toward me. I did that because I began to realize that if I would call him on it or tell those that he cared about, he would watch his words and tame his behavior; it was the only way I felt I could manage his mistreatment of me. During this time Zack was so stressed out with his job that he couldn't control his emotions at all! So I encouraged him to get on some sort of anti-anxiety medication because I had been around my own step-dad when he had a bad temper; and although my step-dad never abused anybody, he would slam or throw things. My step-dad would crash the phone on telemarketers! I didn't want to be around that. My step-dad's temper eventually calmed down and he didn't have such a short fuse after he began to have grandchildren; seems like once he became a *Papaw* he softened *a lot*. This was not the case for Zack. Zack's temper didn't change; it was just on hold!

My suggestion to Zack that he consider getting on some sort of medication was right after he had had an incident in the brand-new home that we had just moved into. That first week he had punched a hole in the wall. Of course, he promised not to do it again and I was surprised that he kept to it. Once he was on the medication, it seemed that his emotions and anger were more under control; he didn't have the desire to punch things that much anymore.

The other thing that kept me going back to the relationship was his apologizing and his promises to do good by me; my believing him, forgiving him, and therefore returning. Around our third-year anniversary, things got really bad again. I didn't want to tell anyone, especially my family—so I played it up as if things were better.

Truth be told, if you were to meet him right now, you would think: "What a nice gentleman," "He's very charming," "A very good-ole boy," "Such a good attitude," "Everybody likes him." No one but me knows who he really is—or how he is—the majority of the time. The other thing that kept me in the relationship was biblical reasoning. At the time, I was *very close* to the Lord and was very much involved in my church. I participated and served in all that I could; I was there all of the time. I was there because I wanted to be there—but it was also the only place that I was allowed to go—the *only* place that was approved for me to be out of Zack's presence. I biblically felt that I should not get a divorce; I

MARY'S STORY

thought it was my job to just stick with him, pray, and hope that the Lord would change him. Maybe when we turned fifty, we would be in love again. I knew I was in an abusive relationship within that first year of our marriage! But, I wasn't willing to do anything about it until about the third year in.

That last year of my marriage to Zack before I requested the divorce, the abuse was at its peak. We were *always* on the verge of divorce. Zack had been having guy's night out once a week and that progressively turned into times when he wouldn't even come home. Zack wouldn't say where he had been. At that point, I believe that he really wanted and was okay with the divorce; but I would've preferred for our family to stay together, for our son. Even though it was bad, I just didn't want to get a divorce. Finally, he decided again that he did want to be married and that he did want to keep it together. But it was like that entire last year, I felt *so numb* to the bad or the good; it got to where the "*I love yous*" no longer had *any* meaning. Zack was frustrated that I wasn't responding to his *trying to do better;* but there was no evidence of trust there.

Zack was the type that never had calls or text messages recorded on his cellphone—he had erased it all. Zack's rationalization was that that's just what he did; he just erased his phone daily. Yet, if he was at work and I was at the grocery store and I wouldn't answer my phone, he would just repeatedly call me until I did answer. Then he would inquire, "Where are you?" "What are you doing?" When we would get our monthly phone bill, there would be seven hundred texts to another woman; I would call the number and *ask* whose number that was. Zack would then rationalize that it was just a friend or ex-girlfriend.

I became isolated from my family who only lived an hour away, because Zack demanded that I be home all of the time and said that it was selfish of me to go see them and waste gas. Zack wanted me to be home even when he worked late hours. Zack wanted me to fix dinner and have it ready for him. If I had to work late or went to see my family, he didn't want me to stop and bring something home for dinner; he said it was selfish of me not to fix dinner. Zack probably thought that I would continue in this encaged relationship with him because he would make it up by buying me anything I wanted, and he encouraged me to spend money any way I wanted to (he would never complain if I had shopped for something or about what I bought). I think he thought that he could be really awful to me, but justified it with the nice lifestyle he gave me.

Whenever I asked if we could go to marriage counseling, he refused. When I asked for a separation, he said that he wasn't going to leave his house and that if I wanted a separation I should move out. During this time, his parents had already paid for a family vacation, so we went on a week's vacation, and we slept in separate beds. As soon as we returned, I moved out. Once I was away from him, then I knew I was never going back. As I thought back about the many reasons I stayed, amongst them was that he was such a manipulator of the facts on what had really happened. I finally accepted that he was never going to be willing to admit to how he treated me; I think it would have been easier to forgive him if he would have been willing to admit his responsibility in making our relationship so bad.

If I would address the bad things that had happened in our marriage, he would turn the focus on me and would talk about the things from my teen years (which I had shared with him when we were dating) he would say that the reason he couldn't trust me was because of my past. Zack would say, "There's no way I could ever put you on a pedestal because look at the things you have done in your life!" They weren't even things that were that bad; I certainly had never had a one-night stand or slept with a ton of people. I had only had a couple of relationships before him, but Zack managed to use those stories against me.

MARY'S STORY

They weren't perfect stories, but they weren't as bad as he made them out to be.

I knew then, that if I ever left him, I was going to have to deal with his version of the truth to everyone. We lived in a small community and Zack's family was all there. They were all involved in my church (which is where most of my friends were) and I knew I would have to face them with what he would be saying. But I finally got to where I didn't care. I was just so low, so unhappy in the relationship, and so unhappy with myself—I had such little self-esteem. I felt like, "This cannot be all that God has for my life; this cannot be it..." So at that point, I made my *final* decision to move out. Fortunately, my employers had seen most of what my life was like. One of the female employers who knew my situation more than anyone else did was able to understand (when I was going through the worst of it). She herself had seen Zack out on the town with other women.

Once my employers knew I was serious about permanently moving out, they helped me find a place to live. It was just a little trailer, but I had left a corporate job to work nearby at a tiny company, and Zack was the primary bread winner now; I had to work with my lower salary. Zack and I had a new home and nice cars; I think he thought that having all the nice stuff would always keep me there, because I grew up really poor. But I just got to where none of those things mattered. I didn't care if I had to live in a trailer; at least I would know what was going to happen next in my life. I think he thought, based on the way his parents dealt with their relationship, that I would just be gone for a little while and then I would come back.

After I left this last time, Zack did some partying then he decided he didn't want that and wanted us to get back together. Zack did agree to some couples counseling at this point; so we went to counseling for a couple of weeks, but I was just so broken by then. Even the counselor said, "I don't know how you could start over unless you're just honestly willing to totally wipe the slate clean and allow Zack to start from the bottom." The counselor didn't see how we could repair the marriage. I said that I would have to see and experience things being a different way (I now knew better). I knew Zack was just a manipulator and that he would do good just so he could then do some bad.

I also thought about our son and how I didn't want him to live around Zack full time. I thought about how my parents divorced when I was very little and how I didn't remember much, so I thought, "Our son's only three. Our son is not going to remember much either." I wanted more for my son; for him to grow up knowing what it's like for a husband and wife to live in a faithful, loving relationship. I knew my son would someday become a husband and a dad; I just wanted so much more for him... I knew in my heart of hearts what the Bible says about divorce, but I felt God loving me and saying, "This is not it." I didn't know what it was that He had planned for my life—I just knew that small voice inside of me was saying this is not the rest of your life. That was enough for me to jump out of there!

When I declined to continue with the abusive relationship, Zack began to give examples of all of the good things about him and all the good that he had done recently. My response to him was, "If you could call the phone company and have them print out the last six months of text messaging on your phone and show *proof* of what you just said, then I would *consider* trying again." Zack just completely lost it. Zack was not just angry—he was *mad*! Zack said, "This is the way you always try to control everything; you snoop to catch me doing things!" I proceeded to get a lawyer, which he thought I wouldn't do (because a couple of days after I moved out, he closed our joint bank account). I was blessed that an attorney who was a colleague of my employer offered me a payment plan that allowed me to pay him a minimal fee, *as I got paid*. I believe this attorney saw how Zack was holding over my head the fact that he had money and I didn't.

From then on, I latched on to my employer's support, my family, and my mom's family who had been very influential in my life. They stepped in *right away*. It was difficult to obtain overall support from my church because Zack's family had been very prominent there. They took sides with Zack and his family. But I did have a small group of church friends who saw evidence of my genuine walk and love for the Lord, and they were accepting of me. There was one older lady that mentored me; she met with me for coffee and Bible study during my son's visitation weekends. She was always very affirming of me and allowed me to be the woman that God had called me to be. She recognized and affirmed my commitment to the Lord. Unlike some of my church family *who knew* how Zack had mistreated me and *expected* me to stay, she did not judge me if I spoke of divorcing Zack. She neither condoned nor condemned.

Three months after my divorce was final, I met Jason. I met him while I was vacationing at a resort, which happened to be his home town. Jason was only there that day for his grandfather's funeral. Jason was (and is still) an officer in the military, so after the funeral he returned to where he was stationed. However, I was with a girlfriend and my battery kept dying on my phone while we were trying to take a photo—Jason offered to take it with *his phone* and to send it to me. Jason got my contact information and that's how we began to keep in touch. We continued to text and became friends through our social media accounts; a month later we went on our first date and went to church together the next day. I believe the Lord sent Jason to me because I was very insecure about relationships—I had *no trust* for anyone. Jason's name means *healer;* the Lord sent healing through Jason. Jason is the opposite of Zack; he wanted to nurture and heal. Jason cared about my past and my growing up poor in the projects. I would cry as I shared my past, and he encouraged me to go deeper; he wanted to know all about me. Jason said he loved my past; he loved my story because that is who I am, and he loved *all of me.*

Jason had been married for eight years and divorced due to his wife's infidelity. Jason's wife married the man she had an affair with. When I met Jason, he had been divorced for a year and he was raising his two daughters while his ex-wife was deployed. At about my third or fourth phone contact with Jason, he asked if he could pray for us; that was something I had *never* experienced before as a couple. It was just so amazing to me, not just for my relationship with Jason, but in my relationship with the Lord because it confirmed that the Lord did have something *more* for me. With Jason's leading, we prayed every night—whether we were together or apart. We got married exactly a year from the date that we met. We have been married for four years.

Zack was very unhappy when he found out I was re-marrying even though he had started dating various girls after I left. Zack lied and told everyone that I had met someone online to marry. When it came to parenting our son, he was quick to say, "I'm his dad. Don't you let anyone else be his dad." Zack *says that*, with his mouth, but ultimately he wants to do what he wants to do; it soon became apparent that he didn't want a three-year-old tagging along with him. Zack would either be a no-show or call to cancel bimonthly visitations. Or he would call during visitations and ask if I would come get him because he had tickets to a ballgame or other place to be. It was very difficult for me to release my son to him two weekends a month because I had raised him primarily by myself. When I re-married, Zack became more demanding of his visitations.

Our son would come back from visits saying, "I want to go back to my dad's. I love it there." Well, Zack would splurge whenever he had our son over and took him to all kinds of places and got things for him that I couldn't afford. Our son didn't have a bedtime there, and he could eat junk food, whereas at home we ate healthy. I have done the best I can to *not to talk badly* to our son about his dad; but I believe our son has already gotten to experience what his dad is really like through an unfortunate experience. One evening at about eleven, Zack texted me and said, "Come get your son." Evidently, our son was missing me and wanted to come home, and this made Zack very angry; he had put our son out on the porch and closed the front door.

My married life is so different now; my husband would do *anything* to make my life easier or better as a wife and mom. Jason actually wants me to be happy. If I ask him to pick up a gallon of milk on the way home, he doesn't hesitate. If I asked Zack the same, that was an outrageous request to make of him! My needs didn't count *at all* with Zack, not even a little bit. Jason is so much more mature than my former husband, and they're about the same age. Because of all of the past infidelity that I had experienced with Zack (with alcohol being a large part of it) Jason initiated a commitment to never drink alcohol apart from each other. Jason wants me to trust him, *that he's going to come through* in our relationship. Jason made this commitment and did not ask the same of me, but I offered to do the same.

Very early on, Jason wanted me to have the password to his email and once he proposed we joined our social media accounts. Jason sees it as an honor for me to put my trust in him. We have a wonderful fifteen-month-old daughter of our own now. We are a blended family, and he doesn't see me as a non-working wife; he sees me as *his wife* who is willing to *trust* him to provide for our family (while putting her career aside) in order to home school our children. Jason sees my stay-at-home role as valuable; he also values and encourages my creativity and spiritual growth. It was always so discouraging when Zack would disapprove of my desire to do crafts. Or whenever I wanted to participate in or lead a Bible study, he would say, "Why would you want to do that?"

My past abusive relationship was one of being very controlled. I was always so sad—so unhappy. It was a depressing, miserable, dark life. I lived in shame, I couldn't believe that this was my life and that I was taking it. I never thought that I would be in that kind of a relationship! I lived in fear that something bad was always about to happen—constantly having to be very careful about what I said, how I said it, watching what time I got home, hyperaware of every move I made. It was like walking on thin ice. I knew that this was not who I was, and that my alternative was divorce. I felt really stuck; but by faith, I elected to move on.

My *entire life* changed! My life now is one of feeling secure, content, and living a joyful, honest life without all of the lies and falseness—no longer living a charade. I should have ended my abusive marriage early on when I saw the signs, but I was afraid to leave; I didn't want to become an outcast or be shunned. It's important to have faith and realize that no matter how good one has it materialistically—looking in from the outside, I lived a nice lifestyle—there is a better life without *abuse*. I had no idea that God had a better plan for my life until I was able to get away from the abuse and look back at it. My life is so much better in so many different ways—by just trusting that God *does* provide. He provided healing and restoration beyond the physical circumstances in ways that I never even could have imagined.

PART III

THE VICTIM: EVERYTHING YOU EVER WONDERED

Victim Characteristics

WE HAVE DISCUSSED THE typical characteristics of your abuser. What about you as a victim? What characteristics are typically exhibited by you as a victim? What symptoms are most noticeable in you as the victim? Take a moment to answer the following questions:

1. Are you spending a lot of anxious time worrying about how to improve and fix your relationship with your spouse?
2. When you think about the problems in your marriage, do you feel like it's your entire fault?
3. After an argument with your spouse, does it feels like your mind has been played with but that you're unable to discern how this happened and why?

4. Since your relationship has become abusive, has your self-image been on the decline?
5. Have you been feeling like you can't seem to measure up and do anything right in your relationship, so you go out of your way to prove yourself?
6. Since you have been in this abusive relationship, do you feel stressed, sad, hurt, near-tears, angry, or depressed most of the time?
7. Have you nearly isolated yourself from family, friends, and/or church fellowship because your abuser creates conflict over those relationships?
8. Is the most relaxed part of your day when your abuser is not with you, and do you look forward to those times?
9. Are you intimidated and afraid of your abuser? Do you protect him and rationalize his abuse?
10. Is your focus always on your abuser, and as a result, have you lost your energy and enthusiasm for daily activities including the things that you used to look forward to?
11. Do you have extreme difficulty setting limits (boundaries) for yourself and others?
12. Have you ever been emotionally, physically, economically, spiritually, or sexually abused prior to this relationship?
13. Are you suspicious of others and can't seem to trust anyone?
14. Do you feel like you *can't* live an honest life and be yourself?
15. Do you feel like you have no control over your own life?

If you answered "yes" to most of these questions, you are exhibiting the characteristics and symptoms of a victim of abuse. It is strongly recommended that if you find that you are a victim of abuse that you seek support and/or professional counseling. If you decide to seek counseling, it would be to your benefit to make certain that your counselor has a background in working with victims of abuse. Beware of counselors who restrict their practice to marital counseling as you may come across a Reconciliation Advisor (R.A.) (definition of R.A. is expanded on in Volume III Part II). A R.A. is the person your abuser wishes that you would tell about the abuse. A professional (defined in Volume III Part II) is the person your abuser warned you not to tell (for fear he would help you).

If you have come this far by reading this book, you have begun your path to freedom from abuse. Remember, if you do not use the courage that you have mustered and used to read this book, to take the next step(s), then there's a chance that you may lose your freedom from abuse. When a victim discovers that there is freedom from abuse and she does not use her freedom to defend her freedom, she loses her freedom. You need to learn to feel the freedom from abuse in order to be able to use the two-letter word "no" to abuse.

Abuser Dating Warning Signs
We will discuss at length victims that are involved in a marital abusive relationship, but it is just as important to do some ground work on the dynamics of victims that are involved in a dating relationship with an abuser. This information is beneficial for general knowledge of what an abusive dating or romantic relationship profile looks like. It is also especially important for an *Overcomer* of abuse to share this data with her daughter(s) and female friends that are at risk for victimization. Teach your daughters, female friends, and relatives to have zero tolerance for abuse. Remember that your sons and male relatives are learning from you as well; they are learning how females expect to be treated and how they command respect. Learn these abusive dating principles and teach them to your loved ones so that none of you become victims by default. Becoming aware of abusive dating relationships is not only useful prevention for those that are

not married, but it is also for those recovering from an abusive relationship that need to refresh their knowledge on not dating an abuser so that they don't repeat the same destructive pattern. Also, be aware that there is evidence that some former victims who become involved in exploitive, abusive relationships do so at a time in their life when they are feeling vulnerable after a life transition, lonesome time, or a sad state after they have experienced loss or life crisis. The point is to be *choosy*. Or, not. Those are the only options.

Let's begin this discussion by addressing some of the typical dating relationship scenarios and conclude with a list of the most common symptoms of controlling men which women have to be observant of and be on the lookout for if they are to protect themselves from becoming a victim.

Typically, in the beginning stages of a dating relationship with an abuser (first weeks or months) you may be in a state of bliss, not suspecting that he's an abuser. The abuser may be interesting—even fascinating. An abuser may appear full of enthusiasm with your presence and so energetically entertaining. One of his features may include that he's *all* about you—he himself is fascinated by you! This intense, quick disclosure of affection can make you feel good. But as you watch your date charming you and others, watch for his subtle or overt vanity that is not about you. When working with abusers, their smugness is so intense that it's obvious that their pride is their entire make up. While doing the abusers' intake, most practitioners note that they are oblivious to their ignoble character, for their focus is on their "perfect" self and "imperfect" mate.

At the same time, they voice looking for a mate that has the same qualities as they view their own self to have. It's been said by colleague researchers that abusers are the happiest when they can date someone like their own person (as they see their self). It's all about their perfect person, and when they discover their

THE VICTIM: EVERYTHING YOU EVER WONDERED

victim's human flaws and imperfections, they become very unhappy—and when an abuser is unhappy, nobody is happy! Total control is the name of his game, and if he can't control the victim's characteristics, he's not a happy camper, and then there's trouble in doggie land. Some spouses talk about being "in the dog house" when they have an occasional quarrel with their wife; once the abuser is disappointed, the victim is *always* in the dog house. If he's not instantly the abuser-pursuer, he can be the other type that puts on a subtle charm. So if he's not falling head over heels in love with you, then you will be powerfully drawn to his sweet and timid nature that you get to seduce. This quietness *is* his manipulative heart that is seeking someone to pursue *him*, someone to take care of his needs. If you can prove yourself (while dating) to be able to draw him out of an introverted state into an extroverted state, then he foresees you as his potential caretaker-to-be.

All abusive relationships have an idyllic beginning during the dating stage because if they didn't there would be no abusive relationships. Think about it. If a woman goes out on a date(s) and the man starts off their dating relationship by ranting and insulting her, will she feel like he's a gentleman and express that she can't wait until their next date? No, most abusers don't operate that way; their manipulative controlling nature is *always* coming into play, so they are *not* going to reveal their abusive nature during the early dating stages of the relationship. The abuser's charm *so* transports the victim that most of the victim's recollections of when she first met her abuser are full of spark! The victim's initial memories of those first dates are about those first blissful impressions; the victim speaks about the dreamy abuser with a positive lilt in her voice. Those dates at the beginning are reserved for entrapping the victim into the abusive relationship.

After the first few dates, the woman may feel special because he builds her up and she sees him as a great guy. She proceeds to tell her friends and family all about this fantastic guy that she has been dating. An abuser may even hold off being unkind to her until he gets her to accept his marriage proposal. Then one day he gradually begins to disrespect her and mistreats her along the way. This can happen before, during, or after their honeymoon. As with any woman who has fallen in love, she's now feeling committed to him yet is confused about his own disclosure that he loves her. She begins to feel a sense of shame about the way he treats her and keeps his offenses to her private. A period of time goes by, and she makes excuses for his abusive behaviors—she rationalizes that something has happened that has suddenly changed him; after all, he's not the wonderful guy that she dated. The woman is now a victim who proceeds to spend her time wondering and searching for the cause of his mistreatment of her. She wonders if she herself possibly caused him to become abusive. As time goes by, it becomes incredibly difficult for her to let go of the precious romantic and loving memories of their dating relationship, and it's especially painful to release this very special man that was non-abusive when he came into her life.

It is hard to detect an abuser in a dating relationship because his love-bombing is difficult to identify, and with the newly-ignited hustle and bustle of all of the scheduled rendezvous and the excitement for a potential new relationship, everything gets convoluted and glossy. The social bonding oxytocin hormone is released and percolating. There is the hope that dating will develop into a commitment. In the beginning, getting to know someone you like can be pleasant but also nerve-wracking because it surfaces feelings that have been dormant, and you are vulnerable. Some victims are distracted and are wrapped up in the emotional highs and giddiness, which are normal when there's a mutual attraction and not altogether a cause for a *yellow flag*.

THE VICTIM: EVERYTHING YOU EVER WONDERED

What's abnormal, however, is to immediately make a commitment into a serious relationship whereby the abuser demands a lot of your time. Texting, email, social media, and instant-messaging make easy access for the abuser to use and constantly contact the prospective victim. An abuser can easily use social media to love-bomb you off your heels! You may have thought of entering the dating relationship with the intention of keeping an open mind and balancing your life around him, but somehow now you find yourself forced into doing the exact opposite. You're in contact at great lengths daily, your agenda somehow gets reorganized, and you begin to believe you've found your soul mate.

Unbeknownst to you, he has declared you as "the one." Your new date mate may even approach you about moving in together or is already making plans in his mind to marry you. This offer can seem appealing to a victim that is susceptible to engaging in a relationship with an abuser. What makes you vulnerable as a prospective victim? Simply put, the abuser's suave characteristics do. The traits and tactics of an abuser make a good first impression with their charm that, even if they're not physically attractive, lures the victim into seeing them as good-looking on the outside because they carry themselves with an air of confidence, leadership, ambition, and independence while maintaining a kind and gentle air at the same time. Love-bombing words melt the victim's heart and make him desirable. An abuser appears attractive to the victim because he sees himself as a great catch, and that influences how the victim sees him. Abusers subtly and sometimes openly brag about themselves (they believe in their own value as a front), so people look up to them. They use this charisma to attract the victim. This powerful charismatic air doesn't reveal the vanity, pride, heartless, self-entitled nature, arrogance, and controlling, aggressive characteristics until the victim is already hooked.

One way to take care of yourself in a dating relationship—to prevent being spellbound and to protect yourself with a suspected abuser—is to become informed that an abuser will use tremendous amounts of flattery at the beginning of the relationship so that the victim will feel as if she matters and is the center of his world. However, in the true vision of the abuser, he sees himself as the most valuable, smartest person in the room. In the beginning, an abuser will profusely compliment the victim and even boast about the victim to his family and friends, confirming that the victim is worthy of his attention and showing off that he was able to conquer getting the victim's attention. However, this showering of support can be withdrawn just as fast as it developed; it's all a matter of time as to when the abuser will no longer value the victim. If the victim is not meeting whatever need(s) for which the abuser selected the victim, his positive interaction with her can come crashing down, replaced by his discontent and wrath for not getting what he chose her for. She is no longer useful to him because she's not meeting his purposes (his conditions) for the relationship.

A prospective dating victim can come from a functional family but may be lacking in confidence nonetheless and may admire the abuser's confidence and feel that void being filled by his presence. On the other hand, she may come from a dysfunctional family through which attachment or other needs were not met and may subconsciously gravitate toward a reminder of someone that traumatized her in the past. The toxic relationship with the abuser may be a comfort zone because this is the only type of relationship she's ever known. A victim may be seeking to improve her relationship with a parent(s) or other significant relationship and believes that if she was unable to work through that relationship that perhaps she will be able to fix the past through this dynamic new person in her life who she believes completes her.

THE VICTIM: EVERYTHING YOU EVER WONDERED

Just know that in a dating relationship, no one purposely seeks to find an abuser. The choice for an abuser is subconscious. The dramatic cover-up that the abuser does on his prey is difficult to spot unless a victim is knowledgeable of an abuser's character and schemes. If a victim has had a dysfunctional or a functional family but a low self-esteem and a pattern of choosing a dating mate who delves out disapproval or bombards her with compliments, it may seem normal, to her, to seek out such dating prospects. If this is the victim's comfort zone, then there will be a tendency to seek and end up in abusive relationships because she is seeking to be comforted through a relationship. But that is only a prescription for an unhealthy, unbalanced relationship. The victim's seeking to be nurtured attracts the abuser as a comforter, and when he discovers her dependency, he turns his interest elsewhere and may want out; after all, he's the one that wants to be taken care of. Regardless, a victim must know before dating an abuser that he's incapable of meeting her needs, short-term or long-term. Abusers are unable to love unconditionally. Love is a decision; it is a choice that has nothing to do with feelings. An abuser can say he has feelings for her, but that's just a chemical reaction. Chemical reactions are temporary and come and go. To love her is to choose to value her consistently and long-term. She must enter a dating relationship with the goal of having a healthy relationship, which can only be born and developed out of unconditional love.

If you have been in a dating relationship(s) with an abuser(s) and you're ready to end this pattern, it's important for you to return to the healthy foundation for an intimate relationship. Maintaining an abusive relationship is enabling a superficial relationship (which is insubstantial). This applies to all relationships whether they are dating, spousal, family, social media contacts, or general relationships; if it's not based on substance, then it's not a true relationship. A genuine relationship is mutual. Unconditional love, respect, boundaries, and acceptance as an individual person of your own are not to be compromised. Although an abuser appears to fulfill all of the requirements of a healthy relationship, it won't be long before his real self will show up; that is why it's so very important not to be impulsive about getting seriously committed in a dating relationship that's relatively new. You deserve the time to get better acquainted through a dating and engagement period—and to expect a healthy foundation—for a lifetime relationship.

It's still painful, but less complicated, to end an abusive dating relationship or engagement before marriage. Knowing before marriage that abusers don't change is helpful data for the victim. Recognizing that it is not a victim's responsibility to help the abuser mature or heal from any of his past or current issues is of utmost importance and, above all, that it is not the victim's fault or lifetime calling to restore the abusive relationship to health. Depending on the victim's personality, the level of persistence and determination to fix the relationship can vary because in some victim's families, giving up is not an option, and in others' there will be family's or friends' support to dispose of the abuser. However, the goal for the dating victim of abuse is the same no matter what her personality is and what support she may have or not have. She is not to invest her precious life hours on the abuser; true love does not require undergoing severe stress and spending every day working toward fixing the relationship.

Knowing what your healthy expectations are from a romantic relationship is all you need as your ammunition to tell the abuser that you have been dating that the relationship is over. If you have repeatedly shared your expectations, and your abuser has voiced or demonstrated through his actions that he is disinterested in fulfilling them, then there's no need to tell him again. It is now time to move on, and as with all self-entitled abusers, they're unable to receive your termination notice in person because they

THE VICTIM: EVERYTHING YOU EVER WONDERED

can't fathom that you would end such a good thing and will guilt-trip you or threaten you for your decision. Spare yourself any further pain and just focus on taking good care of yourself by remaining consistent with your healthy expectations, and this will protect you from this abuser and future abuser maltreatment. Most victims that overcome their abuse eventually develop healthy relationships and end up having to choose those with whom they want to share their lives (if they want to share their lives with someone). At some point, the victim who overcame her abuse is puzzled about how on Earth she got pulled into an abusive relationship(s) in the first place.

It's easier for the woman to fantasize that whatever is wrong while dating is pure immaturity and will change and get better and fixed when married. It is not about the wedding; it is about what will happen with time into the marriage! It is in God's plan for you to marry, but it is not in God's plan for you to marry an abusive man. Whatever is abusively wrong before the wedding just gets worse after the marriage. Many women ask the very important question: If abusers are hard to detect during the dating relationship, how are women able to tell if the man is going to be an abuser? The good news is that even though abusers don't come with warning labels, most abusers inadvertently put out *both yellow* and *red flags before* their abusive nature kicks in.

The following is a list of yellow warning flags to be aware of before accepting a date or considering the continuation of a dating relationship with an abuser:

1. Notice his eye contact, facial expression, and demeanor when you are talking. Watch for his attention span. If he is listening and attentive to what you're saying, he's truly interested in and cares about you. If he's not paying attention to your conversation and consistently redirects the focus on himself and what he has to say, he's giving you a signal about his selfishness and self-entitlement.

2. If your date uses sarcasm or condescending remarks while you're alone with him, ridicules your opinions alone or in the presence of others, makes rude comments directed at you or impatiently demands immediate attention or gratification, he is disrespecting you.
3. If you address his abusive behaviors toward you and how they affect you and he becomes defensive and denies these behaviors, he is controlling you. Control can be difficult to identify at the early stages of the relationship because the comments or actions are rather subtle. However, notice if he chronically interjects negative comments about your thoughts, actions, clothes, body, friends/family, and if he acts upset when you don't agree with his comments. Control can be exhibited by the abuser when he gets upset if you don't participate in an activity he insists on or if your opinion is different than his on education, religion, politics, recreation, food, and relationships. Control can also be visible if he structures your dates or activities to do only the things that he likes to do. Everything must go the way that he plans; he gets very frustrated and moody if you're not up to following *his* plans.
4. Listen to *how* he speaks about other women in his life (family members, co-workers, former girlfriends). It's normal for an occasional remark to be made about a disappointment with someone that just happens to be a woman, but be *warned* if he expends time venting his resentment or ongoing frustration by women in his life—especially if he talks about these women in derogatory terms and blames them as if he's their victim. Go from a *yellow warning flag* to a deep *red flag* if he alleges that a woman has falsely accused him of abuse. Most reports of abuse are an accurate representation of the situation. More than likely, you will not be able to verify what the abuser says about

THE VICTIM: EVERYTHING YOU EVER WONDERED

another woman because abusers that have been previously abusive make certain that their former girlfriend or wife has no contact with the new victim for fear that she will tell about his abuse. Be careful. If he's already telling you his negative attitude toward the women in his life, what makes you think he won't eventually see you in the same way?

5. Your date constantly comes bearing gifts. These gifts can be in the form of material, favors, or overly generous gestures. Be forewarned that he's building up indebtedness in your relationship with him. This is collateral that he can use later when you resist his abusive tactics and he manipulates you to feel sorry for him as he reminds you of how generous he has been toward you.

6. Watch out for his declarations of love that are wrapped up in jealous and possessive dominance of you. If he's threatened by your conversation with other men at work or social activities and indicates that he prefers that you limit your interaction or better yet *not* talk to them, he wants total ownership of you. This possessiveness may involve constantly calling, texting, or showing up wherever you are. You don't have to stop your social life because he's insecure and fears losing you. A man can be madly in love with you and still trust you to be an individual and not his possession under his domain. A man that loves you in this way does not love you—in time, his jealous and possessive behavior will imprison you.

7. Be leery if he's planning your future together, rather prematurely, before you have even gotten to know one another. Abusive men tend to want to own their victim quickly so they can take the lead as soon as possible. Their love overtures not only pressure the victim into committing to a long-term relationship, but the abuser then also wants to

show his love and wants the victim to reciprocate through sex. Let him know you prefer to get to know him and his family better before committing to a serious relationship with him. If he does not respect your request, then it's time to realize that he is exploiting you, and you're better off calling it quits while you still have your dignity.

8. Depending on the age and upbringing of the man you're dating, he may treat you with respect in front of others and abuse you when you're alone; or, he may take pleasure in degrading you in front of his peers and act lovingly when they leave. Either way—it is abuse. An emotionally-healthy man will respect you all of the time (while with peers or when alone with you).

9. Double standards are common with abusive men. They have their own set of standards that they expect the victim to adhere to; some of these standards are even unspoken expectations or rules which apply to the victim but not to themselves. Beware if he tends to become loudly impatient with you when you say or do something that he typically does himself. For example, he can date others while he's dating you, but he's offended if *you* do.

10. Some abusers prey on emotionally or chronologically much younger women than themselves. The abuser is aroused by the idea of having power over a younger woman that allows him total lead, a woman that admires and looks up to him to take care of her. Abusers can also seek to become unhealthy protectors through their attraction to needy women that come from dysfunctional backgrounds. Other abusers seek the opposite; they pursue women that are older, strong, and successful or have the potential for success. Regardless of whichever type of woman he's attracted to, he's pursuing someone that's vulnerable whom he can overpower and dominate.

THE VICTIM: EVERYTHING YOU EVER WONDERED

11. An abuser uses intimidation as one of his favorite tactics. It may appear while on a date that the intimidating behavior was due to stress or some other unexpected circumstance, but intimidation is *never* acceptable. Intimidation is a form of emotional abuse. If your date intimidates you, go from this *yellow flag* directly to a *red flag* because intimidation leads to physical aggression. What is considered intimidating behavior? Intimidation tactics include but are not limited to: he gets in your face, points a finger at you, blocks your path, grabs your arm forcefully, escalates his tone of voice, scolds or shouts at you with threatening remarks, acts in ways that frighten you even if he doesn't say anything, drives recklessly, throws objects that may miss you but scare you, and he may kick or punch things.
12. Some abusers pressure their dates into using drugs or alcohol. Abusers are manipulators at making you believe that you're only going to try it just this once. When and if you do, he will be hostile and demand the next time for you to join him in substance use. When you refuse, he will be angry and tell you that you no longer have anything in common that you can enjoy with him. Abusers are proficient liars; it's not about enjoying something together. So, take your abuser-manipulator *yellow warning flag* and walk away from this relationship because substance abuse just adds an additional problem to the problems of an abuser.

None of the aforementioned *yellow warning flags* are indicative that a *red flag* is on its way (exceptions include condescending speaking patterns about women, intimidation, and control). Some non-abusive men may have traits of these *yellow flag* warnings which they sporadically, unintentionally, humanely exhibit. Regardless, a woman can intentionally protect herself from getting involved in or being conned into a destructive abusive relationship. If you're on a date with a man that is indeed displaying *yellow flags*, your duty is to quickly develop your exit strategy and discreetly make your way to your proximate exit. Affirm your mind and silently repeat to yourself, "I am valuable. I must exit now!" Don't wait until you're over the moon in love with him to set your boundaries. There is no shortcut to ending an abusive relationship whether it is a dating or an established relationship. When an elevator is malfunctioning, you must take the stairs. Exit now—otherwise you're headed toward the devil's pig pen! Once he cons you into falling in love with him, the temptation to give him too many chances is more than a victim's soul can contain. Know in your heart that in dating relationships, a balanced *Overcomer* (opposite of victim) will always know when there's a *green light*!

Where is your heart right now? If your abuser has already captured your heart and you're feeling entrapped, then you've reached the stage of *trauma bonding*. **Trauma bonding** happens when the victim becomes emotionally and biologically addicted to the abuser's cycles, which the abuser keeps the victim spinning on. A person that has never experienced an abusive dating relationship may have difficulty comprehending why a victim would date an abuser let alone give him so many chances and stay in her abusive relationship. This person may even ask, "If you're being treated so badly, why would you continue to date him?" It's tough for a lot of folks to understand why a victim would remain in a relationship with an abuser. Unbeknownst to the person with the query, the victim may not be tuned-in to the fact that she's in an abusive relationship. The victim may be totally unaware that she's engaging in *trauma bonding*.

Trauma bonding can happen while dating because the victim is desensitized about what the abuser's tactics and her own symptoms are. This circumstance mainly occurs because our society has portrayed abuse in one context: physical abuse. Abuse is displayed on the news, social media, movies, and TV

THE VICTIM: EVERYTHING YOU EVER WONDERED

as aggressive acts toward the victim, such as manslaughter and murder. While abuse can progress into violent behavior toward a victim, it is not a full representation of the many types of other serious mental abuse that a victim can experience while dating or in a committal relationship. Therefore, when the victim is exploited by other forms of abuse, aside from physical, she may brush off all of the cruel, inappropriate, disrespectful behaviors. Victims tend to go back to the beginning phase of the abusive relationship when everything was romantic and grand. They remember when the abuser was kind and appropriate in his behavior and was anything but evil. The victim believes that that was the true self of the abuser and blames herself for making him angry. She makes it her mission to win back his affections. The abuser has now become the centerpiece of the victim's life. By now, the victim has become biologically attached to his mood and temper swings.

She gets reprimanded and treated punitively if she misbehaves (according to his standards), and if she behaves as the abuser wants, she is cherished and receives love. Her body, in the meantime, is producing increased levels of cortisol (stress hormone) when told she's misbehaving, and intermittent levels of dopamine (pleasure hormone) when she receives loving affection. As a result of the large-scale stress, the victim's mind and body become addicted to this fluctuating dependent pattern of emotions and can even progress into the development of physical illness(es), including similar symptoms to brain injury. This addiction sets forth the pattern of a victim attempting to break free from the abuse, but by then she's biologically bonded to her abuser and returns to him.

Most victims remain in the abusive relationship because it's unclear to them that the problems that they have are classified as abuse. It's only when the victim is able to be physically separated from her abuser that she's capable of stepping back and looking at the truth that she was abused. Separation is a must, because when a victim removes herself from her abuser she's able to compare the quality of her life to an *Overcomer's* life which is second to none; once separated from her abuser, the choice is very visibly obvious. She can now see the reality that it was not her fault. Grief follows the recognition of the trauma that was inflicted upon her, and she can now begin the recovery and healing process.

If you're wondering whether you are in a trauma bond with the abuser you are dating or are in a relationship with, you can check off a list of signs of trauma bonding:

- You go back and forth feeling love and romance or anger or hurt toward your abuser.
- You have become who he wants you to be.
- You believe that your abuser will change in time; he just needs your understanding.
- You feel trapped by the relationship and can't see a way out.
- Your friends or family comment on the way your abuser mistreats you, but you ignore it or defend him and tell them to stay out of it.
- You feel like you get into trouble with your abuser if you don't behave in certain ways, so you seek your abuser's approval.
- You believe that the abuse is your fault and you deserve it.
- You feel connected to your abuser, yet you want to leave when he's mean, but it hurts too much to leave.
- You're latched onto your abuser even though you don't like him anymore.
- You want out of the relationship but feel unable to detach from your abuser.
- You experience the non-abusive days as your abuser being kind to you.

THE VICTIM: EVERYTHING YOU EVER WONDERED

- Your abuser corrects you if you disagree with him and twists what you said to confuse you and so you don't bring up the subject again.
- Your abuser keeps promising a harmonious life together, but all you're getting is the opposite.

If you have concluded that you are in a trauma bond with your abuser and you want to break away from the bondage and heal, there are some steps you must take if you want to fully recover your identity and your life:

1. Create a support system for when you decide to end your relationship with your abuser and for when you're feeling tempted to have contact with your abuser. Include God (the Father, Son, and Holy Spirit) in your support group. Pray to God in His Name and ask for His mercy and help. Remember what God's Word says: "Let us therefore come boldly to the throne of grace that we may obtain mercy and find grace to help in time of need." (Hebrews 4:16)
2. Pay attention to how unloved you feel. Make only decisions that truly matter. You and your life matter. Make and review a list of positive affirmations, or listen to audio-visual affirmations.
3. Terminate the abusive dating relationship.
4. Make a commitment not to live in the past image of how your abuser was when he was intermittently kind and respectful. Live in the truth of who he truly was when he mistreated you and the reality that it was not a harmonious relationship.
5. Stop compromising your self-respect and identity for the abuser. Notice that your relationship was all about him; no longer even think about exchanging your goals, talents, job/career, and interests to build on his life alone.

6. Pamper yourself with the self-care that you need to recover and heal. In addition to pampering yourself, journal your feelings if you're not up to processing or interaction.
7. Be honest with yourself when you feel grief; experience it and do things to soothe your moments or days of feeling the loss. Identify exactly what you believe you lost as a result of being in and ending the relationship (Even if it was a dream that you thought could be fulfilled if you stayed in the relationship). Knowing the culprit of your grief keeps you in reality.
8. Keep a list in your phone or with you at all times of the reasons you refuse to have a relationship with an abuser. Also, keep a reminder list of your personal positive characteristics. If you are uncertain what those are, ask your support group to refresh your memory.
9. Develop a plan for your new abuse free life; include travel, education, hobbies, exercise/wellness, or activities that you've always wanted to partake in.
10. Live in the present and make new, healthy relationships. Do not dwell on what could have been in the past or the fantasies and promises of what could have been in the future; notice what has never happened for weeks, months, or years through your abuser.
11. You, _____(Fill in your name), can do this! God would never expect _____ to take on anything in His Name without equipping and granting _____ the divine ability to do it.
12. Keep in touch with your Creator (God) daily—the possibilities for strength and for overcoming your abuse are literally endless!

If you have previously been involved in an abusive relationship, you are probably asking how you can know if you can trust the person you are dating. You will know if you can trust to date someone if you have acquired the ability to trust your own self. If you have set standards (boundaries) for whom you will date, then you will have crossed off the standards list before dating the person; you will be confident that you can trust him not to be an abuser. If, after you review the inventory list of *yellow warning flags*, you notice that your prospective date's interactions or his beliefs sound like will-o'-the-wisps, it's safer for you to terminate the relationship. In life there are no guarantees, but knowledge on what is known about an abuser is the best way to protect yourself. Know what non-abuse standards you have set for yourself beforehand and stick with them before accepting a date. It's best to dispatch clear boundary lines as opposed to waiting until you have crossed the *yellow flag* and now you have a *red flag* in your path! Don't wait to be over-the-moon-in-love with him to set boundaries. Obviously, the abuser will always be sweet on the victim during the initial dating stages, so watch out and don't become smitten by his charms because once moonstruck in-love, the temptation to give him just one more chance is just too great.

If by chance you meet someone that you trusted to respect you, and it turns out that he attempts to overstep your boundaries, do the following:

1. *Set a boundary immediately* when his attitude and/or behavior is unacceptable to you. Let him know that if the behavior is repeated you will not continue in a relationship with him. If you have made it clear to him which attitudes and behaviors are unacceptable, and he ignores your request and continues to exhibit some of the *yellow warning flags*, there's a strong indication that he's an abuser. Follow through with terminating the relationship when he violates your boundary, or you will regret not doing so.
2. *Do not continue to see him periodically* with the warning that the next time you will *really* end it all. More than likely,

since you gave him several warnings and you didn't follow through, he will probably think that you will give him one more chance. The more seriously involved that you become with an abuser, the more difficult it will become for you to end the relationship. Escaping from an abusive relationship once you're entrapped is extremely difficult and complex. Do not set yourself up to be entrapped.
3. *Do not listen to friends or family* who encourage you to continue to see him. Set boundaries with both him and them. Remember Mary H. Waldrip's quote: "It's important that people know what you stand for. It's equally important that they know what you won't stand for."

All victims have friends, family, or people that would rather see them "work things out!" Doing so makes perfect sense to them, so why not to you, right? Wrong. You know better because your safety is at high risk—it's a safety factor! So, when others are anxious for you to "just deal with it" and are driving you into your own ditch, keep your faith and concentration on God alone and the support He will send. You give power to Whomever or whatever you focus on! Ask God to order your steps, knowing that when you focus on His power, He will give you hope and peace—while He protects and designs your future—and bring you to safety! News flash: God is your Designer; no one can redesign you or your life unless you allow them to.

Abuse is progressive. When an abuser gets well-adjusted to a certain level of disrespect and maltreatment of the victim, he feels less guilty; this allows him to move up to higher levels of abuse—guiltlessly. As the abuser progresses to more serious acts of cruelty, he moves on to more aggressive abusive behaviors that he would not have previously considered. Meanwhile, the victim increases her level of resistance, which then further increases his abusive tactics because she now requires higher

THE VICTIM: EVERYTHING YOU EVER WONDERED

levels of intimidation and control than at the beginning of their relationship.

This point in our discussion warrants a review of the risk of date rape when dating an abuser. This type of abuse will come without much warning and may at times be drug-assisted. The date victim may not even see herself as such because she does not feel physically injured, may have even been under the influence of alcohol during the unconsented sexual abuse, and blames herself as if she "should have known." Some date rape victims also believe the myth that they were at the *wrong* place at the *wrong* time and said the *wrong* thing. This type of myth-believing about victims being responsible for their own rapes has its roots in either believing societal myths or believing that the victim is already conditioned from previous abuse to think like a victim—that she's responsible, *not* the abuser. The myths that undermine sexual assault are just that—societal myths. Whether violence, coercion, or force was used or other means to *rape*, the unconsented sex *still happened*. The abuser's method does not exonerate him from having committed an unconsented sexual act—a crime against his date.

Any victim of date rape will experience the same symptoms as stranger rape with an increased *level* of feeling completely invaded. The increased feelings of being intruded upon come from having trusted the individual they dated. A date rape victim's feelings of intrusion affect her Spirit, Mind, and Body profoundly. For some date rape victims, they mourn the loss of control over their virginity, which they had reserved for their future spouse. Many date rape victims suppress their symptoms so as not to be found out for fear of their abuser's threats. Amongst the threats to further harm the victim and add loved ones to the list (if she's not *silent* about the rape) are the threats to post profane material and/or sexually explicit/nude photos of her on the internet, which he alleges he has (and *may* have) of her. Before undermining her date rape and assigning blame to herself, a victim needs to put the reality of her trauma into perspective by asking herself: "What has changed in my life, in comparison to the way my life used to be, before my date rape?" Your date rape *is not your* fault. If that self-blame thought keeps lurking in your mind, take a 3x5 card or use your phone to write a note: "You're not to blame; it is not your fault!" Reach for your note-to-self and read it to yourself or out loud. Soon you will be able to repeat this affirmation in your thoughts without your reminder note.

Stop reading again—we're going to make another list! Fold and divide a sheet of paper into three folds. Again, this may sound very basic, but it works with eye-opening results. In the first fold/column make a list of all the ways that you notice the person you are dating is abusing you (*yellow* and *red flags*). Next, on the fold beside it make another list of the ways you feel emotionally, physically, and/or economically dependent on this person. Jot down how you already feel entrapped in this dating relationship. Lastly, on the third fold make another list of the small or big steps that you can take to start becoming independent of him. If your first fold list indicates that you are involved in an abusive dating relationship, use this list as a guideline to redirect your focus and energy to leave this destructive, abusive dating relationship—get out while you can!

If you're still troubled as to whether you're dating an abuser or what additional signals an abuser date prospect may show, take a look at his symptoms of control when you attempt to stop dating him. One dictionary definition of control is as follows: To exercise restraining or directing influence over; to have power over. What happens when an abuser begins to exercise control over his date? The answer may seem innocuous enough since the word control is certainly thrown around a lot in our society, and it has its meaning in various people's lives. But, with a victim of control, safety is at stake and it needs to be fully understood

THE VICTIM: EVERYTHING YOU EVER WONDERED

what this word means relating to an abuser. Some well-meaning people know the word control and may have experienced it in some form, but it may have been undermined in their lives; this failing to comprehend the meaning of the word control and the act of control with an abuser places the victim at a serious safety risk. It becomes evident that when relating to an abuser, there needs to be clarity about the implications for the victim in regards to the meaning of control. The *yellow warning flags* are sometimes not readily visible, unless you know what to look for (because the abuser is such a confidence man). The abuser may initially be able to swindle you into a point of exploitation. However, the *red flag* signals (such as the symptoms of control when you decide to stop dating him) are always *very* visible. Red is known as the color signal for *stop!*

The following are red flag signals which I will leave with you. You have the right to self-determination in all of your life decisions and choices. After you read the list of red flag control symptoms that an abuser exhibits (when you tell him you will no longer date him), it is totally up to you to form your own conclusion about whether you are dating an abuser—and if you're going to stop the abusive relationship or not.

1. Apologizing profusely, even becoming tearful, and begging for you to reconsider while promising to change.
2. Demanding to date you because he has already changed.
3. Alleging that you are abandoning him by not dating him.
4. Manipulating others to talk you into reconsidering.
5. Suddenly becoming very kind and considerate toward you.
6. Becoming very open to you having equal individuality where he had previously expressed a double standard.
7. Being attentive to favors you had previously asked for.
8. Spreading lies about you, attempting to sabotage your relationships and reputation.

9. Beginning to date another person, flaunting it, and attempting to make you jealous.
10. Disclosing personal information about you that you trusted him with.
11. Stalking you wherever you go.
12. Threatening to kidnap you or to sexually assault you.
13. Threatening to harm anyone you date, friends, or family.
14. Insisting that you will be miserable without him.
15. Inducing guilt for stopping the dating relationship and threatening to commit suicide.
16. Becoming self-destructive to worry you.
17. Becoming destructive toward your property (car, pet.)
18. Offering to enter therapy or a support group if you date him.
19. Saying that no one else would want to date you anyway.
20. Threatening to kill you if you won't date him.

All of these *red flags* are alert alarms, but number twelve and number twenty are *red sirens*! If you're threatened by an abuser, you *cannot* adhere to the abuser's *must* rules—that you *must* hold your tongue and *must* never tell this secret message he has given you. Instead, you *must* find your tongue to regain your power of speech, knowing full well that if you remain silently threatened, the abuser will be walking away freely, repeating this with other women, and all with a sardonic grin. Holding your tongue is blindly agreeing to the abuser's maltreatment of you and the false identity he has given you of your worthlessness. What a victim views as the best for her is determined by the standards she has set; she will never reach higher than that. If her expectations for a boyfriend or spouse are low, then it will be an unproductive relationship.

Most victims' horizons are limited with reduced ambition for more; they're easily satisfied with low objectives for a relationship. As long as their abuser makes them intermittently

THE VICTIM: EVERYTHING YOU EVER WONDERED

happy, they accept the brief tale of sorrow it brings as opposed to the eternal satisfaction that they can attain in their life story. It is completely up to you to decide *how* you want to be treated, and it's totally up to you to set dating and relationship boundaries with others. You are the one who decides what's unacceptable. You set the standard for what you will tolerate or not. Psychologist, professor, and author, Lenore Walker, says, "The first time a woman stays with an abuser after an abusive episode, she tacitly agrees to accept his behavior."

What is it like when you terminate a dating relationship with an abuser? Ending a dating relationship with an abuser can feel like you're experiencing a personal tsunami. You're not. It is emotionally, mentally, physically, and spiritually exhausting to be romantically involved with an abuser; the tsunami you're feeling is a result of all the havoc he caused when you or he left the relationship. It's normal for the end of a relationship to cause sorrow, but when you've been involved in a relationship with an abuser who has used you, and others, is obsessed with himself, and has no empathy, it can leave a wound. It makes it more difficult to end it with the abuser because of his love-bombing that may appear real on the surface, not to mention his engaging, charismatic nature with all who know him. The break up almost seems unnecessary. The tsunami feeling is because you fell in love with the charismatic aspects of the abuser, and now it feels as if your heart was stolen; your whole world was centered on his universe, and now it's all crashing down upon you.

Here's what to expect post-tsunami. If he's the one to ask to end the relationship, it can seem impromptu and brutal. You may be in shock because you know you have given your abuser everything he's ever wanted, and you're left stumped as to what in the world happened here. That's because abusers are experts at playing the part only while they're getting something out of their source—the victim—you. By now, you should have already experienced his tendency to be unpredictable in his moods. And yes, everything was wonderful for a while, but over time the abuser no longer sees any value in his victim because he has become aware that she's just as human as he is. The abuser has no use for her if she's flawed; he no longer views her as his prospective commodity. This disappointment causes him to yell at her relentlessly and blame her for his everyday circumstances; he blames her and sees no solution other than to let her figure out what led to his leaving her.

When an abuser is done with the relationship, he has no trouble casting the victim aside and discarding her. The abuser will be neither apologetic nor remorseful or engage in any form of empathy for your investment of your devoted life to him (regardless of how short or long your relationship was). If the abuser returns with apologies, it's usually because he has realized how good he had it and has realized that he can still gain something from you. If he ever insulted the victim, this is the worst of the insults, making her feel worthless. Usually an abuser that leaves has no trouble moving on to a new source of supply from a brand new victim. Abusers that leave don't have a grieving period, and that's because their feelings for the victim were not sincere to begin with. It's not uncommon for the abuser that leaves to have already secured the new victim; his exit strategy is usually accompanied by a new target. Keep in mind that you are not worthless as he exchanges you for a new interest. Even if your abuser said via his actions and words that you are worthless, he lied! Truth be told, it is quite the opposite: he selected you because you had so much to offer. You are more than worthwhile—you are enough!

However, when you turn the tables, and if it's the victim who chooses to terminate the relationship with the abuser, the abuser demands an explanation and does not even listen to the victim but simply begs, pleads, and attempts to negotiate for just

THE VICTIM: EVERYTHING YOU EVER WONDERED

one more chance out of the hundreds which he's already bargained for. Some abusers become tearful and once again promise to change and do some of the things that had been previously planned for the relationship. Another abuser may become highly agitated, put the victim on the center of the wrestling ring and explode with the fight of his life because the victim has obstructed his plans for their future, and he's not done with her yet! The victim sometimes gets tricked back into the relationship through induced fear and love-bombing. This is prime time to remember that in between the love-bombing, he is a ticking bomb. Abusers loathe losing their victim—their life supply system—and will not let go of the victim very easily, so it's the victim that has to let go.

The only solution to terminating an abusive relationship in a healthy way is to have no contact whatsoever once you have made a choice to live an abuse-free life. No contact requires a termination of all communication with the abuser in person or on the internet. If you don't allow your abuser to have contact with you there's no opportunity for him to make his manipulative presentation as to how he's going to change and run the risk of you being persuaded by his glib self-talk into feeling obligated to return to him. Learn to forever say *no* to the abuser. The word *no* is a complete sentence, no further explanation needed. This means removing your abuser from your social media friends and followers list and those that you both are interacting with through social networks, deleting any of his information that you may have saved on your computer (PC), removing his email address from your contacts, and blocking his number on your phone—better yet, get a new phone number. When a victim ends her relationship with the abuser, he will go out of his way to track her down, find her, and tell her what he knows he can say to make her return to him. Therefore, you have to be fast in removing him from your contact stream, and you have to remain strong or you will be manipulated back into the relationship.

Knowing that he may attempt to con you back into the relationship, prepare a list of the reasons you left your abuser so that you can remind yourself to stay firm on your decision. Include in that list the following question for you to re-read: "Why would I allow him to return to hurt me again?" Don't allow the abuser to bombard you with the few selective positive memories, inducing confusion and regret on your behalf; those memories are not representative of the entire relationship.

It's helpful to keep in mind when he attempts to brainwash you back into the relationship that it is not because he feels badly that he hurt you that he wants you back. Abusers don't genuinely care; they don't feel your pain when you're in pain. They, in fact, gain pleasure and victory after knowing they have brought you down; it makes the abuser feel powerful and superior over the victim. Abusers are incapable of empathizing, and they solely want the victim back to restore their ego and validate their person and sense of control over the victim. It may sound like a hopeless attitude, but the abuser-victim research confirms that it's best, for safety purposes, to start life afresh without the abuser. If you're still feeling attached to the abuser you have been dating, read the section on *Divorce and the Victim of Abuse*. Why? Because terminating a dating relationship for a victim is like an emotional divorce.

Although abusers heal quickly from the end of a dating relationship, it is not the case for the victim who had genuine intense feelings for him when the relationship began. She now has to grieve, having had to terminate the relationship, losing the good person she thought he was when they first met, and accepting that she was swayed, blindsided, gaslighted, and love-bombed. The healer for the victim is facing the painful reality that the feelings for the abuser were built on a false image of who he was not. Did she really lose a good person? Probably not. If she stayed in the abusive relationship, would she be losing more of her person and her life every day? Probably so. The victim must encourage herself or be held accountable by her support group to do some self-care during her grieving process. She may become uncontrollably weepy for a period of time. It's okay to have a good alone-time, purifying cry; tears alleviate stress, comfort sorrow, and hasten the healing of the heart. It's the natural way to de-stress. Jesus showed us the purposeful sanctity of tears when He wept after his friend Lazarus died. Emotional and physical exhaustion elevate during a grief transition process; rest and purposeful relaxing activities must be increased. Self-care brings solace and softens the pain of grief; making it bearable so that joy can be restored.

Grief exists whether in losing a good or bad relationship. Some victims don't know what it means to take good care of their person (and may even need to give themselves permission to take time for themselves). They may need to be asked what brings joy and relaxation to their life. For some, it may mean curling up with a book, doing the art of nothing by resting, having a cup of tea or coffee, taking a nature or trail walk, hiking, or getting a massage. It's especially spiritually uplifting and comforting for victims to engage in nature or travel after being forced into isolation because it restores their ability to see the outdoors from a different perspective—noticing the wonders and attributes of God in His creation. The important thing is that she does what works for her; for example, getting a mani/pedi may be enjoyable for some and a task or expense for others. She may need to experiment with what's most relaxing to her; the self-care should not be allowed to add stress.

Many therapists recommend aromatherapy via a pampering shower or fragranced candle-lit bubble bath. Aromatherapy can transport the brain into a relaxed state of mind within seconds. Applying an essential oil in pulse points afterward allows the aroma to stay with her. Lavender is good for depressed mood and calming anxiety. Eucalyptus, mint, and citrus uplift and re-energize. Add another layer of uplift by reading an inspirational book or devotional and soak up some encouraging truths that will linger past the bubble bath! Aromatherapy can be experienced in silence or along with music that has been especially developed for healing. This music may have subliminal affirmation messages or other sounds which are created for self-healing, rejuvenating, and relieving stress.

A daily method that the grieving victim can use is the DEER approach: D—Drink plenty of water; E—Eat only nutritious and balanced meals (do not skip meals or eat junk food); E—Exercise (even if it's just a walk around her neighborhood); R—Rest, lie down, and relax or nap. If she has insomnia, she can take an herbal melatonin, pray, and affirm Scriptural promises which are hidden in her heart (instead of counting sheep). Purposely inhale and exhale three times when sad thoughts occur. Remind her that rest, naps, and sleep are a gift from God. "*It is* vain for you to rise up early, to sit up late, to eat the bread of sorrows; *For so He gives His beloved sleep*" (Psalm 127:2).

The victim was deprived of enjoying her life for a while; now it's time to enjoy the life she missed out on. It's not uncommon for victims to have gone for extensive periods of time without any proper rest. Some victims do not know what it's like to take time off because if activities were meant to be leisurely, the abuser would always be there to make that time intensely stressful or she would be deprived of any down time with all of his demands. It's important for the victim to keep in mind that not even God requires us to work nonstop outside and/or inside the home seven days a week. God's gift of the Sabbath (meaning *rest* in Hebrew) was for the very purpose of restoring one's spirit—working only six days and taking the Sabbath for rest on the seventh day. Christians used to take the Sabbath on Saturday in the Old Testament days, but after Christ's resurrection, they now do so on a Sunday; this day has become a day of worship and rest. There's no rigid rule that the Sabbath must be taken on Sunday, there are many folks who take the Sabbath on their day off from work.

A victim may want to consider creating a Grief First Aid Kit. In that kit, she can place 3x5 cards or Post-It notes with ideas of things that she can choose from to partake in, things which she can do to lift her spirits up and inspire her. When she feels disappointed with her past relationship, or sad, the kit can have ideas for favored hobbies, activities, tickets, brochures, or other outlets that provide rest and make her happy. There will be days that she may want to go on a grief retreat, to revitalize her mood. But, as she reengages with her community, she will make new friends, friends that will treat her properly. Returning to the real life the way it is supposed to be will bring on new meaning now that the victim realizes that romantic and other relationships aren't supposed to be abusive—this deeper understanding comes from the new boundaries that she has set in place for expecting respect.

Identity Theft

In spousal abuse, the victim is stripped of her identity and arrested in her own home, slowly but progressively through a depraved courtship with her abuser. Initially, the abuser's controlling, possessive nature is interpreted as passionate love. The victim feels complimented by his intense interest in her and even feels warmly toward him for looking out for her. Whenever he appears domineering to her or others, she undermines this observation because she cares for him and believes she loves him. Even when she becomes frightened multiple times by his behavior, she excuses it. She believes at that point that this is just a series of unfortunate events.

A victim sometimes enters the marriage while she's not yet emotionally mature and with an incomplete sense of self. Therefore, she values the abuser's and others' opinions of herself and allows others to dictate who she is based on their evaluation of her. Not having an established sense of self-worth, a victim can easily accept the abuser's and others' inappropriate verbal and non-verbal behaviors toward her. The abuser is proficient at conveying to the victim that no one loves her and cares more about her than he does. The abuser can even convince her that her closest family or friends forget about her, whereas he always remembers her; he states that they would betray her at any given time. The abuser amounts his *caring* about her to his jealous surveillances of her; he denies stalking her and justifies it as protecting her, and he "accidentally" opens up her correspondence, checks her purse/devices and phone log, or eavesdrops on/intercepts her telephone calls with loving, manipulative gestures.

The abuser expects the victim to tolerate his relentless accusations of her infidelity *and* his exclusive attention to her, which he says shows his love for her. The abuser professes his *faithfulness* to her and voices comparisons, accentuating her want to "always be involved with some friend or family as if I'm not enough." The abuser demands that as an expression of her loyalty to him, she give up her friendships, family mingling (ultimately family ties), school, or work (which depletes her of her own independent income). Some abusers don't verbally demand but through their passive aggressive or explosive episodes make it known to the victim that having a connection to others outside of their home is not an option. The victim suffers his abusive tactics if she doesn't prove her loyalty to him by giving up her connections.

In some cases, the abuser demands the attention that the victim gives to her children and makes it known that she has to sacrifice (ignore or give up) her children as well, or he threatens and/or proceeds to abuse them, too. Some victims defend their children even if they are afraid to defend their own selves; they will be silent about their own victimization but will not tolerate their children's abuse. Other victims are so programmed into the abuser's possessiveness that they don't interject when the children are being emotionally battered and ignore or deliberately stay away when their children are being physically or sexually abused. The silence that hovers over the victim begins to extend to the children's silent abuse. At worst, the victim enables the children to accept the abuse and rebukes them for opposing it.

The abuser goes to great lengths to deprive her of relationships and, at times, destroys any objects that are of sentimental value to her because he wants her all to himself and feels threatened if she attaches herself to anything or anyone but him. This is the traumatic process that disrupts the victim's ability to attach herself to others and isolates her to a point that she loses her ability to even imagine connecting to another person. The victim begins to believe that giving up her attachment to others is only a small concession compared to how he reacts when she doesn't do what he expects. The victim knows how he reacts and how he threatens to react if she does not "mind the step!"

How *does* a victim tolerate this possession of herself and everything that she cares about being taken away from her? The answer lies in the fact that she doesn't lose everything at once. The abuser does not initially come on like a cyclone; he works his way gradually through her to take her person and all that is a part of her. The abuser starts to rob her of her autonomy one step at a time in such a way that the victim does not sense or suspect his motive; his pattern is not obvious until time passes, and he has destructively detached her from her loved ones, demoralized her, and has completely taken over her identity.

Victim Isolation

Now that she has been forced into solitary confinement in her own home, the victim then becomes more dependent on her abuser. The abuser is her source for communication, feedback, emotional support (none or twisted), and finances, for his is the only relationship that he permits without giving prior approval. The more that she fears her abuser, the more attempts she makes to try to understand his destructive ways. Unfortunately, this only lends itself to the victim taking on his ways of being, as if his relational skills and ways are acceptable. The victim at this stage of abuse may lose sight of her pre-abuse values and morals and join the abuser in his ways and adopt his point of view (smoking, cussing, drinking, watching porn, lying for the abuser, doing illegal behavior or exposing and subjecting her to humiliating acts). Victims are sometimes coerced into sexual acts that they find repulsive or immoral. It is as if the victim's values have become jumbled.

The victim being in constant fear and terror is not sufficient for the abuser who wants to break her. The abuser's desire is to have her completely surrender her soul, and he succeeds through intermittently romancing her, alienating her, rewarding her with a kind word or affection, blasting her, or temporarily taking her off his "hit list." The abuser offers affectionate hugs after his verbal outbursts and ignores the gash in her heart. For the victim, hugging her mean, prickly abuser is like being forced to hug a porcupine, fearing the next time when she'll be shot full of his quills. Even if she forgives, how can she feel safe if she keeps getting pricked and pierced by his quills? These tactics are not the final steps he takes in attempting to control her mind and identity; the final steps are to force her to disown her treasured relationships and to violate her own moral principles. The abuser's underlying goal is to totally demoralize her. The most powerful of all of the tactics that the abuser uses are the losing

THE VICTIM: EVERYTHING YOU EVER WONDERED

of her relationships and morality, which reduces her to a level of despising her own self for succumbing to him.

This *is* the stage of the abuse in which the abuser feels he has truly "broken" his victim. For some abusers, breaking their victim and keeping her docile means coercing her into unwanted sex, total demoralization—raping her. Rape is the abuser's ultimate invasion of the victim's boundaries and private space. Whether she's married to the abuser or not, this is an invasion of her personal space and her mind. The rape raises questions in her mind about her own responsibility in the incident(s). This kind of victim thinking is a result of her traumatic loss of self. If she had her own identity, she would not question her own self but would instead realize that it is the abuser who made the choice to sexually attack her; he is totally responsible for her rape.

The only victims that escape the development of a dependence on their abuser are the ones that consciously preserve their identity through using all of their known resources. Some victims are able to preserve their future safety by secretly protecting their negative independent view of their abusive circumstances. These victims have to actively, in the privacy of their own mind, be able to contradict the belief system of the abuser. This is extremely difficult for the victim because most victims begin their abusive relationship through a courtship of genuine love for their abuser, and with love there is empathy and at times sympathy for the abuser. Many ask the question: "How can a victim love her abuser?" It is no different than when children are abused by their parents; children still love their parents in spite of being abused by them. It's also important to remember that most victims fall in love with their abuser before they discover his seriously disturbing behaviors. They do not fall in love with the abuser because he is an abuser.

Women are raised to be nurturers, helpers, and caretakers; the abuser's persuasive talks and argumentative allegations about her lack of love and cooperation penetrate deep into the core of the victim's heart. This is what plays into why so many victims are persuaded by their abuser and at times by their advisers to return after attempting to escape from their abuser. Women are wired to want to take care of and sustain relationships; this is one of the ways that the abuser is able to entrap his wife into staying in the abusive relationship, by playing mind-games with one of her most cherished inner values—relationships.

To Love and To Cherish—'Til Death do us Part
In order to avoid emotional attachment to and dependence on the abuser, the victimized wife would have to suppress the love and affection that she has for her husband. She has to suppress her love for him when he persuasively argues that one more sacrificial act of love on her behalf will save the marriage and will prove her commitment to him, and then he will end his abusive ways with her. After prolonged abuse, time has a way of making it easier for the victim to suppress her love for her abuser—fear takes over. Sometimes the abuser's slew of jabs at the victim's heart end with one final jab, which kills her heart for him. Her heart hardens; he manages to kill her soul. It is at this point that she is willing and able to consider choosing to seek safety over the empty promises that he makes. This is not to say that a victim doesn't experience *any* sense of loss when she decides to pursue safety and a way out of the abusive relationship. The victim indeed *does* go through a grieving process as she admits to herself that she has been totally victimized. She grieves as she leaves her victim role behind, realizing that the abusive marital relationship will never work out because the abuser is *not* willing to change.

THE VICTIM: EVERYTHING YOU EVER WONDERED

Spousal abuse can be debilitating. The victim's grief at this stage feels like a depressed darkness, as if she will never see daylight again. When the darkness abates, she will be able to look back on one of the best decisions she has ever made; she now realizes that she was on the wrong track and that it was wise, and safest, to resign from being a victim. In the meantime, her support system can be there to help expedite her healing from those dark and dreary days. It is at this level of awareness that the victim begins to realize that her abuser is gaining something out of maintaining her as a victim. In some cases, the victim has even experienced the realization that her particular abuser rather enjoys inflicting vicious fear and pain upon her and appears to get excited about the thrill of being hard-hearted. It's apparent through his comments and facial expressions that he's amused by tormenting her. This type of sadistic abuser that outwardly demonstrates finding it entertaining to act wicked has *usually* experienced a history of having been mistreated (but this does not apply to all abusers). No matter the type of abuser that she's emotionally attached to, it is painstakingly difficult for a victim to accept that she cannot be the one to assist her abuser in healing from his past, present, or future! She herself must face and come to terms with this reality.

This is a rude awakening for the victim with an abuser who plays the victim role because all her energies have been devoted to the hope of helping him to overcome his pain. Focusing on *his* need to heal has been what has helped the victim to survive living a life of terror with him. An abuser who plays the victim role (or even has a deep-set painful past) is *not* someone that the victim will be able to help heal. A victim's healthiest strategy with such an abuser is to redirect her focus into seeking healing and safety for herself and her children. Investing any more time and strength in helping the abuser with *his* problems will only profoundly affect the victim's ability to gain insight, discern, or strategize a safety plan. If your energy has already been zapped by your abuser and you can no longer think clearly about your past or current abuse, safely make a phone call or call an abuse hotline (see Resources) as soon as you can. Speaking to someone who is trained on victim abuse trauma can help you to learn to protect yourself as you are guided into unraveling what he has done to your state of mind.

A victim at this stage in the relationship has already become vulnerable to acquiring some of the abuser's futility characteristics. This is why support is so strongly necessary for the victim if she's going to make any progress in regaining her pre-abuse identity. The abuser's confusion that has been projected on the victim hinders her ability to strengthen herself into the capable person that she is. The abuser prefers that the victim remain in his shadow; his attitude is one of considering her role as his wife as one of playing a supporting role to him including the acceptance of his abuse. Her spouse has become her prig and foe. She's now sleeping with one eye open and both ears wide open.

The abuser does not want her to relax or have peace of mind. The abuser's fear is that the victim will gain insight into his abuse, and if she separates from him, she will return not wanting to be bullied. The abuser is afraid that she may begin to think on her own without his interjecting views and confusing desires of her. An abuser realizes that while apart from him, she may be with others that treat her with respect and that she may feel loveable and discover what it's like to live without his constant control. The abuser does not want the victim to have a respite because he wants total control. In his view, she's only to be around him, to be at his beck and call, because if she does this, then he thinks he can disrupt and get rid of any thoughts to leave him. An abuser's loaded anxiety is that she won't have him there to distort, reverse, and confuse her as to what happened in the relationship and she may have time to reconsider.

THE VICTIM: EVERYTHING YOU EVER WONDERED

The abuser perceives time away from him as an unwanted separation because it may establish some sense of solace for her. The abuser realizes that perhaps the victim wants to think over the relationship and that she may think more clearly about the abuse. The abuser becomes suspicious that she may be considering an end to the relationship. If the victim reveals that she can no longer tolerate being his daily target and asks for a reprieve through time apart, he objects in the worst form. Abusers very rarely honor a victim's request for "time-out." If he agrees, it usually comes with contingencies. Her abuser still wants control; he invariably interrupts the time away that was agreed upon. The abuser does not give her room to think over the abuse and to work out her well-being. The abuser manipulates ways for her to return to him. It's very typical at this stage of the abuse that the abuser will refuse to allow the victim any time away from the relationship when she requests to visit a friend or family member without him. If she doesn't lovingly comply with his requests for her to return home, he may escalate and demand her return, threatening to hurt her or to kill her. This is one of the main reasons victims have to be the ones to leave their own homes as opposed to the abuser who's causing the problems to be asked to leave; he will continue to wrap his control around her as long as she lives with him.

Children as Secondhand Victims
We've all heard of the health risks involved in living directly or indirectly with a smoker; there are visible health hazards for the victims exposed to the smoker. They call this "secondhand smoke" exposure. So is the case for children that are being directly or indirectly exposed to family violence. These children are at risk for PTSD from being abused or watching their mother and/or siblings being abused. In some cases, the children, thought to be protected by the abuser and/or victim who prevents them

from hearing or seeing the abuse, are not really spared from this supposed indirect, invisible family violence. The children, regardless of the attempts made to cover up the abuse, are still aware that family violence exists even if they are not directly exposed to the abuse. Learning that their mother and siblings were injured or sexually violated by the abuser has a traumatic effect; they are affected as secondhand victims.

When children endure the trauma of abuse directly or indirectly, they are subjected to the symptoms of Secondary Traumatic Stress just by being exposed to the inflicting of emotional/physical injury or overhearing the disturbing cruelty of their mother's abuse. Symptoms of Secondary Traumatic Stress mimic PTSD and include hyperarousal, nervousness, anxiety, flashbacks, or ruminating thoughts about the trauma, a negative despondent outlook, and avoidance of emotions or reminders of the trauma.

Children are like sponges; they can saturate, soak up, and internalize what they hear and see (whether positive or negative). A child learns what he lives through his senses. When my oldest daughter was three, we were at a store and she noticed a comic poster and asked, "Who's that?" I responded, "That's Wonder Woman." She then inquired, "Oh, what does she do?" I said, "Well, she has special powers, and she fights for good things." My daughter then asked, "Mommy, are you a Wonder Woman?" I quickly thought of God's power within me and answered, "Yes, I am." She sighed deeply and said, "Well, then I'm a Wonder Child!" as she covered up her mouth and giggled. Later that afternoon when she was on her knees exploring over her toy chest, I noticed she was wearing a pink towel tied around her neck simulating a cape. I never asked her about the meaning of her new cape, nor did I scold her for making a mess in the linen closet. I complimented her on her new cape that symbolized her power and strength and just allowed her to be a super heroine.

THE VICTIM: EVERYTHING YOU EVER WONDERED

Had she elected to emulate negative superheroes, I would have intervened. Currently, she is a Wonder Woman to her own three children.

Parents, or other role-models, can become your children's superheroes; it's up to you to determine those with whom they identify and take after. A father and a mother are the first and most influential sources of gender roles and other identification. Besides God, parents are the first role models of the definition of love. Love is the foundation of attachment to God, parents, caretakers, and others. Love and attachment in a relationship are influenced by role models. Our children are within our sphere of strong influence, and we can always choose at any point to change how we interact with them and what they are exposed to by way of ours and others' interactions with them. Yes, there are cases whereby the negative influence of a parent can strengthen the resolve of a child to be determined not to grow up to become like their bad parent role model, but this doesn't always happen. It certainly can happen that an individual is thankful that they didn't turn out like their parent or significant other and that they did not repeat the circumstances which they grew up with. But, if we have the opportunity to influence our children positively, why not choose to do so? Even our silence and subtleties can influence for the positive or negative. This doesn't mean that we have to feel guilt-ridden when we are not able to supervise them 'round-the-clock. Many single-parent homes and dual income couples have to designate good caretakers in order to work and provide for their families.

You are able to be selective and to protect your children from unhealthy influences (even if it means temporarily not receiving your children's approval of you). Sometimes your children are unable to discern peer and negative adult influences. It is your duty to intervene and guard them against such influences (whether they like your intervention or not). Some parents stay neutral and don't intervene for fear of losing their friendship or popularity with their child. That is parentifying the child into role reversal with you, a process in which he becomes the parent and makes the decisions for how your home life is going to be run. It is worth it to lose the child's approval and instead further develop their good values and principles in order to prevent bad choices or even juvenile delinquency. Someday your child will become a parent and will have to make the decisions you are making in child-rearing; will he allow his children to be exposed to unhealthy influences? Will he be worried about being considered an overprotective parent and not much of a friend? Or will he set guidelines and boundaries for his children on choosing healthy influences?

We can choose to bond and to become a positively attached influence in the lives of our children. The key in becoming a healthy attached influence is balancing God, work, responsibilities, recreation/hobbies, and quality time with our children. Some victims feel compelled to make up for the time they're away by spending all of their free time with their children, and in the long run, they end up over-compromising on time for themselves and/or other responsibilities. Studies validate that children of working parents can fare well and become productive citizens just the same in comparison to the children of stay-at-home parents. In actuality, children have been found to grow neurologically and improve their motor skills while having alone playtime. Toddlers in particular increase their verbal skills and vocabulary as they play pretend and interact with their toys. Perfect parenting is not the goal, but it is instead an awareness of when children need our affection, attention, direction, and re-direction. There's no gain in child-rearing if a parent beats their own self up when they're unable to be the perfect parent. God the Father is the only perfect parent.

THE VICTIM: EVERYTHING YOU EVER WONDERED

I have had parents in my office that are dumbfounded by how their child "turned out!" These parents viewed themselves as "perfect parents" that did everything right, including raising their child in the Lord; yet their child chose the ways of the world, opposite of their upbringing. This is where it becomes important for parents to recognize that while it is a healthy desire to want their children to be obedient to the Lord, it's setting themselves up for a disappointment as parents to make it their own personal goal. If a parent sets a goal for the child to become an upstanding citizen and to be a Christ follower, it requires the child's enthusiasm, cooperation, and participation. No one can monitor another individual's goals twenty-four-seven, including one's children. In goal setting, we have no control over anyone else's actions; we can only monitor and manage our own. Your child has his own free-will and authority to thwart the goal you have set for him to be upright and to follow God's commands.

The only goals you can make a committed effort toward and monitor are your own personal life goals. How can you still be responsible in raising productive citizens and godly children? By turning your *goal* (to raise a fine Christian citizen) into your *desire*. By reading God's Word and finding out how He wants parents to raise their children. The parent's goal then becomes to obey God's Word. A parent's obedience to God's Word (on how to raise children) is a realistic, doable, and obtainable goal; a child's obedience is not. God always knows those who desire to be obedient to Him. Children are free moral agents and they will stand, or fall, accountable to God; just as their parents will. The emphasis when we desire to raise godly citizens is then the parent's obedience, not the children's. Are you as a parent a true Christian who lives a righteous life looking to Christ daily for instructions? Your child can get a taste of the sweet life you live simply by you being obedient to God's instructions for your own life.

The reality then is that raising children in a Christian home does not guarantee righteous children. How your children turn out does not depend on everything that you do to raise them well, but rather on what *you* are and who *you* become. This doesn't mean that you as a parent should throw the towel in with a disgusted attitude (since there's no warranty on your children) and allow your children to run loose in the world. As a parent we can't force our children to obey God's principles and commands; but through our way of life we can witness to them how to be obedient to the Lord and they can be eyewitnesses to the joyous fulfilled lives that we live in Christ. They are able to note that our honoring God obediently has resulted in life going well for us. God's Word does not only give us the parental instructions, but in Ephesians 6:1-3, it also commands children to *honor* and *obey* their parents so that it will go well with them (and so that they shall enjoy a long life). Though, as parents and children, we don't obey God so that it will go well with us; obedience to His Word and reverence to Him does bless us and those around us. We can protect our children from evil influences and guide them while they're still living at home, and continue to pray for them when they leave home. Should they ask for our guidance when they're grown, all we can do is remain consistent with our answers and continue to be godly examples in their lives. If you did not have an opportunity to accept Christ until you became an adult, it's never too late to demonstrate to your teens or adult children the obedient abundant life which you live.

In Deuteronomy 6: 7 and 11:19, God has asked us to not just honor His commandments but to teach them to our children day and night as a part of every opportunity that we get to share God's Word with them. It doesn't have to be a formal teaching session because when God is a part of our daily life it's easy to talk about Him all the time. That's what people do when they love someone, their love feelings for that person just spill out.

THE VICTIM: EVERYTHING YOU EVER WONDERED

I talk about *Him* all the time (Or, had you noticed?)! Needless to say, if there's spiritual abuse taking place with your abuser, you will have to balance out when you are able to safely speak to your children about God. Our love and obedience to God does not always have to be expressed in words but can naturally be spoken by our actions. Whether our children accept or reject Christ, He will continue to work in our children's lives just as He has worked in our own spiritual walk with Him.

One fine spring afternoon, while my daughters enjoyed Disney movies in our family room, I was in my office grading sociology midterm papers when my middle daughter walked in and began to comb my hair. The next thing I knew, my husband was standing at my office door, home from work, asking, "What's for dinner?" grinning and saying, "You look cute." *Suddenly*, it occurred to me as I felt my fingers run through my hair that my daughter had braided my hair with pipe cleaners, and I had two wild Pippi Longstocking braids sticking out of the sides of my head! Yes, it's okay to become focused on our work while parenting, as long as we balance it out!

The sons and daughters of abusive relationships (unless they are consciously exposed to counter-examples) will inherit the abusive and/or victim mentality and can become victim or abuser-prone. These children who are raised in the presence of an abuser learn to love in a distorted, non-attached way. They begin to believe that being disrespected and controlled, or to disrespect and control, is the way to give or receive love. This, in turn, makes it almost impossible for these children to grow up being able to set boundaries or discern when they are being maltreated. They have only experienced feeling unloved, so they are unable to identify when they themselves are being loving or disrespectful.

Children that live with or are being exposed to an abusive parental relationship also experience role confusion as the victim does. Similar to the role reversal that the abuser does with the victim whereby he places her either in a parental role to take care of him or as a child dependent on him, the abuser also does the same with the children in that he feels entitled to the children meeting *his* needs. Children of abusive fathers are like the victim, just grateful to receive his attention and seek his approval. Abused children crave and want that special alliance with their father. This can be at the detriment of the relationship with their mother, who is always available and can be counted on. The children operate on the supply-and-demand principle and value their father's attention over their mother's as it's more on-demand and low on supply.

Children that live in abusive environments generally wear their melancholy facial affect as they don't know how else to be—good times are sporadic. Many of these children are referred to the school counselor due to their depressed mood. Children may have limited social and verbal skills depending on their age, but observing facial expressions is a good barometer for parents and caretakers. One of my fondest memories of my oldest daughter was picking her up from school all the way up until she began to drive herself; she wore the biggest smile from ear to ear as she walked over to my car. Her smile was so contagious that even if I was having a very hectic day, it restored my joy to greet her. Children will reveal themselves to you and others through their facial affect.

Whether children are abused directly or indirectly, children that live in abusive homes are usually distracted at school *and* extracurricular activities. They generally have difficulty with social skills and in their interpersonal relationships with peers and/or adults. Many children are misdiagnosed when referred to school counselors or even therapists; they are labeled as having an Attention Deficit Disorder, when in reality these children are just victims of abuse who need to break the silence! And you guessed it—when the children are reported as having behavior problems and it's brought to the abuser's attention, he blames it on their mother's parenting skills or the children's flawed character. Abusers *love* having the label of father and the status that fatherhood has attached to it, but they refrain from accepting the responsibility it brings. Some abusers simply see the children as a possession such as they perceive the victim. These abusive fathers don't experience their children as having any rights to be individuals.

Healthy parents encourage dialogue with their children, and whenever problems arise, they are open to discussion and compromise with a respectful, conflict-resolution attitude. The majority of abusers see their children as objects that they are entitled to own, manipulate, and control. All of this disrespect toward his children is bestowed upon them while keeping the abuser's good public image intact. In a healthy functioning family, the father and mother are mutually respected, and the father and mother are *both* admired as leaders and providers of their home (whether the mother works in and/or outside of the home). Parents in a healthy functioning home are not seen as the authoritarian dictators of the family. In healthy families, the mother is not berated by the father or children; the father does not work diligently to damage the mother-child relationship. A non-abusive father is not threatened by the mother's love and devotion to her children; he is secure in his own separate role as their father.

Let's talk about what is meant by the hidden victims of domestic violence. It refers to children that have either witnessed their family being abused or are victimized as they tag along with their victimized mother. I can't tell you how many times victims have recounted to me the experience of finding their children sleeping under their bed, in a closet, or behind a couch or stairway after an encounter with their abuser (which was thought to be concealed while the children were safely tucked in). Children do have sensory perception and are able to sense tension even when camouflaged efforts are made to conceal the abuse. This is why it becomes important for the victim to make a decision as to whether or not she's going to choose to continue to expose her children to family violence. An adult victim can make a choice as to *where* and with *whom* to live; children are unable to make such responsible decisions as to their living conditions.

All that children living in an abusive home can decide is if they feel grateful, nurtured, and safe. Parents and the environment to which the children are exposed have a deep influence on their children's perceptions. When my middle daughter was preschool age, she would always bring me roly-polies from her outdoor adventures in our back yard. I usually temporarily collected them in a Styrofoam cup with soil and a bit of grass then let them free after her bedtime. One day, when I thanked her for bringing me yet another roly-poly, she said, "You're welcome; I knew you would take care of him." I notice today as a sensitive young woman, she openly and enthusiastically nurtures and expresses her gratitude to her multitude of friends.

Relationships have to be nurtured to protect and develop them. There are so many different ways of intentionally nurturing children. Think about each one of your children for a moment. I am certain that as you visualize each child, you can come up with ideas on what you can say or do to increase their sense of your nurturance. The beauty of nurturing is that it's contagious, and when you nurture, receivers are compelled to reciprocate. When my girls were school age, I would place love and specific encouraging Post-It notes in their lunchboxes. In turn, they began to do the same. I would find notes from them in my home office, kitchen, books, and anywhere they knew I would find them. Today, I still have a treasure chest box full of notes written on napkins or any piece of scrap paper they could

THE VICTIM: EVERYTHING YOU EVER WONDERED

find, sketched with pencils to crayons to dry erase markers, filled with hearts and messages from long ago, saying, "I love you, Mommy." Children will learn from you and will interchange with you and others what is given to them. It's important to periodically evaluate our choices and interactions with our children because as adults, they will be interacting and making exchanges with others in the same way we interacted with them as children. Children, just like adults, have different personalities. Aim toward attaching and bonding with your children according to their individual personalities (even if your abuser is attempting to drive a wedge into your relationship with them). Children will learn directly or indirectly from you, so teach them what you want them to learn!

Regardless of children not having been physically inflicted with pain, they can decide that they hurt inside (emotional abuse) and can determine if their parents are nurturing or not. Children can decide that their direct or indirect exposure to family violence threatens the safety of their mother whom they count on to nurture and protect them. They can also decide to make themselves invisible as a coping mechanism to keep the peace in the family. Some children say that they "pretend" to be busy with homework or asleep when their abused mother or the abuser checks up on them. Some children have told me that they purposely kept silent and practiced especially good behavior for fear of their mother and/or themselves being abused if they made any noise (ordinary, playful children's sounds). Other children have voiced during play therapy that they don't think their mother cares if she or they get hurt by their father.

Most children living in abusive homes can't even begin to understand the price that their mother would have to pay if she were to stand up to her abuser (or how she actually protects *them* from paying the price). Instead, these children learn through the abuser's role-modeling to look at their mother with disdain. This disrespectful outlook and attitude toward their mother can be transmitted to the children while growing up around their father's abuse of their mother (or during visitations if their parents have separated or divorced). Children can absorb the abuser's derogatory opinion of their mother even if they defend the mother in the abuser's presence; the children still treat her as less than themselves and others. These children from an abusive father, whether raised by him or having occasional contact with him, see their mother through their abusive father's eyes.

It's not only about the abuser's opinion of their mother; the children's opinion is also formed by observing the abusive relationship's parental roles. The imbalance in the sharing of household responsibilities creates the children's view of their parents. The abused mother is always seen in the eyes of her children as the boring, routine-structured, hygienic parent, homework guard, and policing disciplinarian. Whereas they associate their father as the fun parent and their friend. Despite how many times they have observed his irresponsible nature, heard his put-downs of their mother or his yelling, and noticed his perfectionism and controlling ways, he still comes out as the pleasant one to be around because he has time for lounging, and they view her as rule-based and isolated. This is the division between the mother and her children which the controlling abuser has created!

When a victim decides to leave her abuser for her sake and the welfare of her children, some children are relieved and begin to believe that she *does* care. Living without the abuser gives them an opportunity to discover what it's like to not be constantly on edge, and they may actually begin to appreciate living calmly without their abusive father's presence. Becoming appreciative and having an attitude of gratitude is an important trait for children to develop. It's especially important to train children early on that being grateful is not just reserved for the good times; it also means that we can have a spirit of thankfulness as we look around in spite of our circumstances and take in the simple blessings that we do have. For example, children that have experienced the loss of their abusive father through a Safety Escape Plan can be asked to name the things that they appreciate such as the love that they share with siblings, friends, or mentors at school. Or, it can be as simple as being thankful for a rainfall on a hot, drought-filled week.

When my youngest daughter was a toddler, I always noticed that she said "thank you" for the slightest kind gesture she received, and I also noticed how that thanks was reflected in her joyful eyes and laughter. One of the ways that she expressed her *gratitude* as a preschooler toward God, nature, and myself was to bring me dandelions which she called, "flowers for you, Mommy." I never told her back then that they were weeds as she was so proud of them, and I so appreciated her loving gesture; they too went into a Styrofoam cup, but one that was filled with water. Sometimes I would place those "flowers" in my Bible; which are still there today. She eventually figured out on her own that dandelions are weeds. However, up until this week as a young lady, she still brings me "flowers" from the fields, for she loves and appreciates wildflowers (over store-refrigerated ones). She's grateful for those simple flowers and just wants to tenderly spread joy by sharing them.

Children that are taught to express appreciation, develop their inner feeling of gratitude, which influences their capability to express love and tenderness. Gratitude is not just about saying a ritualistic "thank you;" it is the foundation of genuineness, generosity, politeness, sharing, concern or empathy for family members and others. Gratitude develops other virtues. Gratitude inspires both the giver and the receiver and promotes the ability to pay it forward. The giver or receiver doesn't have to experience gratitude over a major deed; it can be a simple word or act that the person expresses appreciation for. Teaching children directly or indirectly through example to verbalize their gratitude of others in their lives provides them with the ability to acknowledge the contribution that others make in their lives. This, in turn, is beneficial in not raising children that feel a sense of entitlement. An ungrateful spirit negatively affects the attitudes and behaviors of the self and others. When children are taught gratitude (yes, taught—children are born selfish like all humans), it can have a tremendous impact on the happiness and growth of every family member. A child that learns to express gratitude can grow into adulthood distributing unselfish, random acts of grateful love.

Children from abused homes *do not* have to carry with them a demeanor such as the abuser's, who is perpetually disappointed at everything his family life brings him. These children can be oriented to the truth that it's not always about them but that there are others that dole out the work to help make things happen for them (providing meals, shelter, clothing, school supplies, education, toys, time, skills, and affection). You are not bragging to your child about your provision when you teach them to be thankful; you are teaching them a courteous, respectful response to receiving a blessing. It doesn't come naturally for a child to recognize his blessings. As these children grow up, the benefit of learning appreciation affects their view of life and ends up being one of the keys to personal and family happiness for their own lives. Gratitude taught to *all* children is essential: it becomes the core of who they are. Studies have concluded that people with a spirit of gratitude for their blessings enjoy higher levels of optimism and lower levels of stress and depression.

Children who are grateful for their safe lives and blessings usually choose to separate themselves from their abusive father; this allows the time for the process of healing into healthier family living. Some children, of course, are too young to make such a choice and have to go along with their mother's decision to protect their safety. Naturally, the abuser is not up to this plan of distance from his victims of abuse, and predictably, he blames their mother for breaking up the family. Who else could it be? Children can decide that their mother and their well-being feel threatened, and they can either begin to accept their role as a victim, such as their mother, or take on the role of an abuser, such as their father. The latter lends itself to continuing the intergenerational family violence within the family and in our society. Your words and actions as a parent can either bring darkness or light into the life of your children. If you are a loving, godly parent, there will be light in your children's lives. God's presence and illumination within you will be sensed and visible to your children and then transferred to them.

The Victim and Self-Defense
In some cases, victims of abuse don't believe they are victims of abuse because in the midst of a knock-down-drag-out fight, they have stood up for themselves, and they too can confess to having slapped, thrown something, or swung at their abuser. These victims of abuse have been led into the abuser's keen and adept way of reversing reality. The truth is that the victim attempted to aggressively protect herself from her abuser in self-defense, and her abuser's reaction is that she is the one abusing him. Reminder: the abuser's intimidation tactic is to twist what has actually happened. Remember: your main goal as an *Overcomer* is to restore your identity and become the opposite of what the abuser is; don't listen to his lies.

Physical aggression on the part of the victim does occur in some abusive relationships; generally, it is the result of an exasperated victim who has been tolerating long periods of nonstop, severe, volatile verbal scolding and/or violent attacks. In most abusive relationships, the victim uses minimal force, sufficient enough for self-preservation. However, I do not recommend (and neither would other mental health professionals) that victims use physical aggression against their abuser except when the victim is in life-threatening danger and, without a shadow of doubt, has to defend herself.

Using physical aggression on an abuser has *never* worked to de-escalate the abuser's attacks; it simply *does not* serve the victim's intention, which is to communicate that *she is in control of her person* and can hold her own. On the contrary, remember that he turns situations around as opposites! Your abuser's reactions to your physical aggression (in his realm of thinking) will be to take revenge, calling it self-defense for him to justify injuring you back, and therefore taking stronger control of you. In most abusive relationships, the abuser is physically stronger and overpowers the physical strength of the victim. This means that when the victim uses physical aggression to defend herself, she ends up badly bruised, while he dusts off his minor scratches and ego humiliation. God has instructed us *not* to take revenge into our own hands. That translates to leaving your abuser in God's hands. God has reassured us that He can take care of *any* situation that we are angry about; therefore, we don't have to resolve to take vengeance. "Beloved, do not avenge yourselves, but *rather* give place to wrath; for it is written, 'Vengeance *is* Mine, I will repay,' says the Lord" (Romans 12:19).

Rest in God's Word, which says that the judgment of those who harm women, children, and any of God's people is certain and guaranteed. God loves you immensely, and you are eternally safe in Him. No single persecuting abuser escapes God's indictment. While it's not up to us to delve out the judgment, consequences, and penalty for the evil doings, we can rejoice in the righteous justice of God as it is meted out to those who choose violence over Him. Be encouraged—God does reign over victim violence!

THE VICTIM: EVERYTHING YOU EVER WONDERED

It is true that a victim of physical abuse does feel as if she's in a daily war zone in her own home. Nevertheless, physical aggression has never been an option in a marriage; it is the epitome of serious disrespect for your spouse. If, out of defense for yourself or your children, desperation, and/or anger, you were physically aggressive toward your abusive spouse, confess and ventilate that sin to the Lord right now. He is not looking down on you in a judging, condemning way; He is looking at you in a loving, merciful way as *your Parent,* as His Child. Ask Him to not only forgive you, but to also encourage you in His strength. It is impossible to be weak in the Lord's strength! "The LORD *is* my strength and my shield; My heart trusted in Him, and I am helped" (Psalm 28:7). Then, forgive yourself and ask the Lord for His strength to be able to ask for your abuser's forgiveness, and make a firm choice not to ever take your abuse out on anyone. Remember that the Lord loves you and understands that you're oppressed and brokenhearted. "The Spirit of the Lord *is* upon Me, He has anointed Me, He has sent Me to heal the brokenhearted, to set at liberty those who are oppressed" (Luke 4:18).

Speak to Him in prayer; He is always ready to listen and to hear your oppressive pain, because your pain is His pain. He already knows abuse is not something you can resolve on your own strength, and He does not expect that of you. When you come to Him depleted of your own reserves, ask for His relief from pain and for the strength to take the road that you must follow. Remember that it is satan who wants you to remain in pain, but *He* has already overcome satan—so that *you* can do the same! In the face of suffering, God gives the victim the prospect of life as an *Overcomer*. His desire is that you will live instead of just exist. In place of a life of weakness, He offers you His strength, and in your darkest victim hours, He sheds His innermost Light of Wisdom and guidance. The Bible says that it was God Who put wisdom in King Solomon's heart. Go ahead; ask Him for wisdom in your heart! The strength He provides is unlike human strength; He's the only One Who can give you that superlative strength. It's okay to admit your feeble weakness without Him and to realize your humble dependence on Him. To ask for His strength is spiritual growth. He and only He is your Source of powerful divine strength. Turn to Him to be renewed daily with His unmatchable strength.

Jesus the Great cross-bearer Himself has suffered the pain of abuse that you have suffered. "So then Pilate took Jesus and scourged *Him*. And the soldiers twisted a crown of thorns and put *it* on His head, and they put on Him a purple robe. Then they said, 'Hail, King of the Jews!' And they struck Him with their hands" (John 19:1-3). He himself has experienced anger: "The LORD has been very angry with your fathers. 'Return to Me,' 'and I will return to you,' says the LORD of hosts" (Zechariah 1:2-3). Jesus has actually shed tears like you and I: "Jesus wept" (John 11:35). He acknowledges that it is *not* wrong to experience anger; like all of our other human emotions, He created that one too. It is *what we do* with our angry emotion that determines whether that emotion is being used appropriately or inappropriately. If, in a state of anger after several bouts of abuse from your spouse, you have lost your temper on your children, it's best to nip it in the bud and to stop repeating what abuse has been done to you.

Forgive yourself, ask for your children's forgiveness, and make a conscientious decision not to procreate your abuse. Learn not to model abuse to them, but don't blame yourself if they allow your/their abuse trauma to direct their lives with dysfunctional choices. Should they decide to lead derailed, misguided lives, all you can do is pray for them to heal from their trauma and for their paths to be redirected to God, Who is the healer of all diseases (Psalm 103:3), which includes the healing of mental health and any other unhealthy stronghold that satan implants! Pray

THE VICTIM: EVERYTHING YOU EVER WONDERED

that they would have a personal relationship with the Lord so that they too can become *Overcomers* of their abuse! Abuse does beget abuse—but you can make a willful choice not to reproduce abuse and to leave your victim and abuser pattern behind and instead re-channel your energy and leave an *Overcomer* legacy for your children to follow!

As we have already discussed, the victim is an unaware prisoner, unbeknownst to her during the courting period or early part of her relationship with her abuser and underneath her abuser's charming exterior. It is only when she becomes *aware* of her incarceration and enters into her commitment to seek an *Overcomer* lifestyle that her chains are released as she begins to live an *Overcomer* life of freedom from abuse. However, an *Overcomer* life is impossible while remaining in contact with her abuser. The abuser's presence makes her more vulnerable to him as his easiest access to prey. The abuser's contact only serves to further deteriorate the victim's mindset and their relationship.

Although busy with responsibilities, over time, the victim's days are filled with lingering depression, which borders on despair. Upon awakening each day, she does not feel well-rested; she only feels the weight of her burdened heart—her body even feels achy as she drags herself out of bed for another unpredictable, guarded day. It could be a day in which her abuser will be kind, generous, romantic, cruel, explosive, or neglectful.

If you've not read the story of Job in the Bible with interest, this would be a good time to do so in order to encourage yourself throughout your longstanding suffering. During your abusive cycles, have you ever gotten angry at God for being what appears to be an absent Father? Have you ever been tempted to succumb to unstoppable weeping or caved into depression and just shut down? Or gotten into a pity party rut? Notice in the story of Job that in his darkest, longest days, Job chose to worship God instead of resorting to anger or depression. In your most grievous abusive days, you, like Job, have a choice as to how you will react or respond. Job suffered intensely, both emotionally and physically; he, like a victim, experienced a tragic, traumatic experience. Never did Job get into the spiritual sulks or spiritual hysterics. It is written in the Bible that when Job lost his dignity and everything in his life, he bowed his face before God and worshiped Him.

As a victim, when you're faced with your world falling apart, and your abuser and everybody else has turned against you, you too have a choice. You can turn away from God and leave the only hope that you have, or you can bow your face before Him and pray, "Loving Lord, have mercy upon me. Give me grace. I don't understand why I am experiencing all of this suffering, but I do believe that You are the powerful living God, and I want to commit myself and be closer to You more than ever before. I believe that You have the power to end my abuse, I now release my abused life to You. In Your Merciful Name, Amen." If you allow your abuse to lead you to return to God, you will reach an experience with God that is richer, deeper, and more intimate than you've ever known before. Job chose to remain faithful to God and worshiped Him regardless of his suffering and God's appearing to be absent; in the end, God blessed Job abundantly.

I am not saying that Job did not ever experience a dark cloud of depression and despair; the Bible says that he did (and so did Moses, Jeremiah, David, and others). But the difference is that instead of succumbing to their pit of pain, they remained faithful and turned to their God of hope, and that perspective kept them from focusing on and giving into a broken spirit (or death) and restored their strength and revealed God's purpose for their lives. You'll notice that God maintains His mysterious Ways through keeping low-profile and remaining invisible during our most suffering days. We must make good use of His humility, our faith, and our hope and be satisfied with His Holy Spirit's presence within us during such times. While suffering, we can experience His Being manifested through those people that do bless us! God's love living in our souls and in others is evidence of His invisible presence. This is how He remains as *God*.

As a victim, you have a choice of living your entire life suffering with your hazard blinkers always turned on or turning on your bright lights and driving through the darkness until you can dim your lights and reach your peaceful, *Overcomer* destination. This can be accomplished over a period of hours, days, months, or years—the choice is yours. One of the major reasons why victims stay in abusive relationships and elect to just keep their hazard lights turned on while in the relationship is that they believe, due to religious or family reasons, that they have to tolerate the abusive maltreatment. It's hurtful enough when a person is bullied by strangers, classmates, employers, co-workers, or online harassers, but it's especially traumatic when the abusers are a spouse or a family member. It's wise that a victim would be seeking to respond to her abusive relationship biblically, rather than just reacting to her hurt feelings and foolishly taking it into her own hands.

However, abusive relationships do not respond to hazard lights, and the bad news is that this strategy, or treating them with biblical respect, will not always achieve the abuser's mutual respect for you. The good news, however, is that God doesn't expect you to have to put up with being mistreated. Honoring a spouse or family does not mean that you have to sit around cautiously while they emotionally and verbally bully you. You have an obligation to your spouse and family in treating them with respect, and that can be accomplished simply by acknowledging their worth as human beings as being created and loved by God. It does not mean that you have to tolerate being oppressed or obey your spouse's or abusive family's requests of you.

When abuse is involved, actually, the respectful approach *isn't* to allow the abuse to continue, but to prevent the abuser(s) from continuing the abuse and removing yourself from the situation. Otherwise, you *can* indeed, biblically, get to a place where you yourself are enabling the abuse by condoning and allowing the sinful behavior. Proverbs 17 is entitled "The Lord Tests Hearts." It is God's take, His wisdom, as to how He views and handles those whose hearts are contentious and how *we* are to manage those relationships in our lives. God warns us not to release strife and to put a stop to contention. "The beginning of strife *is like* releasing water; Therefore stop contention before a quarrel starts" (Proverbs 17:14). God has asked us to address and work out relationship problems. "Moreover if your brother sins against you, go and tell him his fault between you and him alone. If he hears you, you have gained your brother" (Matthew 18:15).

It's generally impossible to explain to an abuser why you must remove yourself from his abuse because of his escalated denial and defenses. In some cases, you may be able to directly share the truth in love about your relationship with family members that are being abusive toward you. This can be done by approaching them politely, unemotionally, firmly, but gently and succinctly, explaining your choice to remove yourself from the relationship. You begin by asking for forgiveness for anything you have said or done on your behalf to cause strife. Calmly acknowledge that although you love them, you cannot allow them to continue to mistreat and hurt you. "He who has knowledge spares his words, *And* a man of understanding is of a calm spirit" (Proverbs 17:27). If he/she insists on continuing to argue or a grudging separation, let it go—and let it be. "He who covers a transgression seeks love, But he who repeats a matter separates friends" (Proverbs 17:9). "He who loves transgression loves strife, And he who exalts his gate seeks destruction" (Proverbs 17:19). You may have had this

THE VICTIM: EVERYTHING YOU EVER WONDERED

peacemaking conversation multiple times already. You may have even written out your boundaries via a letter to them. It may not be necessary then to repeat and say any more about their abuse and refusal to treat you with respect.

However, if you feel you must address it one last time, just be certain that your request for rectification of their tone, attitude, sarcasm, condensation, oppression, control, or maltreatment of you is presented out of a concern for your relationship with them so that your abusers don't allege that you're just enjoying being accusatory. The motive should include a goal to establish boundaries in your relationship with that person; and forgiveness regardless of the decision the family member makes after you address the problem. For example, "I've spoken to you and even written you about how your aggressive tone and your continuous rudeness toward me have hurt our relationship; I would like to have a relationship with you, but it doesn't seem to be happening because each time we have contact, I experience your offensive behaviors toward me. I cannot allow myself to have my high hopes for reconciliation with you and be so disappointed every time we have contact. For this reason, I will not be spending as much time with you." Or "I will have to remove myself from your presence when you are rude to me, until you let me know that you have decided to treat me with respect and honor our relationship," etc. Use your own words but with the same message; you want to have a relationship, but you have to draw the line and set limits and boundaries on any further abuse.

How you address the truth about the inappropriate behavior is most important when defending your position in an abusive family relationship. It does require you to speak the truth about the disrespect of which that person does not want to acknowledge. No matter if you speak that truth with love or not, it will still stir up hurt feelings. Since this is the case, you must choose your words and be extremely careful how you express those words. It is the spirit in which you deliver your words that matters. *Overcomers* who understand the huge impact of words will use words that are helpful and encouraging with a proposed solution and mention what they do like about that person or their relationship with them (if that's the case). Regardless, there has to be compassion and comfort toward the person's disappointment or outrage over the delivery of your message. Use words that suggest or promote healing in that person or the relationship. Painful things have to be said at times, but they can be expressed with empathy and kindness. This, in turn, reduces some of the hurt that will inevitably be felt.

As an *Overcomer*, when you must speak the truth in love, it's always advisable to spend some alone time with the Lord beforehand to seek the Holy Spirit's leading and guidance. By doing so, you will be able to present your own painful, stressful thoughts clearly with grace and dignity toward that person. As an *Overcomer* who must say the appropriate words with a healing touch in a fractured relationship, you can definitely trust the Holy Spirit to lead your words. How that person responds or reacts will be based on that person's emotional and spiritual maturity and functioning, and that is solely their responsibility. An *Overcomer's* attitude is to be inspired by the love of Christ, which has the ability to rise above the contention. Heart-healthy relationships enrich the spirit and mind of a person. God and that type of heart-healthy relationship are precious above all things and matters. If this person does not want to have a heart-healthy relationship with you, seek relationships with those that do.

Sometimes, no matter the appropriate approach you used, the person may elect to stonewall you, bad mouth you to others, threaten you, taunt you, use projective identification (saying you said or did what the person is doing to you), accuse you of not being a real Christian, rally for friends or relatives to conspire and break off their relationship with you, attempt to confuse you, or call or contact you via social media to verbally attack or disown you in response to your talk with them. That person, just like you, is accountable to God; your only duty and responsibility is to speak the truth in love with an effort toward a healthy, balanced relationship. You need not continue to repeat your request for proper honor and respect. Respect is defined as "having differential regard for, to esteem, or to treat with propriety or consideration." Respect, like love, is a verb; an appropriate action is required. The person doesn't have to agree and can choose to remain disagreeable and abusive, and you can choose to hold onto your peace and move on, for *you* have done your part. "Even a fool is counted wise when he holds his peace; *When* he shuts his lips, *he is considered* perceptive" (Proverbs 17:28).

It is totally acceptable to take a stand on respect and contention. It sets a boundary. Even children set boundaries. I'm certain you've heard a child tell another child, "you're not the boss of me!" It's okay if a person rejects the choice against contention which you have made based on God's Word. He will declare blessings-upon-blessings on you when you take a stand against contention in His Name. What can you do when you're hurting over the person's thoughtless choice to continue to disrespect you? Move on and pray. Christ set the protocol for us. While hanging from His cross, He prayed to the Father for us, the very ones who persecuted and crucified Him.

Speaking the truth in love is not child's play it is about adulting; it is the mature, grown-up thing to do. Sometimes, even with your nonthreatening choice words, that person will only hear from their perspective: an emotional personal attack on a loved one or their person. Do not counterattack. That person may not *ever* notice, hear, or recollect your choice words and may even change your words into an exaggerated version. Ephesians 4:15 calls us to speak "the truth in love," not just about the gospel, but so that we, "may grow up in all things into Him who is the head—Christ." Setting boundaries is an act of love and personal growth. Even God the Creator of the world sets limits on the way we are to treat Him and others (love God with all your heart and mind; love one another). God is a God of *peace*. Christ came into this world so that we may receive peace. We are incomplete without Christ and without His peace. God promises to be with us when we accept and practice His peace. That peace is not only for victims of abuse, it is a gift of peace which God wants us to have in our relationship with Him; it is a peace His Word instructs us to have with one another. It is a peace that brings comfort to our hearts no matter what our crises may be. "Finally, brethren, farewell. Become complete. Be of good comfort, be of one mind, live in peace; and the God of love and peace will be with you" (2 Corinthians 13:11).

God's unfailing love, peace, and commandments will not allow our rebellious hearts (disrespect) toward Him to go unnoticed and free from His discipline (consequences). You were created in God's Image and are called to follow God's standards and character (His principles). God's standards and expectations for Himself are not any less for each of us. Why would *you* allow a family member's disrespect to go unnoticed and undisciplined (without boundaries)? Why would you allow *any* person to destroy your peace?

Divorce and the Victim of Abuse

In most cases, due to the abuser's choice not to stop abusing the victim, she not only separates from him but ultimately decides to divorce him so that she can be completely set free from his abuse. Past and current research literature results indicate the same as Ellis and Stuckless found in their study of 362 separating spouses. Their report concluded that more than forty percent of the wives said that they were injured by their spouses during their relationship, and fifty-seven percent said that abuse by their spouse was the major reason for separating.³ By providing this information, I am not suggesting that you should divorce your abusive spouse. I can't tell you what to do regarding divorce—that is a solid decision that only you and your Heavenly Father can make. But, what *I can* tell you about is God's grace, mercy, and forgiveness, should you decide to divorce your abuser. I can also provide some information that can clarify and spell out some truths about God's priorities regarding you, your abusive relationship, and divorce.

What follows now are some pieces of information and facts that you need to seriously consider when contemplating whether divorce is an option for your safety and peace in your life. I am going to primarily focus on those victims that struggle with the idea of separation and divorce due to their deep concerns about religious beliefs forbidding divorce. Over the years, my colleagues and I have had the disappointment of listening to victims who obviously were misunderstood by an R.A. (reconciliation advisor) or their clergy who did not, at any moment, recognize the gravity of the pain, danger, and hopelessness of an abused woman—leading to religion's and the Church's contribution to the victim's burden.

If you have misgivings and are struggling to free yourself from the hands of your abusive spouse (because of religious-induced guilt), read on, because the truth will always set you free. Have you ever felt either by reading or direct counsel ostracized by religious leaders who instructed you to return to your abuser and to just stop your spouse's abuse by being a better Christian wife? Have any religious leaders used Scripture (which, unbeknownst to you, is being misused) to justify the abuse your spouse has committed? I have spent endless hours undoing some of the damage done to victims who have been blackballed to their abuser in the name of God. At the same time, my colleagues and I have also witnessed numerous instances whereby the true God and His true thoughts about the victim are revealed, and the power of faith is awakened in the victim to enable her to no longer tolerate abuse from her spouse or in her family system.

Before plundering into the controversial subject of divorce, let's delve into your basic profile as a victim of abuse as a refresher. Each day, as a victim, you live with the anxiety of not knowing *when* or *how* your spouse will become abusive again—all you know is that he will. Most of the time, you fear for your life and/or that of your children. Do you sincerely believe that God, the God Who created you, wants you to live in fear? God loves and values you. He *does not* want you or your children to be harmed. He wants you to live without fear. Living with an abuser means the abuser will put fetters upon you. God does not want you to walk around with a ball and chain as a result of this abusive relationship. When God said in John 10:10 that He came that you may have life, and have it abundantly, he meant it! Christ can bring you out of your captivity and give your abundant life back to you.

Ephesians 3:20 reassures us that God "is able to do exceedingly abundantly above all that we ask or think." In other words, when we ask to live a life of peace, He will give us that life of peace abundantly because He does not give it to us in pinches or just the leftover crumbs. Living your life abundantly is *not* about having an abundance of "things;" it is about the spiritual abundance of *peace*. A victim receives this new abundant life of peace and is able to pass it on as an *Overcomer*. Once she has been granted this spiritual peace, she is able to part with her dark past, manage any new darkness which life sometimes brings, and live in the peace of His light.

Abundant spiritual *peace* includes being unafraid of your spouse, not feeling imprisoned, and feeling loved and respected as an individual by your spouse. Your home being a safety

THE VICTIM: EVERYTHING YOU EVER WONDERED

net and haven for you and your children is God's will (what *He* wants for you). God does want you to live in peace; you can find this throughout His Word. Read His Word. It is God's will for you to have a life of peace. God's Word and Will cannot be separated; they are synonymous. God's Word is your life guidebook. You've heard what God's will is for you. What do you want for your life? Trust in the Lord and what He yearns to give you. "The fear of man brings a snare, But whoever trusts in the Lord shall be safe" (Proverbs 29:25).

It does not matter to God what you have said, neglected to do, or have done; God does not believe that you deserve to be abused. I have heard victims talking about being told that the abuse is a form of consequence from God. God is not responsible for your abuse; He did not send your abusive spouse to you as a form of punishment. Your spouse's abuse toward you is not God's fault—it is your abuser's total responsibility. Many victims have been misled to believe that their abuse is *God's will* for their lives, which is erroneous. If you as a victim are carrying burdens in your heart which you believe are sins against your spouse, then just talk *directly* to God about it. No religious leader can relieve you of your conviction or absolve you of any sin; your repentance in prayer to God (directly) will set you free. Resolve to never again condemn God or yourself as being to blame for your spouse's abuse because that is simply *not* true.

Perhaps you have encountered religious counsel that has suggested to you that you be subject to your spouse because he is considered the spiritual leader of your household. Ask yourself if your abusive spouse is behaving as the spiritual leader that the Bible instructs him to be. The position of being a spiritual leader gives the spouse authority in the family, but it *does not* give him the right to abuse. On the contrary, having spiritual authority charges the spouse with tremendous responsibility for the well-being of his wife and children. It's also important to note that the spiritual responsibility with that role is to love and treat his wife as Christ loved the Church. Christ loved and served the needs of the Church (the body of Christ's believers) *and* was willing to sacrifice Himself for it. The Bible also tells husbands that they are to love their wives as their own bodies (Ephesians 5:28).

Has your spouse been demonstrating such love and devotion to you? When you married your spouse, he probably stated some vows that included "to love and to cherish" and *not* "to despise and to harm." More specifically, the instructions for your spouse are in Colossians 3:19, which tells him to love you and not to be harsh with you. If your spouse is being abusive toward you, he is not fulfilling his responsibility to you, to *love* and *respect* you—his traumatic mistreatment does not obligate you to him. Anyone that is given responsibility and authority and instead uses it as a power over another loses that trust and authority. A spouse who misuses the authority (as a spiritual leader) that he has been given by God (as a power to harm his wife and children) basically gives up his divinely-appointed authority in the home.

You are unable to trust your abuser in his role of a spiritual leader as a spouse, or as the father of your children, because he has violated that trust through his authoritarian maltreatment of you. When a spouse introduces abuse into the marriage, it is an act of unfaithfulness to his marital covenant to his wife. The trust that was once a part of their loving relationship has been destroyed. If a vulnerable victim can't trust her spouse not to slap her around with his words or hands daily, what can she trust? The spiritual, emotional, and sometimes physical brokenness that engulfs the victim's trust level becomes irreparable between an abuser and a victim. God deeply grieves this brokenness. This brokenness resulting from the abuse is what leads to the end of the relationship. But take comfort in knowing that Christ understands. Christ had to experience brokenness in

THE VICTIM: EVERYTHING YOU EVER WONDERED

order for us to become the family of God. All *Overcomer* families come from brokenness and loss.

It is the spouse that perpetrated the abuse that is responsible for the ending of the relationship. For example, you don't have to have a wedding to have a marriage; you can be married in solitude by a justice of the peace *or* clergy. The wedding is an announcement to the public that you have made a commitment to marry your fiancé. A divorce, in the same way, is only a symbol and public notice of the fact that your spouse has destroyed the marriage. When a victim considers if she will get a divorce, she is not *actually* considering whether or not to end the relationship; spiritually and emotionally, the abuser has already terminated the relationship. The formal divorce announcement and the paperwork notifies the public that you are now authorized to remove yourself and your children from an abusive marriage that ended when your spouse chose to continue abusing you.

Ask yourself: What is keeping me in this abusive marriage? Is it my spouse's selfless love for me and our children? Or is my abusive spouse self-seeking? Do I live in a state of confusion and a life of being attacked by my spouse's evil words and actions? Does my spouse seek God's wisdom and apply God's guidance to our marriage? Is my spouse seeking and sowing peace in our marriage? Victims and others are quick to look up divorce Scriptures to make decisions or recommendations about abusive marriages, but they fail to review the other Scriptures that instruct how a spouse is to treat their wife, children, and the marital relationship. James 3:16-18 gives guidance as to how the spouse is to behave and relate to his wife: "For where envy and self-seeking *exist*, confusion and every evil thing *are* there. But the wisdom that is from above is first pure, then peaceable, gentle, willing to yield, full of mercy and good fruits, without partiality and without hypocrisy. Now the fruit of righteousness is sown in peace by those who make peace."

If you're a victim that has been bombarded by biblical Scriptures that talk about how God hates divorce and Paul's instructions regarding marriage and divorce, it's important to realize that these passages are referring to marriages in which the marriage covenant has *not* been broken. God does not include in the marriage covenant a right for a spouse to abuse his wife and children. It's the motive (dishonest, no good reason) for the divorce of a marriage under normal circumstances that God hates. The Scriptural verses regarding marriage and divorce do not refer to abusive relationships. Your abuser's refusal to suspend his abuse of you brought your relationship to an end. Your spouse's abuse has already broken his marriage covenant between you and God; by God's authority, *you* are now in charge of protecting the life He has given you and the lives of your children.

Jesus Himself recognizes that for a household to be a home, and a family to be a family, members have to feel warmly welcomed, loved, harmoniously received, unconditionally accepted, nurtured, and protected, or they will be divided and will fall. In Mark 3:24-25, Jesus said, "If a kingdom is divided against itself, that kingdom cannot stand. And if a house is divided against itself, that house cannot stand." When an abuser rejects the victim, he rejects the Holy Spirit that lives within her (Christ). Jesus concludes His discussion about a house that cannot stand, referring to the unpardonable sin in Mark 3:28-29, "Assuredly, I say to you, all sins will be forgiven the sons of men, and whatever blasphemies they may utter; but he who blasphemes against the Holy Spirit never has forgiveness."

If anyone attempts to remind you that God hates divorce and that the only exception in the Bible for divorcing is infidelity, do not rely on this person's lack of education on abuse or their ignorance about Jesus' profound love for you over an unsafe marriage. There are folks who are cruel in their judgment of victims who divorce their abusive spouses who return from the military with PTSD. They don't know the characteristics of an abuser and the difference between a spouse that was an abuser before deployment and then returns with the added diagnosis of PTSD. A soldier that was abusive before military service makes for a lethal combination for the victim when he comes home with PTSD. Jesus wants you to have a safe relationship and to live in a safe household. The Lord's instructions to your spouse are clear: he is to love you as Christ loved the Church. Jesus will take care of the actions of your abusive spouse. Instead of relying on other's comments about divorce and your abusive marriage, rely on the Lord's spoken words in Amos 3:3 through which He cries out and says, "Can two walk together, unless they are agreed?" There will be people who will criticize and condemn you for choosing to divorce your abusive spouse, but remember they were not there in the privacy of your unsafe home. Never mind what people think your intentions are or attitude is regarding divorce. God only cares about your intentions, motives, and the attitude in your heart.

When your attitude is about Him and your intentions are to honor Him, He is pleased. It's very common for some folks to be ignorant of the dynamics of abuse, and this issue coupled with their discomfort about the whole topic of divorce leads to blaming the victim. You may be re-victimized by these people who also abandon you emotionally like your abuser does—because they won't agree with your moving on with your life. Even if you have drained dry all the human support resources that you have turned to for help, God is still standing by you with His undeniable goodness and justice. He owns the Earth and the people you have turned to. He will point you in the right direction where you will find the divinely-inspired help He will provide. "He loves righteousness and justice; The earth is full of the goodness of the LORD" (Psalm 33:5). "God *is* not a man, that He should lie, Nor a son of man, that He should repent. Has He said, and will

He not do?" (Numbers 23:19). Pray to God. Ask Him to send you a divine laborer who will validate your abuse and assist you. He keeps His Word, and He will make it good for you!

The only time that a laborer will not be able to assist you is when you refuse assistance. Usually, assistance is refused by a resistant victim who has become *co-dependent* with the abuser (also known as a relationship addiction). You will know if you have become co-dependent with your abuser if your happiness and identity is defined by your abuser. You've become co-dependent if your total sense of being is invested in your abusive relationship and you cannot function independent of the relationship. Typically, the equation of a co-dependent relationship involves one passive individual and a more dominant individual who is fulfilled by controlling the other and being the one to make the decisions as to what happens in the relationship and how they live. Symptoms within yourself to look for that indicate a co-dependent relationship are as follow: confusion about your feelings toward your abuser, valuing his and others' approval more than valuing yourself, low self-esteem, fear of abandonment, feeling responsible for his or others' actions, inducing guilt on yourself for the relationship breakup and wanting to reconcile even at your own expense, and an inability to make decisions. A co-dependent person speaks in terms of feeling incomplete without the relationship. No one can complete another person; Christ is the only One Who can take a human life and grow it into a wholesome person.

If infidelity is involved, the co-dependent victim may become competitive and will reconcile with the abuser at her own emotional cost just so her competitor will not be the one dependent on her spouse. Some victim's feelings of their life being out of control lead them to compete with their counselor who advises not to return to the abuser; instead they sabotage their own self and do not follow the recommendation and return to the abuser to regain some control. When a victim is unable to make decisions about herself, household, or about the difference between a healthy and unhealthy relationship, she is enmeshed in a symbiotic relationship. That is the formula for an abuser and victim relationship. The abuser has a need to make the decisions and to control her, and she has a need for him to make the decisions and to be controlled. Generally, a co-dependent relationship is drawn as one stick figure plus another stick figure with an equal sign, which equates to one stick figure with two heads.

When you're co-dependent, you may feel unable to make decisions and *lonely* without the abuser and *afraid* that if you leave your spouse you will lose your job/career or even your ministry. You may ask yourself, "What will my employer think or do?" "How will my colleagues/co-workers/peers, friends and family, treat me, after I leave my spouse?" God cares more about you than everything that encircles your life. He can fix your work, ministry, and other relationship challenges, but He's unable to lead you to peace when you choose to remain co-dependent in an abusive relationship. God cares more about restoring your dignity and the person He created you to be (not a victim) than returning you to live with your abuser. Daughter of a sovereign God, in His Word, *you* are His chosen one! God instructs you not to remember the former things. If you let Him, He will do as He has promised you in His Word. God's perfect Will can renew your mind (Romans 12:2) and make a new thing for you; and even make a road for you, in your wilderness (Isaiah 43:18-19).

Most victims want to tell God what to do with their life, which includes keeping the abuser in their life. This type of negotiation with God only leads to a stagnation of growth in their lives. A victim who bargains with God to include her idolized abuser in the plan for her life compromises God from being Who she identifies with. She relies on her identity as being both in Christ and in her abuser. A victim who chooses to stay attached to her abuser does not give Christ a full opportunity to renew her mind and make a new thing; she will never get to experience how God could have re-purposed her life without the abuser. She will never get to experience what it truly means to not be *afraid*.

There will be the people who somehow missed the memo on your decision to divorce; they will be inquisitive and expect you to retell your story, which will feel like ripping the scab in your wounded heart. No matter how many friends, family, or church people forsake you, keep your eyes and ears open for God's presence and *His* perspective because *He* will *never* leave you. And when you're all alone, feeling unloved and lonely (because sometimes you will be) and deserted by loved ones who left you high and dry when they turned their backs on you because of the decision that you made regarding the abuser, remember that your faith does not rest on man's wisdom but on the power of your Heavenly Father. Those who counsel you against divorcing an abusive relationship hurl their own opinions from their own criticizing centers and not from the Lord's perspective. The Lord's perspective is that through His immeasurable compassion and the power of His Love, He is available to help you out of your abuse to rebuild a safe life for you and your children. He views you through His lens of love—no other point of view.

Be on the lookout because *He will* actually answer your prayers when you feel abandoned through those to whom you reached out and raced to in desperation for support. In addition, He will answer you mysteriously in unexpected ways through other people that He will send your way. God will ascertain that you are surrounded by numerous examples of others who have endured abusive episodes and now have more compassion for suffering such as yours; they will be generous and open about God's grace in their lives. You will be able to feed off their renewed joy and vitality of strength. God can *do* in *you* what He has done in them. I'm not telling you that choosing to divorce your abusive spouse is going to be a stress-free stroll through your neighborhood, but you will have your Creator God and other *Overcomers*' support to turn to. They will echo your victim's plea for safety!

Needless to say, you are still responsible as a child of God to love those that oppose your position on your divorce while speaking truth into your conversations or interactions with them. Do not continue attempting to win a crown of approval from those that oppose your divorce status. You may not receive the love and approval that you had hoped for, but you will win the greatest race any human can aspire to—in eternity. In this life, we have three choices: we can be like a vagabond and just pass through our life, it can be a training camp for hell, or a journey to eternity. Be a Paul! "I have fought the good fight, I have finished the race, I have kept the faith. Finally, there is laid up for me the crown of righteousness, which the LORD, the righteous Judge, will give to me on that Day, and not to me only but also to all who have loved His appearing" (2 Timothy 4:7-8).

The suffering that you have endured as a victim of abuse is trauma that has been placed upon you against the will of both you and God. Continuing to suffer as a wife fulfills no good purpose in your life; proceeding with an abusive marriage does not bring forth a greater good. An abusive marriage endangers the life of the victim and her children and ultimately destroys the family system. Abuse in a marriage is like a cancer that is malignant and has aggressively spread and cannot be medicated and cured. To accept an abusive marriage is to allow yourself to continue your life as a victim and ultimately end your life as a victim. Perhaps you have already brought up the subject of divorce to your abuser and he has either become explosive (which speaks volumes about the prognosis of the marriage), or he has become suddenly tender, begging for your pardon with promises to change. Stay strong and courageous; your abuser has broken his marriage covenant over and over and over, and you have witnessed no change.

Always remember that abusers are manipulative about feigning remorse and repentance. They apologize and use the word "forgiveness" to their advantage, knowing that they can rationalize being abusive again to the victim by asking for forgiveness. Repentance executes a conscious, action-based change of spirit mindset and the giving up of destructive patterns in exchange for a new constructive direction (immediately after asking for and receiving God's forgiveness). Repentance in both the Old and New Testament means to turn away from something; the change means never to repeat again. Repentance consists of deep conviction, genuine sorrow, an active turning away from being an abuser—a penitent, contrite heart. Evidence of change in an abuser is noted immediately through repentance and obedience to God; genuine repentance is always followed by obedience.

An abuser's disobedience is an outright resistance to God, separating himself independently from God. It's not only about his turning away from his sin of abuse, but it is also about turning to God. Most abusers are not genuine about changing; their prideful, willful obstinacy keeps their refusal to change fueled. The psalmist gives an example of an evildoer that manipulates with soft spoken, gentle words such as an abuser, "He has put forth his hands against those who were at peace with him; He has broken his covenant. *The words* of his mouth were smoother than butter, but war *was* in his heart; His words were softer than oil, yet they *were* drawn swords" (Psalm 55:20-21). Repentance must come from sincere conviction: anything less than that is not Holy Spirit-led and is just a regret being confessed to the victim, which becomes a repeated painful frustration.

Real salvation repentance comes naturally as a consequence of the abuser's broken spirit for the pain he has caused, and a transformation takes place immediately into the desire to only follow and do God's will. A person who repents through the inspiration of the Holy Spirit now desires to walk only in the path of holiness and to become Holy as his Creator. Is your abuser doing God's will and walking a holy life since his salvation? Repentance means that God's light has entered the abuser's heart; without true repentance, there is still darkness in his heart. An abuser must be real in his repentance. If he has truthfully recognized the seriousness of his sin in the raw, he will not remain self-righteous in hiding his sin; he will admit that he is sin-sick and truly repent.

True salvation includes conviction and repentance—genuine remorse and an admittance that he has sinned. An abuser is unwilling to admit his sin of abuse, other than verbal outrage at himself that he has committed what he sees as a blunder and should be forgiven (entitlement). Be warned. Do not be deceived. Your spouse's conversion may be real *or* based on an abuser's dynamics—it *can* be a fraud. No amount of your abuser's human effort or verbal talk of his reform or placebo effect equals his salvation. Salvation is not just about renouncing his sin in order to unite with Christ. It's also about surrendering pretense. This includes relinquishing his pride, attitude, and how he thinks and views everything. Humility means to suppress one's pride. The abuser is unable to do that. The abuser is like a heretic; he tends to accept one truth to the exception of others; he excludes the truth that accepting salvation is not evidence of his deliverance from being abusive. It is far worse for the abuser to take salvation into his own hands than to refuse salvation by faith.

Most abusers get desperate when the words "separation" or "divorce" are mentioned, *especially* the "d" word. Some abusers get desperate enough that they turn to religion and say that they have accepted Jesus in their heart. Be extremely cautious when your abusive spouse all of a sudden converts upon your mention of the "d" word. If it's indeed a genuine conversion, then his new walk with the Lord will be beneficial to him as he commits to the road of the Abuser's Program. However, his decision to accept Christ *does not* exempt him from the risk of being abusive to you again. He still needs to understand his horrific problem as an abuser and to work on his problem. Your abuser may mislead his pastor or others by saying that he has experienced an instant cure, but I'm here to tell you—along with all of my colleagues, the research, and former victims—that salvation *alone* is not the cure-all for an abuser.

Your presence as an abused wife is not required in order for your spouse to change. The suggestion not to separate by some clergy is based on a Scripture that encourages wives of unsaved husbands to patiently model their Christian lifestyle to influence their husband's conversion. An abuser does not need his victim wife to help him change. God does not need the victim's help to save the abuser. If the abuser wants to stop his abuse, he has to work with a person that is trained to work with abusers—one that can hold him accountable. If it is the sin of abuse that the abuser wants to restrain himself from, the victim's presence, as long as she is there, is actually an occasion for his sin. This is because the victim is the one whom he feels entitled to abusing. As long as she makes herself available, he will abuse her and continue his sinful behavior. Ironically, leaving him can be of more help to him.

I have met many a victim who has elected to stay in the bondage of abuse for a lifetime for the sake of forgiveness instead of bearing the temporary pain of separation and divorce. Some victims have told me that they believe the pain of separation and divorce hurts more than the traumatic abusive episodes they endure daily (even knowing abuse can be lethal). Working through the tormenting injuries of abuse and the damage that has been done to the victim's life is possible—there is a road to healing and recovery into wholeness. But only God has the ability to make the victim whole and complete again through the power of the Holy Spirit and the quality of His love, which is a "to have and to hold" love, a love with a non-abuse standard that teaches her to demonstrate the same to her loved ones and all whom she interacts with thereafter. A victim must allow God and her support system to take over the process so that His full works of love can be done in her life—no matter how much she aches or how long it takes. I am in no way attempting to whitewash the pain of separation and divorce; it is indeed painful. As with the death of a parent, son, or daughter, it *does* puncture the heart.

However, do not be pulled into your abuser's multiple requests for your forgiveness and return to him. Forgiving him and returning to his abuse does not help *him* or *you*. Your forgiveness is *not* what will cure your abuser. You are forgiving him for your sake, not his, and *not* for the act of forgiveness. Yes, you *must* forgive him, absolutely! But that forgiveness does not equate to everything being good between the two of you now; your forgiveness of him does not mean ignoring his abuse, but instead acknowledging it with a healthy perspective. Forgiving him means placing the abusive experience behind you and not allowing it to continue to re-victimize you. Your abuser may have pierced your heart, but God can heal it!

The God of the universe has seen every abusive act your spouse has inflicted upon you—just because no one else saw it does not mean it didn't happen. God knows your abusive spouse's heart and what you have experienced; He is all about loving, respecting, caring about, and protecting *you*. Furthermore, you had best hustle and bustle about your protective role as the mother of your children (if you have them) as they are a part of you in this abusive relationship. Your children are *innocent victims*, and they are unable to protect themselves; they depend on your wisdom as a parent to make healthy choices for their lives. Your children are a gift from God to you; you are accountable to God for them. It is best to remove your children from being exposed to additional abuse—which puts them in harm's way.

If you choose to protect yourself and your children, God will provide the way to safety, but *you* must take the first step. God can use various people in or out of your life *right now* to help you with your circumstances and needs. Don't expend your time and energy worrying about *if* He will come through for you—He will. You have a magnificent, supernatural connection to Him in your heart through the Holy Spirit (see Volume II Part I). You simply can't expect to *not* activate the Holy Spirit within you and still be in contact with God. God is *expecting* your contact with Him; pray to Him and ask Him to open up the doorway to safety for you. He already knows exactly what you're wrestling with. Ask Him to provide guidance—the Holy Spirit is like having a divine Personal assistant. "Now we have received, not the spirit of the world, but the Spirit who is from God, that we might know the things that have been freely given to us by God" (1 Corinthians 2:12). Ask Him to teach you *how* to take care of yourself. Ask Him to show you and lead you out of this abusive relationship. Ask Him to help you to always recall what you have learned about abusive relationships. Pray that God would help you to accept the new life He is offering you. He will answer you and provide you with resources galore so that you can lead yourself and your children out of your abusive relationship. The resources are there (see Resources list); all you have to do is accept the courage and strength that He will provide as you reach out to connect with your resources.

Don't dwell on the people that have induced guilt when you shared your abusive circumstances by saying you could not leave and divorce your spouse because it is a sin to do so. Some clergy will condemn you and tell you that divorce is sinful, that God hates divorce, and divorce should not be considered as an option in any marriage. These clergy even condemn other clergy that understand the circumstances of an abused wife and her children, and they call those clergy "lukewarm Christians" for helping to protect you as a victim. The clergy that are fixated on select divorce Scriptures are the type of clergy that refuse to become knowledgeable about the truths of the trauma of abuse and instead prefer to join the abuser as an accomplice in his denial by agreeing that men are being portrayed as abusers and women and children as victims.

There are numerous folks (Christians and non-Christians) and clergy that take pride in having memorized Malachi 2:16, quoting to you that the Lord hates divorce, and that's their opinion on your situation. Sadly, they only quote the first part of Malachi 2:16 and leave out the remainder of that verse: "For the LORD God of Israel says That He hates divorce For it covers one's garment with violence, Says the LORD of hosts. Therefore take heed to your spirit, That you do not deal treacherously." Being treacherous is being disloyal. It's clear by reading the complete verse that the Lord does not approve of (before or after divorce) the sin of violence or disloyalty—period. Abuse is about violence and disloyalty.

Clergy and people with this perspective on marriage and abuse are *not* operating from the compassionate side of abuse, which is where Christ operates from. Those that reject a victim's need to separate from her abuser further confuse her, violate her conscience of being worthwhile, and impact her wounded heart negatively with what she "should" do. You don't need this lack of support when you have God's and others' support. Behind every abusive act you tolerated there stood, and remains standing, your Heavenly Father Who is still molding the healthy, peaceful life He has designed for you to live. Select a support system that exhibits God's desire to help you and uphold you as one of His precious children. "Fear not, for I *am* with you; Be not dismayed, for I *am* your God. I will strengthen you, Yes, I will help you, I will uphold you with My righteous right hand" (Isaiah 41:10).

The clergy, counselors, and other folks who have a vested interest in saving your abusive marriage are in the same category as a Reconciliation Advisor (R.A.) (see Volume III Part II for descriptive definition of R.A.). If you're faced with a R.A., ask yourself, "If he had an abusive spouse would he return to live with his abuser, and what does that say about him?" Note of warning: A R.A. is not the only one who will not be willing to help you when you ask for help. Even people working in victim abuse organizations can have an uncaring, unhelpful day (burnout or personal problems). Keep seeking help—their unprofessional, inexcusable attitude is only satan's detour, and their offense is not about you. Don't ever give up seeking help; you're on the right path! satan will give you a feast of detours to choose from, making it tempting, confusing, and very difficult to follow God's path to safety. But with the guidance of His ever-present Holy Spirit, you will easily become aware of which path to take. Choose to only surround yourself with clergy and people that demonstrate God's unconditional love, forgiveness, grace, and compassion. Only listen to those that build you up and assist you and your family from being destroyed. Abuse pays no dividends, only destruction. Protect you and your family from being destroyed or experiencing a fatality by investing in the security of support. You need as much support as possible through the separation and divorce process, especially when, in most cases, an abusive spouse has a vicious heart and will not give his victim a divorce easily; he still wants to control her.

Always remember that Christ has never addressed us, his children, with an imperious demeanor. Notice how He spoke when He was discipling. He prefaced His teachings with "if," never with "you should." Christ never used "should" in his teachings to us because He is a God of grace—we as His disciples are to minister to others in the same way. Christ does not have a dictatorial attitude about anything in our lives—including divorce. Yes, He is a God of absolutes when it comes to His Commandments. But He is also a gentle God of unconditional love. He offers you an unconventional, divine love. Christ offers the *"if"* option with compassion and justice on certain matters of life that do not violate His morality commandments—let us do the same for others. Instead of being naysayers, how about saying: *"If* you are being abused...then..."

When Christ walked the Earth, He did not exclude *anyone* from approaching Him, even if they were plagued with sin in their lives. He was *not* judgmental of any choice (decision) they had made in their life. Christ welcomed *everyone* and extended His love and Arms to everyone, and through His charitable grace, He received them openly. In the same way that Christ exhibited His charitable giving spirit back then, He extends it today: "Jesus Christ *is* the same yesterday, today, and forever" (Hebrews 13:8). If ever any clergy, church person, or professing Christian has *not* extended their arms to you and has *not* accepted you to come as you are, I am *so sorry*. Christ does not have any predilection toward any of us. His entire goal is the forgiveness of our sins and bringing each one of us into complete union with Him and one another.

Jesus Christ says that it is fine to come as we are. Rejecting a victim with judgmental behavior is *not* from God. God is actually looking down on you and your abusive relationship *right now,* and His Spirit is grieved as much for your painful verbal and/or physical assaults as He is toward the prospect of divorce. However, God is love (1 John 4:8) and because that is what He is made of, He will gravitate toward you with His profound love and compassion more than and over the prospect of divorce. When you are being wounded, He is looking at you in the process of abuse—like a combat casualty. He is not focused on the prospect of your divorce. He yearns to save your soul more than saving a dangerous marriage. That's one of Jesus' main goals for your life—to save you, the very reason He hasn't returned to Earth just yet (2 Peter 3:9). He's still reaching out to you and our world because His salvation mission is not complete until everyone has had an opportunity to save their soul! And when He returns to Earth as He has promised, and He will, Jesus will not be judgmental of you or the world about their abusive marriages and divorces. He just wants you and the world to be on board with Him!

God's observation of your grief *is* His grief, and as He watches the evils in your life, He is also calculating the lesser of two evils. He *does* hate divorce, and the instructions are clear that husbands are *not* to deal with their wives treacherously: "But did He not make *them* one, Having a remnant of the Spirit? And why one? He seeks godly offspring. Therefore take heed to your spirit, And let none deal treacherously with the wife of his youth" (Malachi 2:15). God does not want to continue watching you suffer when your marriage is deplorably *worse* than the process and act of divorce. God never insists on the greater evil—satan does. God would rather *carry* the pain and burden of divorce than to watch you ruin your lifespan or cut it short through an abusive marriage. It requires *no* faith, supernatural courage, strength, or growth to stay as a victim in an abusive relationship. God's love and value for you—your worth to God—is the same in public as it is in private. He doesn't discount or love you less because you divorce your abuser. The Christian communities that are outraged over divorce are not truly upholding Christ's principles and Image; they are preserving a no-divorce public image of Christianity, the people, and the Church's front.

When you are at a level of pain in your abusive relationship that you would consider a divorce, and you're no longer listening to those that condemn you, you are actually on the threshold of growth. And you can now see God's optimism for your life. You begin to trust His holy optimism because He never gets overwhelmed by ghastly circumstances or deathly relationships. You have learned that one of your Heavenly Father's most remarkable characteristics is that He will always be constructive (at peace) in the midst of destructive relationships. If you earnestly seek His guidance in your darkest days, He will always bring in a flicker of His Spirit's light; so that you may see that through Him there is hope and His peace, which you can inherit for your life. Although you have been valiant in your hope and tolerance for the abusive relationship, you do not have to continue to suffer your entire life. Amongst the many life reasons, God's Word was given to us is to keep us from unnecessary oppressive suffering. If our nation passed a law forbidding divorce under *any* circumstances, our country's statistics for deceased abuse victims would escalate even higher.

That is the reality that God is already aware of and *all* should be aware of. Marriage was inspired and ordained by God Himself; therefore, He has a purpose for it. God's purpose for marriage is *not* for the wife to thrive at her worst self (whom she becomes when her heart is *not* motivated to love, pray, or be with God). A victim, or anyone, is not much credit to God if she lives with depressed or raging feelings inspired by satan. It's not possible to draw a victim close to God when she's exhibiting anything but His image. How can it possibly be God's will for a victim to just die with such agony in her life? His compassion, forgiveness, and superiority over *all* have authority over His eternal purpose for marriage, which is for *her* to become Christ-like (Romans 8:29). His purpose for marriage takes priority.

Marriage is a world institution. It is not like the original marriage that God created between Adam and Eve before they sinned; marriage is a temporary Earthly commodity (Matthew 22:30). When marriage does not fulfill God's designed divine plan for it, to prepare married couples as marriage partners with God (1 Corinthians 11:2), then it becomes purposeless and evil. How's that? If the marriage is making the victim into an unfit bride for her Bridegroom (Christ), it is satan's onslaught of evil. A victim is free to choose between the destructive marriage (evil) and her relationship with God. It's a matter of choosing a *temporary* relationship (abusive marriage) over an eternal one with Christ. What will you choose? One way to discern your choice is to do an evaluative self-study. Simply take inventory of yourself: is this abusive marriage bringing out the best or worst in you? Are you becoming better or worse as a person in this marriage? Ask yourself: "Am I contributing to God's will for my life by staying in an abusive relationship?" When abuse is staring you in the face and you're not even looking in the mirror, it's time to make a decision on how you want to live out the gift of life which God has given you.

Choosing the *temporary* makes marriage out to be more important than God's purpose for it, and it's basically being rebellious of His divine plan. Divorce would be wrong if the marriage is fulfilling God's will for your life by allowing you to grow in Christ and benefitting both you and your spouse as a couple united in your relationship with God. Divorce would be wrong if your reason for divorcing is not pure (honest). If your spouse treats you with respect, but you just don't want to be married anymore, it calls for some marriage counseling to restore the relationship that brought you together in marriage. The question is, are *you* and *your* spouse growing together and exhibiting Christ-like behaviors in this abusive marriage? Your spiritual growth and growing in His Image mean more to God than your personal desires to coexist in a marriage that's damaging your spirit. After all, it is your spirit that ascends into heaven—*or* your person into the lake of fire. Take a good look at yourself: is your marriage contributing to your spiritual growth? Your spiritual growth is God's goal and purpose for your marriage.

If you make a decision regarding divorce, how do you know if it is based on the will of God? Pray. Present your decision to God for His input. Yes, God *cannot* answer you *if* divorce is *His will* for your life if you don't first make a decision and then ask Him to give you feedback or the blessing on your decision, He will communicate with you through the Holy Spirit and others in your path. Ask Him to give you peace in this decision, if it is His will. You will know His will through the Holy Spirit because the peace of God is a feeling that is unmistakable. If something is out of God's will, He will *definitely* let you know through feelings of unrest and discomfort. Just be sure not to confuse feelings of doubt and turmoil with the worries over the questions of: "Is divorce God's will for me?" Or "What will happen to me if I divorce?" When indecisive, choose the answer that is closest to the inward voice of the Holy Spirit. Just be certain that you do not ask the Spirit to support you with an opinion that is not in agreement with Christ's thoughts about you.

The discomfort of safety is a separate matter that you can pray about if you are to receive God's peace; it should not enter into the decision on God's will for the divorce. He will handle the abuse repercussions regarding divorce separately. That is the way God's peace is sensed in our lives—it's always separate from our circumstances. We can experience His love and peace that surpasses all understanding in the midst of dire circumstances! Rest assured that the Holy Spirit will never deceive you in connecting you to God's feelings about a matter. You will know whether God approves of your decision or not—the Holy Spirit is known in God's Word as the Helper and Comforter, and you will sense comfort or discomfort from the Holy Spirit.

I have had many victims state that after praying over their decision to divorce, they feel nothing. Feeling nothing is acceptable, and it means God is allowing you to choose and He will support either decision because you turned to Him in prayer. He is not a pushy God. He is a gracious Father Who has given His children free will. Just remember that when you are in eminent danger, He will let *you* know through His Spirit. That is, *if* you stay in touch with Him. This is the awesome God that we serve! He will use *whatever* decision you make to somehow accomplish His purpose in *you*. If and when you have made your decision based on God's will for your divorce, be at peace and don't let satan's lies overwhelm you through interpreting the natural painful process of divorce as God's condemnation. Remember, satan is the counterfeiter of facts!

Remind satan that God is *not* a prosecuting attorney or a judge sitting in his bench; He is both a loving Father and the King of Kings sitting at His throne, so satan should *be gone* from persecuting you any further. The Bible tells us to resist the devil, and he will flee from us (James 4:7), *especially* if you quote God's Word to him! You will have grief and other turmoil from the divorce process, but that's not from God; those are human feelings dealing with divorce. Know that satan will do everything in his corrupt power to steal your victory in Christ; he does not want you or your children to have faith, be in God's will, or have His power in your life. satan knows that God's power is able to take a victim's despair and transform it into a hopeful and victorious life.

The devil is in the business of sustaining destructive marriages; he is in the reconciliation of abusive marriage business. satan doesn't care whether the victim saves herself from herself; abusive marriages are his doctrine. satan roams around abusive marriages, strategizing how he can maintain the spouses living unrighteous lives, blending their *godly ways* with their *ungodly ways* and ultimately producing unrighteous children which he can devour. The devil knows that children are the most vulnerable and are the future leaders which God has called to lead righteous lives. Corrupting a marriage through abuse builds on satan's plan to create an unrighteous (sinful) society plagued by family violence. Abusive relationships fulfill satan's goal for the nation—to lead future generations away from God and righteousness.

Some states in the USA make the decision about separating the victim from the abuser more feasible by providing victim support. This is based on the research findings that in most cases, a victim of abuse may not be able to decide about her own and her children's safety. These states adhere to the Family Violence Prevention and Response Act. The legislation of the Family Violence Prevention and Response Act is designed to protect women and children involved in family violence. It is very explicit in its safety advocacy instructions and spells out some clear-cut responsibilities of police officers in the handling of family violence between an abuser and a victim. This law includes in its provisions separating the abuser through a mandatory arrest with probable cause, an option for a protective order for the victim, arraignment of the abuser on the next court day following arrest, enrollment in a pretrial Offender Education Program for first-time misdemeanor abusers, *and* the provision of allowing the victim to choose an assistant such as a Family Violence Victim Advocate. This law, *if* implemented by your state, is a national model that requires the supportive cooperation of all individuals, organizations, and agencies that come into contact with any victim of family violence.

If this is not an option in your state, contact Women's Law (see Resources) and learn how you can obtain an *emergency protective order*. This order can go into effect as soon as you apply for it and it lasts from five to seven days to buy you some time to file for a restraining order. When a restraining order is put into place, it can include for your abuser to be forced to leave your mutual residence. These legal protective steps provide you the time to contact either the National Domestic Violence Hotline to get a list of organizations that have contacts with shelters, or The Domestic Shelters organization (see Resources) can direct you to a nearby shelter by you entering your zip code. A shelter would be a temporary safer place to live where you will receive guidance for your next steps as you plan for financial provision and a new residence for you and your children.

There are some risk analysis questions I want to ask you at this point to aid you in your *mindful thinking* about your separation and/or divorce decision. These are as follows: If you decide to *stay* with your abusive spouse, do you believe that *staying* in the abusive relationship would bring out the best or worst in you? How? If you stay in this abusive marriage, is your life going to get better or worse for you? How? If you *leave* the abusive lifestyle, do you believe *leaving* would make things better or worse for you? How?

Not all victims decide to end their abusive relationship through divorce or decide to lead their children into an Overcomer lifestyle. Those that do are marked by the following processes:

1. *Victim Reaches her Limit*—Abuse has accrued and increased; she's worn down with depleted coping skills; affection for her abuser has been destroyed.
2. *Yoke is Accepted*—The victim gives her burden to God, seeks help, and learns from her newly established support system. She's willing to rewrite her life script; she reframes her past and finds rest in her spirit as her burden is made light (Matthew 11:29-30).
3. *Boundaries are Set*—Victim suffers the final tragic episode of *all* abuse from abuser toward her and/or children.
4. *Silent No More*—Seal of silence is broken, trusted others are confidentially informed of abuse and plan to escape; she's officially doing *mindful thinking* and is free of emotional confinement. She receives validation, support, and

assistance in return. This is the beginning of the healing process. Self-confidence is lifted.
5. *Develops Safety Escape Plan*—She clandestinely works with advocates and resources. With supportive assistance, she has a plan in place that she can use twenty-four-seven to escape from her abuser. She has regular *mental safety escape drills* that are realistic and well-prepared.
6. *Fairy Tale Disenchantment*—She has come to realize that she will not be able to *fix* the abusive marriage in order to live happily ever after. She grieves. Although it is painful, she no longer dwells on the loss of her abusive marriage and now focuses on her new realistic script of permanently overcoming her abuse.
7. *Overcomer Peace*—Her strategic escape from abuse plan and spiritual growth pay off; her identity, coping skills, and her *peace of mind* are restored.

This discussion on divorce due to an abusive marriage is *not* a quick fix view or an attempt to downplay or glaze over the act of divorce; it is simply applying God's love and compassion on the decision and the act. *He* is the One willing to bear the act of divorce for a victim and her family's life that's being destroyed. Safety for a victim and her children (if she has them) is an emergency decision. Deciding on a separation and/or divorce is not stress-free. Making a decision about separation and divorce while in the war zone of abuse is *not* like playing hot potato either; it's more like being thrown a ticking bomb which *will* explode, so a quick, on-the-uptake decision has to be made. Most victims are able to (through receiving comprehensive information on the dynamics of abuse and the abuser) *generally* take a leap of faith and ultimately make an astute decision regarding separation or divorce.

Yes, there is a deep grief like a death when divorce takes place. The end of any intimate relationship is always experienced as a sorrowful human loss. There's a feeling of inconsolable deep sadness, but when God's love is involved, there's also His Holy Spirit's infiltrated, comfort, joy, hope, compassion, and peace. Boldly get on your knees before His throne and ask Him to take away your sorrow. While it may seem like wishful thinking that your sadness would suddenly disappear and that your spirit would be uplifted with His joy, don't forget that you serve a God of power and might. You will be taken aback at how He uses this short prayer request to fill your heart with His unsurpassable love and peace. "You have turned for me my mourning into dancing; You have put off my sackcloth and clothed me with gladness" (Psalm 30:11). Your sorrow and sighing will flee—you shall have His joy and peace! When you got married, you didn't sign up for the heart-wrenching daily living you've undergone, but take heed—God will use your pain to give you insurmountable courage and strength that will deepen your faith. He will give you joy in proportion to your former abusive warfare and replace the darkness of the evil days with light and goodness! It's lamentable that a victim has to experience such trauma in her life in order to grow out of the cycle of abuse and become an *Overcomer*, but not a single traumatic moment in a victim's past is *ever* wasted in her future life as an *Overcomer*. Once a victim emerges from her place of abusive darkness into the path of light as an *Overcomer*, she will arrive at a place of peace which she had never known before.

The worst-case scenario for a victim is if she gives up and tolerates the abuse; thinking or speaking about giving up is not an option for an *Overcomer*—it's not in her vocabulary. You are infused with super-spiritual strength! Use it. Through your Spirit, you are strengthened not to give up because the Holy Spirit God has given you that power. When God created you, He gave you power over *all* things. You have dominion (sovereign authority). You have Holy Spirit power over your abusive circumstances—power over every moving, living thing. When God created us, He commanded us to: "Be fruitful and multiply; fill the Earth and subdue it; have dominion over the fish of the sea, over the birds of the air, and over every living thing that moves on the earth" (Genesis 1:28).

The majority of victims come out stronger after the separation and divorce than when they entered the wilderness of abuse. Victims usually come to recognize that the pain and crushing losses that they experienced through divorce can be used to weed out any pre-existing sans identity, pride, and warped priorities. All of the hot tears running down their faces soften their wounded and now scarred hearts so that they can empathize and comfort others. "Blessed *be* the God and Father of our Lord Jesus Christ, the Father of mercies and God of all comfort, who comforts us in all our tribulation, that we may be able to comfort those who are in any trouble, with the comfort with which we ourselves are comforted by God" (2 Corinthians 1:3-4). Victims can become *Overcomers* of abuse who reach a point in their life through which they can look back and actually *thank* God for their past suffering and for whom they have become, *trusting Him* to use their past for their new purposeful life.

Every victim of oppression has been given the power to overcome her abusive world! Christ, the One who keeps our Earth turning on its axis, has the power to help the victim overcome her traumatic world. A victim overcomes her trauma world by faith; she opens up her eyes to the Lord Jesus' character and incomparable love. She realizes that her abusive life is to be renounced and overcome. Her abusive world is engulfing and suffocating but merely temporary compared to what's eternal, so she chooses to look beyond it. An *Overcomer* strives to acquire and emulate the Lord's character while here on Earth, pressing toward living in peace and more abundantly—as He has called her to do—pressing toward what's eternal. She now strives to live in His Image, under *His* example so as to overcome her world. For *if* she doesn't, her abusive circumstances will overcome her to her ruin (1 John 5: 4-5, John 17:1-3, Revelation 2:26, 3:5, 3:12, and 21:7-9). Once an *Overcomer*, she and others will sense Christ's presence within her because she now reflects His radiant personality, and this illuminating light will bless not only her but everyone who comes in contact with her.

Without further ado, I will wrap up this discussion on divorce by reminding those victims that are staying in their abusive marriage because they made the "till death do us part" vow that this vow is *not* found in the Bible; it is a man-made thought and promise. Consider the truth that we humans can't even, through our own strength, endure the pain of minor car accident stitches without some form of anesthetic pain killer, and yet we solemnly vow in court or church the strength to tolerate whatever, even the daily pain of abuse for a lifetime until death? Having no love, mercy, and compassion for a victim of abuse (in the name of religion) when she's contemplating a divorce is acting as if Christ is no longer our forgiving King of Kings, Lord of Lords. Our Father has never lost His position of Grace—as God. He is the only One Who has divine authority over an abusive marriage and divorce because He is a sublimely sovereign overlord! He does not decide on an abusive marriage and divorce like humans do; His compassions are new every morning. God's thoughts and ways are far higher than humans'. "'For My thoughts *are* not your thoughts, Nor *are* your ways My ways,' says the LORD. 'For *as* the heavens are higher than the earth, So are My ways higher than your ways, and My thoughts than your thoughts'" (Isaiah 55:8–9).

When a victim feels duty-bound because she recalls the vows she said at the altar and is guilt-ridden because she said she would stay with her groom *for better for worse, in sickness and in health*, but yet feels a stranglehold at the same time, this is not

THE VICTIM: EVERYTHING YOU EVER WONDERED

God's purpose for her as a wife. Moments like this can be turned into a stepping stone for the victim to undergird herself with the *truth* that the vows were not written and intended to include allegiance to a life of emotional and/or physical torture and for her to endure in order to uphold the vow of *'til death do us part.* God in His Holy writ has left us with His objectives for each of us, and His Word is replete with instructions for living our daily lives; and they do not include tolerating abuse. Bolstered up by faith, the victim can succeed in acquainting herself with the disheartening truth that the toxic, abusive relationship does not have to be suffered out but instead overcome, and through recognizing this truth, the victim can begin to separate herself from a lifetime of abuse and discover hope for herself and offer the same to others who are consumed by their abuse via vow loyalty.

No. Jesus does not expect the victim to tough it out and suffer the abuse—that was His role. He actually suffered an abusively barbaric crucifixion. But, He had a purpose for that suffering (to demonstrate His love for the world, suffer and die for the forgiveness of our sins, and to offer the plan of salvation to us), and He fulfilled that purpose. Yes, there are those martyrs that are called to defend the gospel and suffer to the point of death, refusing to deny God, which is not the same as being forced to suffer victim abuse. It is *not* God's will that a victim suffers. Christ's suffering was purposeful. His death brought victory. The suffering of a victim brings tragedy. Oswald Chambers said it clearly in his devotional book *My Utmost for His Highest* when he spoke on needless suffering:

"To choose to suffer means that there is something wrong; to choose God's will even if it means suffering is a very different thing. No healthy saint ever chooses suffering; he chooses God's will, as Jesus did, whether it means suffering or not."

It is God's will and good pleasure that his children live abuse-free lives, even when it means suffering the loss of a relationship(s). Even though He understands suffering, His will is that we must not suffer heartrending abuse in vain. Christ's ministry on Earth began with suffering. He knows all about it! He has understood the pain of being a victim while still in Mary's womb. His parents had to go in exile in order to protect Him from King Herod who sought to kill Him. Christ was born as a homeless victim because His parents elected to escape harm's way and sought safe shelter for Him. A victim is technically homeless in an abusive home; she must live and sleep under her abuser's forcible restraint and threat for her life. She longs for refuge, a safe shelter. Christ, more than society, understands victimization. On His way to and while on the cross, He was a Man of suffering! There is enough suffering that you and your loved ones will be exposed to or experience as a part of living in this world: terminal illness, mental illness, natural disasters, unemployment/poverty, terrorism/wars, school/public place shootings, death, and the list goes on. You don't need to add the suffering of abuse to your list. Some crises and catastrophes in the world are out of our control, but abuse trauma is treatable, and death from abuse is preventable. A victim has no reason to put herself in the line of fire when an abusive spouse refuses to stop; that's when it's time to forgive and move on.

What does it mean to *move on* from abuse when the relationship has to end through boundary separation or termination of the relationship? It doesn't mean that you don't feel the pain of the loss; it doesn't mean that this is a fair or just resolution; it doesn't mean you forget that person; it doesn't mean you stop praying for that person. Moving on simply means that in time, the pain of your loss will subside, you will realistically accept the reason for the loss of the relationship, and you will be able to experience a peaceful, new normal as you form new healthy relationships. Moving on also means that you have accepted your loss and have genuinely forgiven yourself and your abuser, that you believe that God and the Holy Spirit within you are good even when life as a victim wasn't fair, that you understand both happiness and sadness are a part of the life experiences of this world, and that you will grow spiritually in your relationship with God as a result of this experience.

Pray with me, "Father God, moving on from my marriage seems too painful and impossible to do. Please continue to prompt me through Your Holy Spirit so that I don't have to move on through my own strength, but that I can do so through Your love, grace, and strength within me. Help me to allow Your Holy Spirit free reign in my life so that I can experience Your peace. In the Supreme Power of Your Name, Amen."

Post-Traumatic Stress Disorder (PTSD) & the Victim

When a victim has been in an abusive relationship, there are so many feelings that linger: confusion, humiliation, shame, anxiety, fear, guilt, anger, lack of trust, deprivation, ruminating thoughts about abusive episodes, nightmares, hypervigilance, sadness, or depression. After she has successfully gotten out of that destructive relationship, she assumes that those feelings will naturally go away. When those feelings do not disappear, she begins to believe that perhaps the problems in the relationship were indeed all of her fault; after all, she has the same symptoms whether she's with him or not. She may even begin to long for her abuser and think that she perhaps made a mistake in her decision to end the relationship. She mistakenly thinks she is lonely and misses him, not giving attention to the fact that he has managed to cut her off from significant relationships and this isolation and disconnect is the cause of her loneliness.

At this point, she can become scared that she went out of the frying pan and into the fire. She could even experience feelings of desperation, depression, and hopelessness; she can't imagine how her life will change for the better at this point. The victim wonders *how* she can make it on her own without a loving husband. She begins to think that maybe *she* can make things better, that *she* can replace those doomsday negative feelings with a vision of a faithful husband. She agonizes and asks herself the question: "Is there real living without a good marriage?" She ruminates over those times when her abuser said that she was "a basket case," "crazy," "a moron," "ridiculous," "incompetent," "an idiot," "naïve," "gullible," "heard or saw things differently," or called her by any foul name—and wonders *if* this is true about herself. In a transition state of fearing the unknown, she may tell herself, "Maybe he was right; maybe I am all those things he said I was—*that's why* I'm unhappy." She continues to have that feeling of impending doom in which she fears her abuser will return to attack her as he has threatened and is capable of. This is quite common for victims that have undergone any type of traumatic abuse; it doesn't naturally go away because it is a result of post-traumatic stress disorder (PTSD).

PTSD takes on many forms, depending on the individual; for some, they may have insomnia, intrusive terror thoughts, nightmares, psychosomatic manifestations, clinical depression, anxiety, or panic attacks; or, it becomes chronic, and they never recover and go into states of psychosis. As with all symptoms, they range from mild to severe. The worst fear for any traumatized victim is that the moment of hideous abuse will recur. Chronic abuse does place a victim in the position of realizing her worst fear. Her trauma does recur in her mind, and in some cases, the abuser does return to attack. This, in turn, magnifies her PTSD hyperarousal, hypervigilance, anxiety levels, and overall agitated symptoms.

It is important to note that a victim's anxiety and panic are not the same as the typical anxiety disorder diagnosis. A victim's physical symptoms are not the same as the typical psychosomatic disorders; a victim's depression is not the same as a typical depressive disorder; it's not typical because it's manifested as a result of the abuser's presence in *your* life. These symptoms run parallel to the abuser and are not self-imposed or a result of some other factor or dynamic. The symptoms are *not* caused or aggravated by a mental factor or originating from a mental or emotional cause within you. You'll notice that they're only experienced whenever you think about him, whenever *he* is in the vicinity or *you're* nearby your abuser (Treatment interventions for PTSD resulting from prolonged victim abuse are discussed in Volume III Part II.).

A Safety Escape Plan (SEP)

Are you willing to read about *how* you can develop a plan to escape your abuse and learn to live in safety? You can either create the SEP on your own by using this book or call the abuse hotline to get the contact phone number for a local women's abuse shelter and allow the caseworker to assist you in developing your SEP. Are you ready? Don't just say, "I'll think about it someday. Someday I'm going to break away for the sake of my children." "Someday" has arrived today! By the end of this part of the book, we will have generated a plan of action for *your safety*. Let's begin by soliciting God's help on your behalf. Allow me to pray for you:

Heavenly Father, I lift up this dear one who has come to a point in her life whereby she's exhausted of being oppressed and being constantly in pain, which is inflicted upon her by her spouse. I ask for your deliverance now from her unclear thinking, times of denial, the fears, faulty thinking, and unrealistic hopeful dreams of being happily married, which has further entrapped her in this abusive situation. Provide now the wisdom to help her to protect herself from her abuser's mental and/or physical abuse. Help her to recognize that her body is the temple of Your Spirit and ought not to be dishonored (1 Corinthians 6:19). Teach her that Your Word states that her spouse is to love her as his own body (Ephesians 5:28). Give her the insight that an abusive spouse does not love his wife because love does not hurt others (Romans 13:10). Provide her the strength and courage to remove herself from her danger. Send her trustworthy, supportive contacts that will not betray her confidence. Grant her places of resources with refuge and support. Father, you have power over everything, including abuse. May Your ability to do the unimaginable for this one that comes to You for help fill her with Your hope and peace of mind. I stand on Your Word which promises that You will supply all of her needs according to Your riches in glory (Philippians 4:19). Thank You, Father, for honoring Your Word. It is in the authority of Christ's name that I thank You in advance for answering this prayer. Amen.

If you have become acquainted with The Author and Finisher of your life (God), it is probable that you have come to realize that you're not an accident and that instead you're one of His planned creations with a purpose and that He is here to help you! He's actually here to serve you—it's His good pleasure to do so. While going to a certain restaurant, I have often thought about God when the restaurant staff greets me with, "How may I serve you today?" And, when they repeatedly state, "My pleasure" after I say, "Thank you," I've thought that this must be the way God answers each time we come to Him in prayer. I've thought about His offered friendship with His humble attitude of grace and mercy and how He makes Himself available in service to us. "For even the Son of Man did not come to be served, but to serve" (Mark 10:45a). "No longer do I call you servants, for a servant does not know what his master is doing; but I have called you friends" (John 15:15a). I have not only thought about the fact that God is *always* available to serve us in this life's journey, but I've thought about how comforting it is to feel His presence when our hand is clasped in His. "'For I, the LORD your God, will hold your right hand, saying to you, 'Fear not, I will help you'" (Isaiah 41:13).

He invites us to pray to Him, to tell Him how He can serve us, and He promises to answer when we call on Him: "Call to Me, and I will answer you" (Jeremiah 33:3a). It is both His good pleasure to serve you and to answer your prayers while He takes you by the hand and helps you to safety. Pray to Him; His help is available. Prayer is somewhat like instantly connecting to the internet. When you pray, even though your feet remain firmly planted at your location, your Spirit is immediately released to connect directly with your Heavenly Father. However, the difference is that sometimes the internet is down, but God's connection is never down. Prayer is the super power gift He has given you. It is your spiritual gem. Prayer will uplift your Spirit and quiet your mind. At this very moment, the most powerful assurances of God's presence are already there within your reach—His Spirit and the commodity of prayer. God will not remove your abusive circumstances without you taking the first step, but He will equip you to face your abuse and show you the direction you need to take in order to live an abuse-free life. Just chat with Him in prayer right now and say, "God, about my abuse, grant me the strength to follow You into the unknown, Amen." God has been longing to hear from you, and He doesn't care whether your prayers are confused utterances or blundering, desperate crying words; He is there to quiet your Spirit and to organize your anxiety-producing thoughts into abuse problem-solving strategies. So send up those pleas for help via power prayers; Your Servant and Friend is listening!

That being said, we can proceed to discuss how you're going to trust God's wisdom to guide you through the uncharted waters of a *Safety Escape Plan* (SEP). It is perfectly fine with Him if you seek *Him* to work out this SEP; in fact, He welcomes your prayers for His assistance. Confide in Him through prayer because it will enable you to think clearly and make wiser choices. Even if you don't have the *drive* to create a SEP, together let's develop a safety plan for you (and your children if you have them) so that you can escape your abusive lifestyle (even if you may not at the moment sense or see what your future as an *Overcomer* of abuse holds). This is a good time to consider the aphorism: "The best defense is a good offense." Counter the abusive threats—*refuse* to do nothing about your safety. A SEP is a tool to equip you against your danger; you will at least have a SEP ready to use. Some victims may choose to protect themselves with additional back-up support through pre-arranged persons that can intervene once the escape plan goes into effect. This could be making use of assistance from a police officer or asking for the intervention of a nearby neighbor, friend, or relative. The SEP is a combined formula that is used based on the variety of victim cases and the information that has been gathered on victim abuse.

Since each abusive relationship has the same dynamics but varied circumstances, not every safety strategy applies to every victim; options and flexibility are made available. If there are children involved in this abusive relationship, strategically design your plan to safeguard the risk for their safety too. Incorporate *all* of the elements of the safety precautions for yourself into the plan of escape to take the children with you. Solicit the assistance of a women's crisis center hotline and use the counselor's suggestions in setting up additional strategies to safely get you and the children to a shelter or designated location. There's a *huge* risk that your abuser will attempt to harm the children, manipulate them to betray you, or use the judicial system against you; this needs to be considered as a part of the safety planning process. If you decide *not* to activate the SEP in your life at this time, then that's fine, too. It's whenever *you* are ready.

The purpose for drawing up the SEP in advance is so that it will be ready for you to use when you feel led to follow it. After all, it is your life and your choice. Establishing a SEP is a tremendous leap of faith to consider. Nonetheless, in this safety plan, even if you cannot see the goodness that safety will bring, God and your support system see it, and *He* has it all planned out for you as an *Overcomer*! Trust Him. Ask God to open your eyes to see what *He sees* and your ears to *hear* His voice. Remember that God is all for you. He is not going to judge you; He is actually providing an exit sign for you through the SEP. Sometimes you'll feel as if you're sinking with no foothold. Other times you may feel confused while contemplating the stages of your safety plan. *Confusion* is *not* from God; it's from your enemy. "For God is not *the author* of confusion but of peace" (1 Corinthians 14:33). *Talk to God* in prayer about the SEP. By talking to God, you will eliminate a multitude of worries and confusion because you will begin to realize and recognize Christ's power in our life and that He *is* by your side in every step you take toward freedom from your abuse; meet Him with unfailing certainty over His Hand in your life—and He will meet you there to come through for you.

Ask God to give you clarity of mind to make the right decisions for your life. Ask Him to eliminate the state of fear that lines the path before you. Ask Him to provide you with hope and the courage to confront your future. Ask Him to show you through this SEP His creative vision for your life. Ask Him to imprint wisdom in your mind as to what He wants you to do, which doors to close, and which doors to walk through. An Overcomer's life is marked by Second Corinthians 5:7, "For we walk by faith, not by sight." Focus on *where* He wants you to go and ask Him for the courage to drive your life in *that* direction. Ask Him to help you with the challenges of the SEP. Ask God to give you *His* marching orders for your life. Sometimes, you have to take an unknown route to get there!

Pray that you will seek His wisdom through His Word before you even make a move or not on the SEP. However, common sense does apply as well when considering a SEP and renouncing your victim role. If you and your children are being physically abused, you've run out of options. God wants to love, protect, and secure your safety more than you want it for yourself. Seek His guiding light as you make your rounds through your maze of abuse, and simultaneously inspect and pay attention to your need for a SEP.

Ask the Lord to embed in your heart the truth and assurance that He will always walk ahead of you, lead the way, and never leave you betrayed. "And the LORD, He *is* the One who goes before you. He will be with you, He will not leave you nor forsake you; do not fear nor be dismayed" (Deuteronomy 31:8). If you're still feeling strongly forsaken by your abuser, *and even by God*, think about David's poignant words in Psalm 22. David's words were the same words that Jesus cried out on the cross, "My God, My God, why have You forsaken Me?" (Matthew 27:46; Mark 15:34). David found himself in such a painful situation, such as *you*, that it caused him to blare out at God in this way. His question to God: "*Why are You so* far from helping Me?" (Psalm 22:1) indicates that just like you, he felt abandoned, forsaken, and even ignored. "O My God, I cry in the daytime, but You do not hear; and in the night season and am not silent" (v.2). *However*, for every ounce of David's hopelessness, in this *same Psalm* he goes on to credit God as his deliverer from his desolation!

Through and through, David learns that God is *indeed* holy (v.3), *trustworthy* (vv. 4-5), *a deliverer* (v.8), and *his strength* (v. 19). David learns that *God answered him* (v. 21) and that God does *not* despise or abhor the affliction of the afflicted, nor did God hide His face from him, but that God *actually* heard his cry after all (v. 24)! Are you still feeling traumatized by your abuser's character that did forsake you? Call out to the Lord such as David did; rehearse God's character in your mind and "Trust in the LORD with all your heart, And lean not on your own understanding; In all your ways acknowledge Him, And He shall direct your paths" (Proverbs 3:5-6).

As you work on becoming independent, you'll find yourself wanting to meet all of your own needs. Still, your abuser's swarming troubles hover over you like a plague everywhere. You may begin to feel needy. Most humans, especially those that have been victimized, deplore feeling needy. At this stage, ask God for *His* source of power. Tell Him all about it like the psalmist did in Psalm 109:22, "For I *am* poor and needy, And my heart is wounded within me." The psalmist knew that as long as he abided in *Him,* all would be well with him. Do not be prideful; pride never gets a victim *anywhere.*

Ask Christ to grant you the ability to keep your focus on the SEP and overcoming your abuse, *not* on what you lack. Ask for His reassurance that He's taking care of you. *Fear* is your enemy, and when abuse arrived at your doorstep of life, it disabled you from moving forward and interfered with your doing what is *right* in your relationship to your abuser. Fix your eyes on the One you can trust with your life, and listen to Christ just as the disciples had to when they were on the boat during a tempestuous storm and in the face of *fear* of drowning! He said to them: "Be of good cheer! It is I; do not be afraid" (Matthew 14:27).

You have been through a brutal, unnatural, abusive relationship experience. Your relationship was like a pandemonium you wish had never happened. An excruciating, unnatural relationship justifies an unnatural Safety Escape Plan. Most marital or family relationships don't call for a Safety Escape Plan; in fact, it's totally unnecessary! But we're not talking naturally when we're working with an abuser. A natural relationship consists of *trust*—a factor that's nonexistent in an abusive relationship. Therefore, a SEP, although uncomfortable for some victims, is deemed necessary. I'm not saying setting up a SEP is like a walk through the park. For some it may even appear as taking the lonely path of exile. What I am saying is that you, unlike those that are in a non-abusive marriage, have to be proactive, and you must lay down certain things that others don't have to be affronted by. Right now, as a victim, it may appear as a raw step to formulate a SEP, but it's only those who take that unflinching step that now live abuse-free lives. You may be tempted to run away as opposed to following an intentional SEP. A victim really has nowhere to hide. Running away is not a solution; in most cases, it just amplifies the circumstances. Running away is an emotionally-based decision. Running away to escape the abuse with no strategic plan only takes the danger along with you. When developing your SEP, ask yourself: What are the facts which indicate a SEP has to be created? Creating a SEP does not involve feelings; it is a response to what you know about your abuse—it's a healthy response to what you know about your abusive relationship, not what you feel. Developing a SEP is a pre-emptive approach to mitigate the danger of attempting to escape in the midst of one of your abuser's explosive episodes.

The only way to escape the abuse is to stop hiding the abuse, acknowledge the waywardness of the abuser, and work out a strategic SEP to overcome the abuse. Don't be afraid to proceed with preparing your SEP. Pushing through your SEP is pushing toward your *Overcomer* goals. Remember the old saying that having courage doesn't mean being fearless; it means being afraid but doing it anyway. Even if you're scared, it's okay to just bow down to God in prayer and believe in Him over what you feel (fear) and see (abuse). You may be thinking that you're going to lose your Earthly home, but just think of it as losing a material possession and gaining your life and a heaven-sent dwelling which you will re-establish as you proceed with your new *Overcomer* life. Ask God to give you the willpower and to help you to consider the loss of your abuser and the loss of all things as rubbish compared to gaining Christ's presence in your life.

THE VICTIM: EVERYTHING YOU EVER WONDERED

"Yet indeed I also count all things loss for the excellence of the knowledge of Christ Jesus my Lord, for whom I have suffered the loss of all things, and count them as rubbish, that I may gain Christ" (Philippians 3:8).

Open your eyes, dear one, and see your abuse and how Christ trusts confidently in you to overcome your abuse. See His love and purpose for your life—which will victoriously unfold before your very own eyes—just as soon as you take that very first step of faith in His plan for your life. Once you have a safety plan, you will no longer be walking around numb or like a lost sheep; you're no longer a runaway or shepherdless. Your good Shepherd is looking down on you with compassion as you create your SEP. "But when He saw the multitudes, He was moved with compassion for them, because they were weary and scattered, like sheep having no shepherd" (Matthew 9:36).

If ever in doubt, even after you adapt a SEP, rest assured that God sees *everything* in your SEP, and if anything needs re-direction, He will notice and lead the way! Isaiah 40:22 says that *"It is He who sits above the circle of the Earth."* God doesn't miss a thing, not about your abuse, your new SEP, or *anything* about *you*. Nothing gets past God's knowledge. Remember the psalmist's alert to us all that there's no place we can go without God knowing where we are (Psalm 139:7-8). He will *guide you* on the development and implementation of your SEP. "The LORD will guide you continually" (Isaiah 58:11). Isn't that grand?

No matter what a victim tries to tell herself or others about managing her abusive circumstances, the human condition of abuse only grows worse without a resolve and intervention. The ray of hope is that although she has been enslaved, with a purposed judiciary strategic plan, she can be set free. God did not create humans to be under their own self-willed authority. He created us to seek His discernment, not the enemy's, so that we could live in this world under the safety net of His Holy Spirit guidance and His empowered protection. The purpose of this book is not to outline a safety plan for your circumstances but to guide you into finding your specific plan which will cause you to find your own safety path. God has already implanted the direction and the way within you. All you need to do is recognize the path which He has laid out before you and go forward. "For you shall not go out with haste, Nor go by flight; For the LORD will go before you, And the God of Israel *will be* your rear guard" (Isaiah 52:12).

Some online dictionary definitions of *rear guard* are, "a position at the rear, the rear division of a military unit." God promises that He will garrison His Holy Spirit and be your rear guard such as in a military unit. He will be behind your enemy lines and have your back, to protect you and your conscience, as you step out of your fearful, painful past and as you step up and move forward to be with Him at the front of your warfare. He is your personal Bodyguard! He will become your clearing house for your decision to follow through with your SEP. When you leave your irreparable past in His Hands, He will heal it. As your indefatigable rear-guard protector, He will divinely take over your present and fight for you that He may bless your indescribable future. Yes, you will be able to count on the Lord leading you to safety, for He will go before you and be your Rear Guard, but you won't find safety if you're too scared to try.

A note-to-self reminder: this SEP is between you and your Savior. Using common sense, logic, or reason is not an option with an abuser, so thinking that you will be able to communicate with your abuser about your SEP is not realistic. Needless to say, announcing your planned departure and enunciating the reasons you are leaving him will not be received with empathic understanding.

Before engaging in the establishment of a SEP, remember to take a moment to stop and thank God for the huge obstacles that

THE VICTIM: EVERYTHING YOU EVER WONDERED

He has overcome in your life thus far in order to bring you to this turning point. Your preparation to embark upon the creation of a SEP warrants that you pray continually for the guidance of the Holy Spirit. This allows God's Spirit a closeness that speaks to you regarding His will for your life. Your decision to remain a victim or to take the route of an *Overcomer* will not just influence your present and future well-being but also that of those whose interests you take care of. Working on a SEP only needs faith the size of a mustard seed from you. He will do the rest. There is no doubt that you will need the wisdom and direction from the Holy Spirit to supply you with a new vision and decisive clarity of thought. You need His counsel and guidance because He views all decisions from an eternal perspective while most victims in captivity generally focus on the here-and-now. They are stuck in survival mode. It is your responsibility to turn to His Spirit for assistance; He has already invited you to come to Him. "Come to Me" (Matthew 11:28a); "Draw near to God and He will draw near to you" (James 4:8).

For all declared states of emergency, as well as individual needs such as terminal illnesses, losses, grief, and the darkness of sin—for all these things, along with abuse, prayer and seeking God's presence and intervention is the universal remedy for relief. God's presence and peace can relieve pain under the direst circumstances because He is God. Yes, the One Who calls you by name and says, "Come to Me." He can relieve your pain, in the midst of your troubled abusive world, like no one else can!

God will jumpstart your strength, give you supernatural stamina, and remain with you. And when He does, *nothing* can cast you back into the fear gear. However, He cannot do *anything* for you until you release your despair and your decision to Him— that's your ticket to that realm of the possible. God's sufficiency can deliver you from your abuse and restore your hope; you can trust Him with a SEP. "Not that we are sufficient of ourselves to think of anything as *being* from ourselves, but our sufficiency *is* from God" (2 Corinthians 3:5). There is no hope with despair. Remember that when you've lost your hope in ever getting out of your victim agony-maze and you're at your lowest point, the only encouraging peace to be found is to look to your Heavenly Father for guidance, direction, and remedy—restoration of hope. "Why are you cast down, O my soul? And why are you disquieted within me? Hope in God" (Psalm 42:11).

As your Supreme Protector, God promises you in Second Chronicles 16:9, "For the eyes of the LORD run to and fro throughout the whole earth, to show Himself strong on behalf of *those* whose heart *is* loyal to Him." God's eyes surveil the Earth on your behalf to watch for when you're being hurt and to listen for when you trust Him and call out to Him for help. He does come to the aid of those who place their faith in Him. He will tear down walls for you. Run to Him! When you seek out His Holy Spirit, you will allow the Protector, Master, and Redeemer of your abuse to move in. It is your answer to His invitation that will determine the results of your SEP and your life. Becoming an *Overcomer* of abuse is a divine commitment. If you make this decision halfheartedly, you and your loved ones will be deprived of living in communion with Him in an abuse-free lifestyle.

The result of being unwilling to accept this divine *Overcomer* commitment is living in a lack-of-life. satan offers to steal your life via abuse, and God offers you an abundant life. A victim merely exists. The *Overcomer* lives out her abundant life. In the Gospel of John, Jesus has something to say about satan, the thief. Jesus lets us know what our lives ought to be like; He says that a thief only comes to steal, to kill, and to destroy, but that He has come so that we may have life and that we may have it more abundantly! Jesus contrasted the life He offers with what satan offers. The thief Jesus speaks of is the evil enemy of our Spirit, satan. Jesus gives this as an example of the choice we have with our life. Tell Jesus you're choosing to live an abundant, abuse-free life and ask Him to establish it for you; ask Him to protect you from satan. "But the Lord is faithful, who will establish you and guard *you* from the evil one" (2 Thessalonians 3:3). Fight for your life with a plan because satan also has a plan for you; you must develop a new plan to counteract satan's plan with *His* plan. Take God's plan for your life—take the whole package deal!

To accept His *Overcomer* invitation and to design a SEP is a solemn undertaking. However, you are not doing any behavior that Jesus did not do Himself in order to protect Himself from being abused. Jesus was being abused emotionally, physically, and spiritually, so He took another route by not going through Judea where the Jewish people were seeking to kill Him. "After these things Jesus walked in Galilee; for He did not want to walk in Judea, because the Jews sought to kill Him" (John 7:1). Jesus even hid and in this way took shelter when the Jewish people picked up stones to hit Him. "Then they took up stones to throw at Him; but Jesus hid Himself and went out of the temple, going through the midst of them, and so passed by" (John 8:59). Jesus did seek to protect Himself from harm's way and expects no less from you. Developing a SEP is a vow to your Savior and a ban on your abuse. Jesus *does* ask for a devout commitment to follow Him and for you to accept His will for your life. His Word says that it is His will and honorable that you avoid the sinfulness of strife and stop ongoing quarrelling. It does require a decision from you, but rest assured that because of God's love for you, He would never ask you to give up something without having a better plan for you in its place.

You will not only receive a physical shelter or safe house to temporarily be housed in, and counsel, but remember you also have with you your refuge and strength—He is your shelter, and nothing can penetrate His safe protection over you. "I will both lie down in peace, and sleep; For You alone, O LORD, make me dwell in safety" (Psalm 4:8). "Where *there is* no counsel, the people fall; But in the multitude of counselors *there is* safety" (Proverbs 11:14). He will send encouraging counsel and lift you up through the shelter staff. "He sets on high those who are lowly, And those who mourn are lifted to safety" (Job 5:11). God is the foundation upon which you can build your safe *Overcomer* present and future life. Seize this foundation He is offering you, and begin to live your life peacefully in His safety. As you actively proceed with your SEP, He will revive you from the numb languor of a victim's dormant, half-dead state into the vitality of an *Overcomer*. He will imbue you with the divine aliveness of an *Overcomer*. He will become your oasis of love and safety!

I did not write this part of the book to throw out abuser healing miracles that could happen by replacing them with spiritual platitudes that sound good. I wrote it entirely from the foundation of my spiritual leading, educational training, research, and the depths of client/patient experiences which confirm that the spiritually-lit guided way is the *only* path to take. "For the Lord God will help Me; Therefore I will not be disgraced; *He is* near who justifies Me. Who walks in darkness And has no light? Let him trust in the name of the Lord And rely upon his God" (Isaiah 50:7-8, 10).

While you're working on developing your SEP—to avoid being pulled in by your mind in error—keep a strong grip on the *truth*. The abusive incidents that led you to this point of a SEP are there for your consideration; they are like a wake-up call. Perhaps you have been on your usual victim "autopilot mode," but a recent abusive incident really shook you up and got your attention. Although this is a most unpleasant wake-up call, this is a call to come face-to-face with the danger of your enemy (satan) who's always ready for attack! It's not just about your abuser (as is discussed in Volume II Part II *Overcomer* Principles), it's also about your adversary who wants you to *stay* in the battleground of your abusive relationship. The SEP will offer you *God* as an option to fight your battle with you, for when He's present, there's no entertaining defeat for the victim; her enemy will retreat. "Be sober, be vigilant; because your adversary the devil walks about like a roaring lion, seeking whom he may devour" (1 Peter 5:8); "Therefore submit to God. Resist the devil and he will flee from you. Draw near to God and He will draw near to you" (James 4:7-8).

Do not be overwhelmed by the daunting road that leads you to the path of an *Overcomer*. It may appear narrow in resources at the outset. But, as you progress, following the *Overcomer's* way of life, you will connect with the resources you need and eventually briskly walk and even run to your *Overcomer* destination with inexpressible joy! A SEP will offer you an opportunity to leave the suffering of always being at the hands of your abuser. Allow God to cradle and protect you. He *is* your safe fortress. He will protect you more than a precious gold vault; in His care and within the company of your support system, you are safer than Fort Knox!

If you're experiencing fearful anxiety, believing that your abuser will have an explosive episode and react destructively and possibly assault you for leaving him and for proceeding with a SEP, always go with your Spirit's leading *even* if he has not been physically violent before. Most victims *are* accurate in their predictions as to their abuser's potential reaction to the breakup of the relationship. If you are contemplating leaving your abuser, it is extremely important that you do an inventory of the potential for his becoming violent toward you *or* the children if he suspects or even catches you leaving him. The abuser's potential for becoming assaultive does not mean that you cannot or should not create a SEP; it just means that you have to develop your SEP accordingly. Yes, you are to flee from danger, but it renders a safer escape with a thoughtfully, strategically drawn-out plan of escape for your particular circumstances.

Here is an inventory assault checklist for you to use to evaluate his potential for assaulting you. Again, listen to your own intuition (Spirit) after you review the check-list.

1. Has a history of uncontrollable rage when you discuss separation. Has shoved, pushed, or thrown things at you.
2. Has threatened and has been violent against others.
3. Has been violent toward children and/or animals.
4. Has been isolative and is obsessively jealous and possessive.
5. Has access to weapons and knows how to use them; he has threatened you with weapons.
6. Has a criminal history.
7. Has been depressed and has verbalized suicidal ideation.
8. You have gotten severely ill after he has prepared a meal for you.
9. Has been overseeing your comings and goings and even stalks you.
10. Has been abusive even during your pregnancy(ies).
11. Has locked you in the house and taken your phone.
12. Has forced himself in the car with you or has taken your car keys.
13. Has denied or yelled at you for using the internet to communicate with friends or family.
14. Has insisted on driving you to work and accompanying you everywhere you go including the grocery store; he has requested to download an app on your phone to follow your location.
15. Knows all of your routines and the details of your contacts and where he can locate you.

16. Has been expending consistent time watching violent media, playing weapon-firing video games, or viewing pornography.
17. Engages in substance abuse.
18. Has sexually assaulted you.
19. Has shown up at your school or work unexpectedly.
20. Has threatened to beat you up and/or kill you.

When an abusive relationship ends, can a victim's unique self be restored even after losing most of her identity? Absolutely! A victim who makes a commitment to leave her victim role *for good* and escapes to safety begins to change back to her individual self simply through the empowerment that the experience of seeking and finding help brings. Validating that she doesn't deserve to be abused assists in recouping her sense of self. The victim learns to recognize that it's too dangerous to stay and that there *is* a way out; that realization in and of itself restores her right to be an individual deserving of respect and peace of mind.

What about abusers who abandon the relationship on accounts that "things aren't working out" or "I just don't want to be tied down" or "I don't love you anymore?" Do you still have to develop a SEP? Yes—a resounding yes! Why? Because an abuser's characteristic profile does not change just because he decides to end the relationship. He's an abuser; he reverses and distorts interactions with the victim. When the victim finally accepts his desire to break up the marriage (or his abandonment), he still has the desire to take vengeance toward her for ending the relationship (as if it was her idea). The abuser will return in person or via some form of communication and complain about what the victim has done to destroy the relationship and about how deeply *she* has hurt *him*. The victim must be certain to contact an attorney if there are children involved to file for an emergency custody order. It's important to include custody provisions with your protective order. However, it is typically ignored by the courts in most states when a victim requests to deny visitation because she's unable to provide proof of the severe emotional harm to her children. It is a federal offense to prevent the abuser from seeing the children even if he is an abusive father. Abusers love the opportunity to charge the victim with child abduction.

Bear in mind that the abuser's distorted thinking will view all of the times his victim stood up for herself or the children (even this last time) as attempting to override his role in the marriage; he won't see that the victim was attempting to defend herself and have a sense of identity in the relationship. If a victim accepts an abuser's request to be free of the relationship, he may present to others his lopsided view of the relationship and lie about her character to split her from her relationship with them. Some abusers feel a sense of privilege and power to end the relationship, especially if the victim was strong-willed in her defense against his abuse; he feels his last blow at her will humiliate her, reject her, and make her feel incapable of being loved.

In some cases, the abuser leaves the victim with his financial responsibilities, property settlements, their abused children, or even pregnant. Since he prides himself as the powerful one in the relationship, even if *he* elected the break-up, he likes to leave loose ends so that he can harass the victim when and if she attempts to close the door behind her. Whether the victim leaves the abuser, or the abuser leaves the victim, his abuser trail is left behind, and his *abusive nature* remains on the horizon. This is *why* the SEP is necessary, regardless of who ends the abusive relationship. A SEP is also useful to have in place while seeking or receiving legal assistance.

If you're unable to hire an attorney while creating your SEP, you may be able to file independently and obtain a protective order through the Domestic Violence Act; this protective order can cover both you and the children. This order can even identify temporary financial support and the itemized items that you or a moving vehicle will be transporting out of your home. Most victims that use this approach make arrangements so that when they depart from the home with their children and possessions, the police, along with the victim's advocates, have been contacted and are present to serve legal papers to the abuser. The abuser can either be served papers in your presence (if he's home) *or* you must have papers served wherever he is located. Your advocates must be with you even if he's served elsewhere so that you will be prepared if he arrives at the scene of your move and becomes explosive. The police department states that when domestic violence is involved, "Strategic planning and legal intervention are required to dodge separation violence. Enforcement advocates and battered women must work in partnership to ensure that the separation process is safeguarded against batterer violence."[4]

This strategic moving-out strategy is most beneficial to victims that do not want to escape with their minimum basics and prefer not to make later arrangements to return to recover their and the children's belongings. To obtain information about your rights and to learn the legal administrative steps in order to proceed with moving out safely, go to the National Coalition Against Domestic Violence at *www.ncadv.org* and ask for the contact information for your State Coalition Against Domestic Violence.

There are some abusers who, upon finding out that their victim is leaving, either severely injure or attempt to kill their victim, even with none of or just a few of the inventory assault check-list behaviors. Furthermore, the danger is heightened when the victim has no advocates to assist her. I know of such a case locally where the victim was completely isolated and cut off (other than the victim hotline that she called desperately to secure shelter for her). Her abuser stalked her and killed her right in the shelter parking lot. She never made it in the door to safety. It is crucial to trust your Spirit more than the inventory list as to what his abusive reaction will be if you disclose that you are leaving. *This is the reason most victims leave the abuser without giving him any notice.* In general, *all* abusers escalate when they hear that their victim is ending the relationship, so it is of utmost importance to contact a program for abused women as a part of your safety plan initiative. Listen to their instructions on how to stay safe *before* escaping.

Contacting a program for abused women will give you extra strength and support as you develop your SEP. This support will include helping you to create an infrastructure for yourself in order to break out of your cycle of abuse. Safety Escape Plans are best strategically-developed in advance while living with the abuser in order to better decrease your safety risks on the day of escape. The most successful escapes from abuse occur when the victim has a solid SEP in place. In this book, I only discuss the strategies for a *safety plan of escape* as this is instrumental in becoming an *Overcomer*. For information on a safety plan when you elect to stay with your abuser, contact a program for abused women (see "Resources"). But a word to the wise: should you decide to delay your plan of escape or to stay with your abuser, most victims who postpone leaving their abuser until the eleventh hour often experience their most brutal attack at half-past ten!

Do rest assured that when you contact a program for abused women, your safety is of the highest priority. You can trust that your privacy will be upheld. The abuse hotline will develop a safety plan with you with total confidentiality of the abuse details, and if you prefer not to give them your identity, they will still work with you. Overcoming abuse always starts with crying out for help. When a victim reaches the end of herself and shouts "help," amazing, victorious things begin to happen in her life! By faith, believe that this is the day the Lord has made—for you—don't let it get away (even if, right now, you're unable to see your limitless future).

The following is a basic example of a Safety Escape Plan (SEP) from an abusive relationship. More or different strategies can be added depending on the victim and her particular circumstances.

1. Purchase a prepaid cell phone (see Resources). Always keep it on the silent setting. Program shortcut tools or voice recognition in the phone so that you will only have to dial one number to contact the police or your support resources. Use this phone for *all* abuse safety plan calls. Use the phone to save information such as the addresses to your closest police station, hospital, or other sources.
2. Purchase a Post Office Box (POB) at a post office that your abuser does not frequent so that you can receive your confidential mail from the women's abuse program and other support organizations. If you're unable to set up a POB, do what you can to get your mail through a trusted person.
3. Set up an email account through a library computer or trusted friend's computer.
4. Open up a bank account at a bank that the abuser does not use so you can build up funds for your use upon escaping.
5. Make duplicate photo and hard copies of *all* important documents (passport, yours and his social security cards, birth certificate, health cards, insurance policies, school records, certificates, resume, portfolio, your car registration, Protective Order, photos of your abuse evidence, etc.). Also make copies of house and car keys. Do not take originals from where they are stored, or he will suspect you are leaving.
6. Hide a duffel bag (not necessarily in your home) packed with copies of documents, copies of keys, and a wallet with cash. ATM and credit cards leave tracks, so use these

only with discretion. Pack travel size toiletries, feminine products, underwear, and seasonal layered outfits; take only what is absolutely irreplaceable in sentimental value.
7. Plan where you will stay when you leave. Friends, family, and hotels are convenient but *not* the safest due to your abuser having access to this contact information. The hotline or program for abused women will be able to provide you with information for a safer place to go to.
8. Register (if required by your state) for a firearm permit to carry pepper spray.
9. Never attempt to escape if you're under the influence of drugs or alcohol as your impairment will derail your plan.
10. If your abuser suspects that you are leaving and you believe he will become violently explosive, keep the door or window unlocked for fleeing and exiting quickly. Plan various escape routes from within your home in case your abuser catches you on your way out and becomes violent. Use your prepaid phone to call the police and women's abuse hotline if you get caught escaping. *If at all possible, it's best to leave from work or a regularly-scheduled activity.*

You must *always* have *everything* in your Safety Escape Plan prepared and be ready to leave *any of the 365 days the year.* Some victims have a pre-arranged understanding with a shelter or trusted out-of-town friend or family member (whom the abuser cannot contact) that when in danger, the contacts will receive a call from her. Other victims have escaped to safety at their friends' or family members' homes or high-rise residences that have twenty-four-hour security. This contact should be someone who *knows* that you will be calling if you're in danger *at any hour;* you should both have a code word set up, indicating that you're leaving and are on your way to their place of safety. Another code word may be established to notify your contact that you want them to call the police to come to your home.

THE VICTIM: EVERYTHING YOU EVER WONDERED

It's important to be selective about the type of prepaid phone you purchase. With a disposable phone, there is no contract, and some phones even have features for texting and taking photos (which you may need for your defense attorney). In some regions, prepaid phones, whether disposable or not, have the ability to call emergency services even if the minutes have expired. If you forget to recharge your minutes, this means you can potentially access emergency hotlines as long as your phone has batteries; ask if this is an agreement between your cell carrier and government agencies before you purchase.

If you have purchased a prepaid smartphone, you can go online and download the free Aspire News application (app) which reports top world stories, sports, and entertainment news. This app is of course disguised as a regular icon with a decoy home page, but it's truly from When Georgia Smiled: Robin McGraw Foundation. This app is a useful tool because the Help Section of the app contains resources for victims of family violence. This app features a GO button, which you can activate when you're in danger. The GO button sends a pre-typed or pre-recorded message to your support system (pre-selected contacts) or dials 911 if you prefer. Once you activate the app, your phone will audio record what's happening in the room you're in (which can be used in your legal defense).

Whether you decide to use a women's shelter or friend or family member's place of safety, it is still highly recommended that you report the abuse and obtain a protective order to restrain your abuser from attempting to attack you at your place of safety. The police report and protective order will also serve you well for documentation, which can be used in legal separation/divorce matters and child custody. Be careful not to use your home computer to research abuse resources or to make contacts as your abuser may have access to your information and track you down (use the library, friend's, or work computer). Also, refrain from using your GPS when traveling to abuse resources so as not to leave tracking information in your vehicle. Put your phone on airplane mode and go off the grid!

Once you have safely moved out, take care to protect the privacy of your residential address. Remember that for your safety, *no contact* with the abuser also means *do not* return to your former household lest he attack you there or follow you to your new home. If you accidently left an important item behind, do not return to your former domicile. Whether the abuser is home or not, it is well worth your safety to lose the item and not your life. The extra sets of house and car keys are only for your protection before you escape in case he attempts to lock you and/or your children out of your home or car.

Forgiving Yourself & the Abuser
Your abuser will *always* welcome your retaliation and will *always* call you on the carpet for your display of anger and aggression. An abuser will use every opportunity to label *you* as an abuser so that once again, he can shift the focus away from him and on what's wrong with *you*! A victim needs to actually grieve the loss of her moral integrity while she was in a relationship with her abuser. She must work on finding a way to make amends with herself, forgiving herself and others for what cannot be undone. This act of seeking forgiveness from the Lord, herself, and others does not exonerate her abuser of his egregious treatment of her; rather it reaffirms her as an *Overcomer*. It's to validate her pursuit of living with dignity and her morality in the present; it is to aid her in being absolved from her past—to encourage healing into a state of peace.

Realizing that forgiveness is an extremely difficult but *necessary* act for a traumatized victim to engage in, I am obligated to address this vital step in the healing process. Forgiveness is a *choice*. A victim can either *choose* to hold a grudge and retain that resentment, or she can choose to let go and let God make it up to her. I am not insinuating that the hurt you've been through deserves to be undermined in any way. I'm saying that forgiveness is a recommended choice for a victim's sake. If you choose *not* to forgive your abuser, you are choosing to allow him to have the power to keep you bitter and wrathful. It's normal for a victim to be outraged for the things she has lived through with the abuser. Nevertheless, it is crucial for the victim to forgive herself, the abuser, and others *if* she is to progress into the role of an *Overcomer*. The step of forgiving the abuser(s) is not for the abuser's sake; it is for *your* healing purposes.

Forgiving yourself begins through prayer and supplication *and* by loving yourself and others. When you love yourself, you are also able to ask for forgiveness and to be capable of loving others. In Matthew 22:37-39, Jesus said, "'You shall love the LORD your God with all your heart, with all your soul, and with all your mind.' This is *the* first and great commandment. And *the* second *is* like it: 'You shall love your neighbor as yourself.'" Prayers of supplication are a result of powerful feelings from a broken and contrite heart. It takes sacrificial, shameless humbling (which God does not judge) to get on your knees and ask for His forgiveness. If you do this, I submit to you today that you will feel the intangible freedom of reconciliation in the Lord because His response will be, "forgiven," and "redeemed." Can you hear Him say that to you? "The sacrifices of God *are* a broken spirit, A broken and a contrite heart—These, O God, You will not despise" (Psalm 51:17).

The world may brand this type of prayerful submission to God asking for His forgiveness as foolish or lame, but God calls it wisdom. So, feel free to surrender. Are you still waiting to forgive yourself? Can *you* truly say that you have fully forgiven yourself as a victim? The way to know if you have truthfully forgiven yourself is if you can attest that you are free from any guilt and self-condemnation. If this is not the case for you, then you will be recycling the turmoil of having made poor choices which are now done and over with and cannot be reversed or erased. You will not be able to continuously carry a guilty conscience and correct those decisions. Guilt does not make poor choices disappear. Some victims relive the past and do not allow themselves the release of their past poor choices and attempt to make up for those choices in the present. You *cannot* expect to overcompensate in the present and future to correct past transgressions without ending up making some *new* poor choices. What's done is done and cannot be undone, but it can be replaced by His love, forgiveness, and renewed *mindful thinking*. Has anyone told you today how very loved you are by Him? He loves you boldly and bountifully forgives when you ask for His forgiveness.

You must forgive yourself once and for all without any more self-condemnation. Otherwise you will remain in a victim's deteriorating, sinking path of self-deprecation. God always sees past our believed imperfections, incompetence, and failures. He sees what you can become as an *Overcomer* through the power of His Holy Spirit, if you would just allow Him to lead you. He will persevere with you in spite of any weaknesses you may see or feel. He will not stop loving, forgiving, or leading you into the *Overcomer* purposeful life—if you will just let Him. He is a forever forgiving God. Our Heavenly Father may discipline us when we rebel against Him, but it is only through His holy and purest love of a parent; it is never in the form of harsh punishment or to be received as condemnation (Hebrews 12:6). When we disobey God's commands and disappoint Him, the Bible says that His *favor* for His children remains consistent; God would never allow our misbehavior, or any situation or person, to prevent us from obtaining His blessed favor which He has purposed for our life. There are no worries; God's Word promises that He does not withdraw His favor or any good thing from us (Psalm

THE VICTIM: EVERYTHING YOU EVER WONDERED

84:11), and that's simply because we belong to Him; He is more than willing and able to provide His favor and turn our darkest days (including abuse) for our greater good.

God does not waste any of our suffering but instead uses that pain to bring favor and freedom in Him (peace) with which we can minister to ourselves and others. Pray to God and ask Him for His favor in your life. God covers us with His favor as a shield (Psalm 5:12). Believe that God is not a punitive God that misuses His power by castigating us or our families when we sin. Instead, He offers us His favor to rely on when we need His strength (Psalm 89:17). His Word reassures us that He does not willingly bring affliction or grief to His children. Yes, there are consequences if we or our families deliberately choose the path of disobedience (sin), but that is our choice—not God's. God's consequences are aimed at Christ modifying us through His discipline, but to our Heavenly Father it's always a godly wrath over our offenses.

God's discipline and consequences are similar to when one gets stopped by a policeman while driving, as I was once. I had just had a teaching moment with my toddler, hugged her, shut her car door, and got into my car to pull out from the side road when suddenly, I heard a muted siren behind me. I got stopped because, to my shock, I had watched my child open her car door via my side view mirror (this is before child safety locks), and like with any mother in protective adrenaline mode, I slowed my vehicle down enough to drive with my left hand while grabbing my child's leg and car seat behind me with my right hand before she could be thrown out the door! My child's innocent response to me had been that she was just trying to see the car wheels spin and to figure out how they worked. The policeman's response was that he was only going to give me a warning (God's grace and favor) because he didn't see what happened with my child's door; he had only seen that I was going way below the speed limit and putting other drivers' lives in danger!

About a month later, my other toddler decided to take off her seat belt while I was driving. She said she wanted to see the trees on the road from the *other* window because she could only see cars from her side. Again, like any mother in fight-flight-safety mode, I had quickly slowed down my vehicle to pull over to the shoulder, and just as soon as I did, a policeman stopped me and approached my vehicle; then my other child took off *her* seat belt to check out what all the fuss was about with Mr. Policeman. All this from a simple trip to pick up my oldest child from school. This policeman was *appalled* at how I could be dangerously driving below the speed limit, and on top of that, have two toddlers without their seat belts on! That policeman wrote me a ticket for driving under the speed limit, alluded to reporting me to Child Protective Services (CPS) for endangering the lives of my children, gave me a long wait (as I silently sat in my car praying) while my children sat more quietly than they had *ever* been in their short lives!

When he returned to my car, he let me go with only an under-the-speed-limit ticket because he said he didn't *see* my children undo their seat belts and that he was *not* going to file a report with CPS (big time grace and favor!). Unlike the policemen, *God sees everything;* all dynamics are included in His decision-making. He knows when a situation is a wrongful accusation, a calculated sin, or a time for His grace and forgiveness. He *knows* if our motives and actions are pure, and like a policeman, He determines if you're at a warning point or at a risk for harming yourself and His Kingdom; He decides what the consequence will be for the choices that we make.

By the way, as an update on my children: The one we were headed to pick up at school became a teacher and travel agent; the one who didn't want to see cars on the highway and preferred the trees is now a life coach, hikes for a hobby, and is currently serving as a missionary; the one who wanted to see the wheels spin on the car is an artist.

God is not a condemning God. His Word says that *"There is* therefore now no condemnation to those who are in Christ Jesus, who do not walk according to the flesh, but according to the Spirit" (Romans 8:1). "If we confess our sins, He is faithful and just to forgive us *our* sins, and to cleanse us from all unrighteousness" (1 John 1:9). Our God is a God of favor—an uncondemning, forgiving God of justice!

In addition to praying to God for favor and your forgiveness, our God of justice wants you to believe that He has heard you and that He has unquestionably forgiven you. God's love, grace, and favor are available in endless supply. It's available to anyone who asks for it. Because of God's unconditional, extravagant love, He forgives you when you ask for His forgiveness. Have you received His love, grace, and favor so you know in your Spirit, Mind, and Body that you are free from the shame and guilt of poor choices (sin)? If you're uncertain, forgive yourself *now* and trust God to do the rest in your life. "In Him we have redemption through His blood, the forgiveness of sins, according to the riches of His grace" (Ephesians 1:7).

After forgiving yourself, you will find that this process will open your heart to forgiving others in your life. Self-forgiveness is not only the infuser in forgiving others but the fuel that's necessary in order to forgive your abuser. Genuine forgiveness of others and your abuser originates from your Heavenly Father's forgiveness of you. If there are *any* remaining obstacles that you have yet released to your Heavenly Father, determine today that you will release that obstacle(s) and lay it at the foot of His empty cross—conclusively. Your Heavenly Father will receive you and those obstacles with His love, favor, and unflagging grace! He will forgive it all and remember it no more. So, why should you induce yourself with guilt over and over in your mind? For every moment of the rest of your life, you can go forth and accept a clean slate from Him. "I, *even* I, *am* He who blots out your transgressions for My own sake; And I will not remember your sins" (Isaiah 43:25).

God's Word talks about how He forgives immediately after you confess your sin. Instantaneously your sin that may be as red as scarlet: He promises to turn it as white as snow. Think about the fact that scientifically snow is actually translucent; it's just that it appears white, when it falls on the Earth (due to the way light bends). When something is translucent, that means light is permitted to pass through and therefore is *clear* because one can see through the transparency. Now think about your conviction and repentance of personal sin—it is brilliant red, as is scarlet. However, God is offering the translucence of snow as your insight and awareness of sin; you're able to see your sin clearly, you're now able to reason and distinctly see the sin and His offer. All He asks is for you to allow Him to transmit His Light through the darkness (sin) because darkness and Light cannot be together (2 Corinthians 6:14). He promises to turn your sin translucent—as white as snow! "'Come now, and let us reason together,' Says the LORD, 'Though your sins are like scarlet, They shall be as white as snow'" (Isaiah 1:18).

Now, let's talk about forgiving your abuser. When you forgive your abuser, you're no longer holding on to his wrongdoing and your fury toward him. An added gift of forgiving your abuser is that your forgiveness will reflect on your children because you will not speak badly of their father, and they too can quietly forgive him as you have. By forgiving him, you release his power to continue to mentally hurt you through those reminders of his misdeeds toward you. An unforgiving heart eats at your spirit with feelings of animosity and disgruntlement. Don't allow unforgiveness to permeate in your heart, or it will contaminate the

THE VICTIM: EVERYTHING YOU EVER WONDERED

work that you've done in your Spirit. There is no value and no peace to be had when you carry around rancor toward your past abuser. The abuser is not hurt in any form by you harboring hatred in your heart toward him; he's actually continuing in his life as he usually does, thinking that he has never wronged you. The abuser's not feeling *any* pain by you not forgiving him—*you* are.

It's sad, but many victims continue to experience anguish and crossness even after they have elected to separate from the abuser. These victims continue to hold a grudge regardless of the abuser moving on to a new relationship. The outcome of such unwillingness to forgive is that the victim herself cannot move on and be set free from the abuser; she's still captive through his power and control to keep her angry (separated or not). Obviously, it's nearly impossible for the victim to progress into an *Overcomer* role if her heart is full of bitterness and enmity. Bitterness and an unforgiving heart is the root of the spirit of bondage. Bondage subjects a victim to temptation and the things of darkness (sin). It's a tragedy in itself that the abuser hurt you deeply in the relationship; it's even more tragic if the abuser continues to ruin your life through your unforgiving heart. God Himself, personally, has called you out of your abuse and into an *Overcomer* role—into freedom from abuse. What steps are you taking today to fulfill that role?

An unforgiving heart will only keep you from reaping all of the blessings God has in place for your future. This, again, is not to indicate that what the abuser did to you is behavior that can just be overlooked and that your experiences are not valid at the level of your hurt. Forgiving him does not mean that you are deeming his past abusive episodes as acceptable and that you have to remain on friendly terms with him. Forgiving an abuser(s) just means choosing to purposefully remove the hurt and outcry from your heart so that it won't live there and contaminate the rest of your life.

Forgiving the abuser means no longer giving him the time of your life by mulling over his hateful maltreatment in your mind. Every time you think of him while seething at his injustices toward you, you empower him to remain within your soul. *Stop* rewinding those hurtful thoughts of him; don't give him any more time—you've got *Overcomer* potential to fulfill! As a victim that has decided to overcome her abuse, you can't afford to exhaust your emotional energy focusing on your past abusive encounters. The more that you digress into your abusive episodes of the past and let them consume your new freedom, the longer it will take for your trauma to heal. Reverting back to the abusive, traumatic events only serves to keep your wounded heart from healing and experiencing *peace*. It is like periodically revisiting old wounds when you refuse to forgive the abuser. It's similar to intermittently picking at open wounds; they can't turn into a scab or a scar of the past because you keep picking at them.

Granted, it's tough and toilsome to forgive someone that has tortured your Spirit, Mind, and Body. Nevertheless, *there is no other cure* to freedom from the abuser's ongoing torture of the mind than to simply forgive him and move on to the rewarding *Overcomer* life that God has in store for you. Forgive him, lest you become such as your abuser and live with an angry heart. In abuse, there's always that risk that the victim may emulate what she has loathed the most about the abuser. There's nothing more that the abuser, the enemy, wants than to continue subjecting you to pain for the rest of your life! Living in pain for the rest of your life equals *not* experiencing freedom, healing, and peace of mind. Forgiveness can give you that freedom to move forward with your *Overcomer* life.

Because forgiving an abuser(s) is so burdensome for the victim, and the abuser is so recalcitrant, forgiveness is a *process*. However, it *does not* have to take a lifetime to experience the act of forgiveness. If you sincerely desire to achieve a level of freedom from an unforgiving heart (the kind that only God can give), He will give you the strength and fortitude to gradually, day-by-day, let go of the hurt. You will develop feelings of healthy compassion and forgiveness toward the abuser(s). Don't expect others to be forgiving first; it's not up to them to help you change your unforgiving heart. Look to God; He's in the business of forgiveness. He can work through the Holy Spirit to convert your hardened heart into a spirit of forgiveness. God can work *actively* in your life to keep you from losing the gift of peace of mind. A victim in recovery with a goal of becoming an *Overcomer* must be willing to let go of the past. When you forgive, God will deal with the abuser. He is the supreme Master Judge of *all*—including your abuser.

If you're going to go forward (Godward) as an *Overcomer*, you can't continue to look backward. What happened in the abusive relationship must be mourned through a realistic period of grief, and then God will provide a proper and healthy new beginning. If you *trust* God in that way, you can be cleansed in your heart and heal. Yes, you will feel your wounded heart, and you will grieve and even feel a depression of darkness as if mourning. It may even feel as if you'll never see daylight again. But the darkness will abate, and you will be able to look back on one of the best decisions you have made in your life. For a victim that reaches the *Overcomer* status, hindsight does bring on 20/20 vision.

You will realize that you were on the wrong track and that it was the wisest, safest decision to resign from being a victim. You will continue to add healthy friends to your support system, and they will be there to expedite your healing from those dark and dreary days. Forgive yourself and forgive your abuser and others; only then can you experience deliverance and live in His *peace*. Going forward means now that He has endued you with His Holy Spirit—put on and wear that new garment daily. While the nature of abuse culture around you would make you want to do a U-turn, don't. Instead remember that His magnificent faithful presence is living in your bodily life and you can go forward!

Are you having a discouraging, dark day? The chances are that there will be days when you will feel discouraged about your past and the aftermath it leaves, but never condemn yourself because you're not where you want to be in the process of healing yet. Instead, be grateful, praise God, and commend yourself for how you're coming along nicely! Mindfully think about how far you have already gotten—how each day is a fresh start—to celebrate the new *Overcomer* in you! If you're feeling overwhelmed with discouragement at this point, perhaps you can look back on your highlighted notes in this book to re-encourage yourself or meander through Volume II; read some excerpts of what you can look forward to as an *Overcomer*! You'll be surprised and encouraged by the hope to be had as an *Overcomer*; if you'll just continue to ask the Lord for the strength to carry on.

A victim cannot afford to spend time in a depressed state mourning over a lost past; instead she needs to invest time on what's left of her life. You must—you have to—*rise* out of your pit of victimization. Luke 22:45 states that Jesus was praying at the Mount of Olives and that when He rose up from prayer, He found His disciples *sleeping from sorrow*. In today's society, we call that type of sleeping depression. In verse 46, He makes the solution to that sorrow known; He point-blank asked the disciples *why* they were sleeping and instructed them to *rise* and *pray* lest they enter into temptation (sin). Although it may be tempting, you have to *arise* from that depressed state. "You shall weep no more. He will be very gracious to you at the sound of your cry; When He hears it, He will answer you" (Isaiah 30:19). Pray this prayer to Him now:

> Lord, I need you. I need your strength and power
> to rise above my circumstances; help me to focus

THE VICTIM: EVERYTHING YOU EVER WONDERED

on You, Your Word, and the steps I need to take toward living an abuse-free life. Please deliver me from my own self. In Jesus' Name, Amen.

Not all victims choose to forgive themselves, the abuser, or ask God for His forgiveness. Not all victims decide to end their abusive relationship—the actual death of the victim role is the endgame. The victim no longer drags her hardened heart, her love-deceased heart. If she does choose God and His forgiveness, her new reality becomes an enlivened life of an *Overcomer*! With God, you don't have to live the life of a broken-spirited victim; He offers to replace your broken spirit with His wholesome Spirit.

When a victim turns to God for help in order to forgive herself and the abuser, establishes a Safety Escape Plan, and asks to become an *Overcomer*, it's like she's opening up a life insurance policy. Except, this policy has *extra* benefits; it covers securing *peace* during and throughout life eternally. You don't have to physically die to receive the benefits of this policy. So, in the process of making all of those phone calls to secure your Safety Escape Plan, call on God. A wise *Overcomer* with a Safety Escape Plan in her hands can be assured of *spiritual peace* in the present—and have her future God-covered. It's like operation D-day when a victim decides to surrender her victimization and creates her SEP! Did you create your SEP? Good work! Now, take a second to praise God for that. Ask Him to help you implement it, to maximize the insight you gained in preparing it, and to assist you in internalizing more in-depth information that will be covered in Volume II

Do not be afraid. You are capable of setting boundaries. You are capable of breaking-free from your abuse. You are capable of healing from your abuse. You are capable of *overcoming* your abuse. You are capable! You are the only one getting in your own way of moving forward. *Overcoming Abuse: Embracing Peace* Volume I and II are your unstoppable invitation: to be set free and to experience peace. Abuse is *not* the boss of you! God and you are in charge of you. So read on to Volume II and prepare to break-free!

> "Keep sound wisdom and discretion; So they will be life to your soul
> And grace to your neck. Then you will walk safely in your way, And your foot will not stumble. When you lie down, you will not be afraid; Yes, you will lie down and your sleep will be sweet."
> Proverbs 3:21-24

ESMERALDA'S STORY

MY FIRST HUSBAND, MARK, and I met through my college roommate, who had gathered some friends to go out to eat. Mark and I began to date after that. We fell deeply in love and were married at his church. I was Presbyterian, and he was Baptist; I decided that it made no difference to me which church we married at. I had moved into a small town in the South, where Mark had been raised. I had no friends there; his friends were my friends. Mark had three and a half years of college under his belt, worked as an electrician, and made a decent salary. I had one and a half years of college and worked in a clerical position. Neither of us finished college. I was accepted into his family by his father and sister, but his mother never accepted me because I am Hispanic; she was *very* prejudiced. We have one daughter from this marriage.

Mark's mother became heavily involved in everything that we did; she had even convinced Mark that I was cheating on him. Mark's father remained passive at all times. It was just so unusual to me that his mother was *so controlling*. I just didn't understand what was going on. I thought "Maybe this is the way things are when you're married versus when you're dating." Mark's mother's input on our marriage and her control of our life ruined *everything*—it was the only reason that we divorced. Mark initiated the divorce as we were constantly arguing over his mother's unhappiness with our marriage—he told me *I* had to leave. I got custody of our four-year-old daughter. To this day it is still really weird to me how I got custody. I still can't forget his words. Mark said that if I wanted custody that it was okay with him; he was very nonchalant about it. The thinking behind that just blew my mind! I was very grateful that I *could* have full custody if he was going to be that aloof about her. We were married for six and half years.

Mark said that he took eighty percent of what we owned because his parents had either given it to us as a gift or had provided it. Everything that we had worked for and acquired together Mark kept. I left the marriage with very little; my daughter's bedroom suite, our clothing, and an old car. As I look back on Mark's ways, I recall being emotionally stressed over his rigidity and high expectations. The way he had to have the yard raked and mowed—things just had to be a certain way. I became a closet eater because Mark was always very concerned about me gaining weight and how much I weighed. I would eat small portions in front of him and then when he worked his long hours, my daughter and I would eat together. Mark insisted that our daughter try a variety of nutritious foods, but he would only eat the same six types of meals every week. We never ate out because he was very particular about all of the restaurants' prospective kitchen filth. I didn't piece together all of the eating issues until after our relationship ended. Even when I saw that his mother was abusive in her controlling words and behaviors—and we could *all* see it—it just didn't dawn on me that Mark probably felt that the only thing he could control was how much I weighed. However, he always covered it up as a *concern for me* and not wanting me

ESMERALDA'S STORY

to be *unhealthy*; he was very persuasive and manipulative when talking about my weight.

I met my second husband, Jose, in Chicago about two and a half years after my divorce to Mark. I was working my second job as a bartender; it was the only night job that offered good pay. My day job was in medical billing. Jose had an eleventh-grade education and worked in construction. Jose would come to the bar as a customer and would frequently bring his widowed mother to dance to country western music. Occasionally, he would have a date with him, but he would always be very cordial and very nice toward me—very gentleman-like. I was very impressed by his nurturing ways toward his mother; he took care of his mother a lot, and I admired that quality in him. After six months of his befriending me, we began to date; we got married a year later. Jose was Catholic but not a practicing Catholic, so he was fine with marrying me in my Baptist church.

When my daughter was about to enter high school and was college bound, Mark came back into the picture. Mark offered my daughter an opportunity to live with him, with the enticement of a small town *and* academic scholarship opportunities for college. Suddenly, Mark became a loving father; she re-built her relationship with him. She became his focal point, while at the same time straining my relationship with her, and *somehow* severing her bonded ties with me. Mark planted a seed that I didn't care about her and that I didn't want to spend time with her. I had re-married, and Mark told her to "leave Mom alone—she's busy." She went to live with him. I had given birth to another daughter three years into my marriage to Jose. Whenever my oldest daughter and I were to spend one-on-one time together, it became less and less frequent; something always came up. If Jose and I attended her school activities, her attitude seemed like she didn't want us involved. It's been very hard to maintain a relationship with my oldest daughter because she doesn't want me to be around her father and his family, the relationship heartaches, stress, and harassment. She's *very cautious*—it's like a whole different mentality.

Jose had begun to be *mentally* abusive toward me by this time, but I had not yet realized the extent of it. I came to find out that Jose's father had been very verbally and physically abusive toward his mother and his siblings while growing up. Jose somehow managed to emotionally abuse me in a way that I had never experienced, while he lifted our *daughter* and *me* up on a pedestal! It was always about me and our daughter—taking care of us, sheltering us, and doing things that *I* couldn't do for us. It was like an underlying approach that he used to make me feel that I was getting a security that only *he* could provide. But it was in the midst of *all this caring* that, slowly but surely, he would begin to pick at things—unravel them.

Jose would invariably say that I didn't clean the house like his mother did, and he would begin to lecture me using "we" statements like: "we have this opportunity to have this nice home, and we've worked on it together, but we need to rearrange these things because it's not to my liking." It was always for *his* reasons that we had to move furniture or other things around the house because it was, as he said, to *his* liking and not mine. It was never for the convenience of the family as a whole. Everything in the household was geared toward him. Jose moved the computer to several locations, finally to a corner where no one could see what he was doing on it.

We have been married for twenty years. I'm currently and have been legally separated for five years; I'm on hide out—he has no idea of my whereabouts. I have been afraid to serve him divorce papers because he may then figure out where my daughter and I live, and he could stalk us. Jose's biggest threat if I left him was that he would kidnap our daughter and I would never see her again. I realize that she's of age now to decide, according to our state laws, who she wants to live with, but his threat is frightening and real to me, because I know he is capable of hurting us! I have purposely waited to serve papers until our daughter turns eighteen and she becomes an adult. In just a few more months, she will be free of his parental rights as a minor.

I have tried to leave this relationship several times. The first time I attempted to leave the relationship, we were seven years into our marriage. I called the police because he had grabbed me very hard by the arms and restrained me; he's very strong. I panicked, fearing that I couldn't get to our daughter and protect her. The police offered options to stay and they would patrol the area but said in these cases it's usually best to leave the home. My pre-school aged daughter and I left for a few days and stayed at different friends' homes. We were separated for three years. Jose had been in secular and pastoral counseling, had quit drinking, and was active in A.A. meetings throughout that time. We reconciled for four more years, and then he returned to excessive spending, not taking care of obligations, not wanting to work, becoming explosive at work, and losing his job. Jose would just find another job, he would work for several months, and sometimes would lose that job and switch jobs without my even knowing.

With both marriages, I had just kept telling myself that maybe things were so bad because *I* was being hormonal, or I rationalized that this is the way it is being married, or it was part of becoming a parent. I blamed myself and actually thought it was *my fault* that things weren't working out. My tendency was to keep things smoothed over and justify my husband's behaviors by saying, "oh, maybe he had a bad day." I would look at what perhaps I had done wrong to cause our problems. I've learned since then, through counseling, that I acted as an *enabler*. I have now looked back on my own background and have gained insight into the influence my estranged father had on me; we did not have a good father-daughter relationship. My father's lack of emotional closeness and his overly high standards made me feel that I couldn't measure up. Not only was he detached from me, but he had no desire to become a grandfather, and up until today, he remains uninvolved with his granddaughters.

Now, I have to say that my father has been better at emotionally supporting me these past five years, but the fact that he fathered a child (through an affair) soon after I had his granddaughter had an impact on us. My father prioritized the woman he was having an affair with *and her children* while ignoring his own grandchildren. My parents were married for fifty-four years. My father was very, very, emotionally abusive and controlling toward my mother, all the way up until she recently passed away. She had been sick for a while, but my dad had insisted that it would be too expensive to go to a doctor; he would cancel the appointments that she made. My aunt and uncle had to take over and provide health care for her and take her to her appointments.

Meanwhile, Jose had become so grossly irresponsible and careless in his life. Jose was out late drinking; he would fall asleep on the couch. On many days he would return home, appear as if he had been drinking, and go directly into the shower. Jose was such a liar and manipulator; after heated arguments, I always felt that my daughter and I were in danger. I worried about what he could do to harm our daughter—and only because he wanted to get back at me for not wanting to tolerate his ways! I was in constant fear of his threats; I didn't know if one day he would just pack her up in pretense that he was taking her on an ordinary outing. There was never a good splitting point for us. One of my employers helped me to file for a divorce.

But the judicial system was not in my favor; they didn't believe *any* of my testimony of everything that my daughter and I had gone through with Jose. We ended up staying separated for another three years. Jose had gone to a doctor during that time and had gotten help. Jose had calmed down and was diagnosed as bipolar. We reconciled again. I would remind him to take his medication only because I never wanted it to get back to the way it had been in the past, but he wanted to be in control of his medicine, and I was on pins and needles all of the time.

This final time that I left him was for the same reasons. Jose became enraged when I wouldn't co-sign for a new boat. Jose was angry because I had previously declined on co-signing on other items that he had wanted to purchase. I reminded him that we didn't have the money. I had lost my job because I was emotionally stressed and physically not well; I had been diagnosed with non-alcoholic cirrhosis of the liver. This last time that Jose physically attacked me, he restrained me by the arms and held me against the wall. Our daughter was in her room; she was now middle school age. Jose left the house after that explosive episode and then returned. I stayed in the relationship for another six months. In the meantime, I had earned some money through a summer church camp job. While at that job, I felt the Lord speaking to me saying, "This is it—this is your opportunity to leave—prepare yourself."

My daughter and I went home from the camp, laundered our clothes, re-packed our bags, and hid them in her closet. Our daughter knew I was afraid of him and she would even say to me, "Mom, don't let him talk to you that way," and "Don't let him do that to you." It had gotten to where we could now sense in advance when he was about to have an explosive episode. My daughter and I began to work together to keep things calm. We would make sure the house, laundry, and cooking would be done. If I was going to be late due to job hunting, she would get dinner started so as not to set him off. Occasionally, he would verbally go off on her, so we were both always walking on eggshells;

other than that, he was usually good to her because she's such a good kid.

I had known for weeks prior to the church camp that Jose had quit paying the rent. The rental agreement was under his name, but the landlord had called me. Jose agreed that our family had to move out—perhaps with friends. Therefore, I had started to pack some of my daughter's and my personal belongings in boxes. What Jose didn't realize is that while I packed our household, I was *packing and storing* our daughter's and my belongings separately. Since I had been doing home health care for a church member that had cancer, it was not uncommon for my daughter and me to spend the night or days at her house. Jose was fine with taking care of himself at home while I was doing home health care, but if we were home, we were supposed to have *everything* in its place. One day, we left Jose under the pretense that we were going to stay over to do home healthcare. We only stayed there very briefly for fear that he would come after us.

Jose left a voice message on my phone, saying "Where are you? I went to find you, and you weren't where you said you would be!" I stayed with my parents for a few days. I was relieved that my mother stepped up and said, "This is our daughter, we *need* to help." Jose called again a week later and said, "I'm going to find you!" and then a year later, he left another voicemail. We then fled to move in with a distant relative for a year. Jose has not called and left a message in the past two and a half years. We live where he can't find us. The church has been very supportive of us; they provided a car as a gift because prior to that, I had a car payment through my dad. We have been totally blessed to be able to move into a lavish property owned by a generous church family charging us only minimal rent.

I live my life so differently now. I live nearly every day with a focus on the upbringing of my daughter; I'm working on rebuilding her self-esteem and reassuring her of her security. I attend her school activities and work my job schedule around her. I'm allowing her a balance in her independence and encouraging her to make better decisions than I made. I teach her to learn from my mistakes but in an enlightened positive and uplifting way. I have shown her how you can make it without needing someone to be in control of you. I have taught her to know the difference between someone who is demeaning, someone who makes you feel that you're in a non-sharing relationship, that you're not an equal, as opposed to a fulfilling relationship.

My daughter tends to be shy, so I've also brought to her awareness that you can relocate and be accepted into a new church family and be welcomed with loving arms. I've helped her realize that you can build new relationships without having to be ashamed about all that you have been through—humility. She has become cautious of all relationships but in a positive way. She's now more flexible and accepting of people's differences; at the same time, she can *choose* not to be mistreated by anyone. She can confront inappropriate behavior and set boundaries. She can be independent yet appropriately dependent and allow herself to love and be loved by her friends.

My past life was one of being naïve. It was a very sheltered and private life; it was all an outward appearance—a façade. It was a very controlled life; I was a pleaser and smoothed over the chaos. I've learned to think things through—to soul search. I'm no longer open to misguided advice; I seek discernment and guidance. I don't just settle for what others want for me. It's about what I want for my life and what I expect for my life. I make my own choices for my life. I know that there's always a way out no matter how minor or how major the abuse is. Whether it's during an escalation or lull period—when the time is right—there's an escape point! It may not be through family or friends; it may be through strangers.

My faith has been the greatest factor in living an abuse-free life. It goes back to my basic belief that no matter what I've done, what I do, or what I will do in the future, I have a Heavenly Father that has forgiven me for *everything* that I've done and do. He has granted me grace to be whoever I want to be for the benefit of my girls and to accomplish anything that I need to do. I have been blessed to live. I know of others—even family members—that have not been able to live through all of this as I have. God has allowed me to break away in order to raise my youngest daughter in a healthy environment and has provided us a safe place to be.

My life now is full of *relief*; I am released to all the open possibilities knowing that *nothing is impossible* for my daughter or me. We've made it! We've conquered all the little things and the BIG things. I feel SAFE. It's taken a long time, especially since we're by ourselves, but we do feel safe—we've both reached the point that we're fearless. I have no more relational constraints. I can experience being the designated mother for carpooling or activities now because I no longer have to get home right away. I no longer have the "have-tos." My daughter and I can even take in an evening movie nowadays—no fear—no more pressure cooker! I am free.

ENDNOTES

PART I
SEVEN TYPES OF ABUSE
1. United States Department of Justice. Office on Violence Against Women. *Domestic Violence.* http://www.justice.gov/ovw/domestic-violence
2. A. Littwin, *Coerced Debt: The Role of Consumer Credit in Domestic Violence* (2012) California Law Review, 100(4). Retrieved from: http://scholarship.law.berkeley.edu/californialaw review/vol100/iss4/6

PART III
THE VICTIM:
EVERYTHING YOU EVER WONDERED
3. Demie Kurz, "Separation, divorce, and woman abuse," *Violence Against Women Journal* (March 1996) 2, 67.
4. Metropolitan Nashville Police Department Domestic Violence website (2000).

RESOURCES

The National Domestic Violence Hotline
1-800-799-7233 1-800-799-SAFE Toll-Free
www.ndvh.org
www.thehotline.org

Domestic Shelters
Free national database of domestic violence shelter programs.
www.domesticshelters.org

Break the Cycle
202-824-0707
www.breakthecycle.org

Break the Silence (BTSADV)
1-800-855-BTS (1777)
Mon-Sun. Supportive assistance and connection to resources.
www.breakthesilencedv.org

Final Salute, Inc.
Mission: To provide homeless women Veterans with safe and suitable housing.
One of the factors contributing to female veteran homelessness is domestic violence.
703-224-8845
https://www.finalsaluteinc.org

Military OneSource
800-342-9647 (U.S. or Overseas)
TTY/TDD: Dial 711 and give the toll-free number 800-342-9647
https://www.militaryonesource.mil/
24/7/365 abuse helpline via telephone or on website, click on Confidential Help in the menu; live chat with a prompt response is available for all electronic devices.
To locate resources at your military installation go to:
https://installations.militaryonesource.mil/

Women's Law
www.womenslaw.org
Provides civilian and military domestic violence information and laws.

National Military Family Association
2800 Eisenhower Avenue, Suite 250
Alexandria, VA 22314
703-931-6632
info@MilitaryFamily.org

Operation We are Here
Resource Center for the Military & its Supporters
Email: opwearehere@gmail.com
www.operationwearehere.com

The Mary Kay Foundation for Domestic Abuse
Mary Kay sponsored text-for-help line (for victim or if you know a victim that needs help).
Text "loveis" to 22522

HOPE for the Heart Care Center
Prayer & Christian Counseling referral source.
Hope care representatives are available M-F 24 hrs.
1-800-488-4673 1-800-488- HOPE 4673 Toll-Free

RESOURCES

Americans Overseas Domestic Violence Crisis Center
International Toll-Free (24/7)
1-866-USWOMEN 1-866-879-6636 Toll-Free
www.866uswomen.org

National Teen Dating Abuse Helpline
1-866-331-9474 Toll-Free
www.loveisrespect.org

Childhelp USA/National Child Abuse Hotline
1-800-422-4453 1-800-4-A-CHILD Toll-Free
www.childhelpusa.org www.childhelp.org

World Childhood Foundation Inc.
Mission: To stimulate, promote and enable the development of solutions to prevent and address sexual abuse, exploitation, and violence against children.
900 3rd Ave. 29th Floor
New York, NY 10022
212-867-6088
Website:info@childhood-USA.org

Rape, Abuse, & Incest National Network
1-800- 656-4673 1-800-656- HOPE Toll-Free
www.rainn.org

National Human Trafficking Resource Center/Polaris Project
Call: 1-888-373-7888 Toll-Free Text: HELP to Be Free (233733)
www.polarisproject.org

Battered Women's Justice Project
1-800-903-0111
www.bwjp.org

Brain Injury Resource Center
P.O.BOX 84151
Seattle, WA 98124-5451
206-621-8558
Email: %20brain@headinjury.com
www.headinjury.com

Deaf Abused Women's Network (DAWN)
One in two deaf women experience family violence.
One in three deaf women is a victim of sexual assault.
Email: Hotline@deafdawn.org
VP: 202-559-5366
www.deafdawn.org

Abused Deaf Women's Advocacy Services (ADWAS)
Email: Deafhelp@thehotline.org
VP: 1-855-812-1000 Toll-Free

American Bar Association Commission on Domestic Violence
1-202-662-1000
www.abanet.org/domviol

ASPIRE News
An app that is hidden in a traditional news reader icon with cryptic programming capability.
Smartphone App Offers Resource Contacts & Help for Victims of Abuse: The victim can program the app to alert "trusted personal contacts/resources" of the victim's emergency status.
https://www.whengeorgiasmiled.org/the-aspire-news-app/

RESOURCES

NNEDV
National Network to End Domestic Violence
1325 Massachusetts Ave NW 7th Floor
Washington, DC 20005-4188
202-543-5566
www.techsafety.org

In order to maintain victim safety and privacy through the proper software, The National Network to End Domestic Violence (NNEDV) Safety Net Project, together with the Office for Victims of Crime, Office of Justice Programs, U.S. Department of Justice provide guidance on a Digital Services Toolkit to protect victims from digital abuse. The toolkit is equipped with resources for local programs that offer services via text, chat, video call, and other digital technologies.

TracFone Wireless, Inc.
A pre-paid mobile phone network operating in the U.S., Puerto Rico, and the U.S. Virgin Islands, who also offers several other cellphone brands with services from various phone companies. Monday-Sunday 8:00 a.m.-11:45 p.m. Eastern Standard Time 1-800-867-7183 0r 1-880-378-9575 Press # 4 then repeatedly ask for customer service when the prompts do not apply to you. If the prompts ask for your TracFone # or other information which you do not have, say "other" and a representative will answer.
www.tracfone.com

OTHER BOOKS BY REINA DAVISON

Overcoming Abuse: Embracing Peace Volume II Your Encyclopedic Guide to Freedom from Abuse uses a holistic approach to guide the victim: which includes a renewed attitude, overcomer principles, and techniques for permanently removing their self from an unsafe abusive relationship; the victim gains lifetime clinical and faith-based solution skills, to heal from the trauma of abuse. She learns to stop her abuse and to choose—a curated lifestyle of peace. Surrendering her victimization and accepting her overcomer role is the precursor to a victim's willingness and ability to experience an abuse-free life (that is infilled with peace). A plan of action and a blueprint is laid out for the victim, her support system and society; to maneuver the healing, prevention, and stopping of victim trauma and family abuse. To bring the message of ***Overcoming Abuse: Embracing Peace Volume II*** to your organization, church, or event, visit: www.overcomingabuse.info

Overcoming Abuse: Embracing Peace Volume III An Encyclopedic Guide for Helpers of Abuse Victims is a guidebook that brings to light the historical gravity of the problem—victim abuse. Detailed treatment strategies are provided through clinical and faith-based approaches for the victim and those interested in helping the victim in civilian and/or military jurisdiction. Case scenario self-told stories of triumphant victims that have overcome their abuse are cited. Interventions for the victim of trauma are circumscribed: including working with the immediate needs of the victim, assisting with safety decisions, modeling trust and self-protection, dealing with victim regression, using cognitive behavioral and reality therapy, neurological interventions, and treating PTSD. To bring the message of **Overcoming Abuse: Embracing Peace Volume III** to your organization, church, or event, visit: **www.overcomingabuse.info**

OTHER BOOKS BY REINA DAVISON

Overcoming Abuse: Child Sexual Abuse Prevention and Protection: A Guide for Parents Caregivers and Helpers is a parent's handbook to learn the dynamics of Child Sexual Abuse (CSA), the sex offender profile, and *how* to prevent and protect a child from being a target of CSA anywhere, including the internet. This book guides the adult on initiating conversation to help the child gain an understanding about the precious gift of his body; and walks the adult through introducing a healthy, age-appropriate, biblical perspective on human sexuality. The concept of overcoming Child Sexual Abuse is fully addressed to encourage and strengthen the parent/caregiver and child as they come together to empower the child against CSA (whether he/she has never experienced CSA or has already been a target).

To bring the message of ***Overcoming Abuse: Child Sexual Abuse Prevention and Protection*** to your organization, church, or event, visit: **www.overcomingabuse.info**

Overcoming Abuse: My Body Belongs to God and Me A Child's Body Safety Guide is a book written for a parent, caregiver, or helper to read to children from pre-school to fifth grade. Trusted adults can teach children how to identify *no touch people* and how to distinguish "good touch" (God touch) from "no touch" in a non-frightening way and non-threatening environment. A series of possible scenarios with no touch people (including the internet) are presented, and the child is guided as to how to respond in a similar situation. The child is emboldened to stay away from no touch people and is strengthened and encouraged that most touch *is* good touch!

To bring the message of **Overcoming Abuse: My Body Belongs to God and Me** to your organization, church, or event, visit: **www.overcomingabuse.info**

www.ingramcontent.com/pod-product-compliance
Lightning Source LLC
Chambersburg PA
CBHW071657170426
43195CB00039B/2219